Travels with my Father

A South American Journey

Travels with my Father

A South American Journey

Daniel and Feliks Topolski

ELM TREE BOOKS: LONDON

First published in Great Britain 1983
by Elm Tree Books Ltd
Garden House 57–59 Long Acre London WC2E 9JZ

Published in the United States of America by
Elm Tree Books in association with
David & Charles Inc, North Pomfret, Vermont 05053, USA

Maps by Janet Fahy

Topolski, Daniel
  South America.
  1. South America—Description and Travel—*1951*–
  I. Title   II. Topolski, Feliks
  918'.04   F2224

ISBN 0–241–10874–8

Phototypeset by Tradespools Limited, Frome, Somerset
Printed in Great Britain by Richard Clay, The Chaucer Press,
Bungay, Suffolk

When the description of countries and civilisations
had not yet been inhibited by a multitude of taboos
arising from the compartmentalised division of knowledge,
authors, who were usually travellers, did not disdain
continuity as it is written in the slope of a roof, the
curve of a plow handle, in gestures or proverbs. A
reporter, a sociologist, and a historian used to co-exist
within one man. To the mutual detriment of all, they
parted ways.

Czeslaw Milosz
(From *Native Realm*,
Sidgwick & Jackson Ltd.)

To Feliks, Daniel
To Daniel, Feliks

Acknowledgements

We are grateful to old and new friends encountered
throughout South America for their generosity, their time,
hospitality, advice and active help. And to those at
home for their invaluable help in the preparation of this
book.

CONTENTS

Passages printed in italics and the drawings are
by Feliks Topolski.
Photograph section by Daniel Topolski

Santa Marta
Barranquilla
Caracas
Cucuta
Ciudad Bolivar
El Dorado
GUYANA
NORTH ATLANTIC OCEAN
Bogotá
VENEZUELA
FRENCH
GUIANA
Cali
Popayan
SURINAM
Boa Vista
Esmeraldas
Equator
COLOMBIA
Quito
GALAPAGOS
ISLANDS
ECUADOR
Belém
Guayaquil
Manaus
Amazon
Santarém
Iquitos
Leticia
Itaituba
Teresina
Cajamarca
Porto Velho
1982 Journey
Recife
Trujillo
Pucallpa
BRAZIL
Lima
PERU
Machupicchu
Salvador
Ayacucho
Cuzco
Pisco
Lake
Titicaca
Coroico
Puno
La Paz
Brasília
Arica
BOLIVIA
Iquique
Belo Horizonte
Ouro Prêto
Calama
PARAGUAY
Rio de Janeiro
Antofagasta
Asunción
São Paulo
Capricorn
CHILE
Iguaçu
ARGENTINA
La Serena
Andocollo
Viña del Mar
Valparaíso
Santiago
URUGUAY
Buenos Aires
Montevideo
PACIFIC OCEAN
SOUTH ATLANTIC OCEAN
Temuco
Puerto Montt
Bariloche
Esquel
Commodoro Rivadavia
Gregores
FALKLAND
ISLANDS
Lake
Argentina
Rio Gallegos
Punta Arenas
Rio Grande
Tierra
Del Fuego
Ushuaia

The Route
Flight
Overland

Scale
0   150   250   500   1000 miles
0   300   600   1200 kilometres

PROLOGUE

Ever since I first visited Brazil in 1962 on a school expedition to film the Vaqueiros, the cowboys of the north east, I had longed to return. Journeys to China, India, Africa, the Middle East and North America had distracted me from doing so, but now I had a purpose. I wanted to show my father a continent he had never seen. In all his years of travelling the world, and recording it in his unique style of draughtsmanship, Latin America had always eluded him.

We planned a six-month journey, from the southernmost tip of Tierra del Fuego – an indulgence of my childhood curiosity in extremes – to the northern Carribean shores of Colombia, and thence down the Amazon to Rio. It would be a dual voyage of re-discovery, the one of a whole continent, and the second, of each other. And we would try to record it in all its anticipated drama and excitement, its colour and grandeur, its humour and its squalor: through Feliks' drawings, through my photographs and through our complementary words. In short, it would be a sketchbook-cum-diary of an adventure. In addition, BBC Television decided to film the venture, dropping in on us at strategic moments during the trip, in Peru, Colombia and Brazil.

How we would blend our travelling techniques, how we would bend the one to the other, to accommodate our diverse whims and wishes, were to be part of the unfolding story. How we each reacted to events, to people, to panoramas and to each other, was part and parcel of the project. How a thirty-five-year-old 'rough voyager' who revelled in the day-to-day details of local travel and contacts, would partner a seventy-three-year-old companion and father, whose speed and flexibility might be tempered, but who delighted in the grand event, the centrepiece, rather than the miles of travelling in between, was something we would discover en route. What we agreed, however, was that we would concentrate on incidents, and conversations that were our unique experiences, and hope that through these we could create a portrait of the South America we saw. We agreed from the outset that it would be futile, and perhaps offensive, to attempt an authoritative 'study' based on such a fleeting visit. So a sketch in words and pictures became our aim.

Yet at the same time we recognised that the passing observer with a keen eye and an enquiring nature could often discover more through his energetic prying on a short visit, than the long term resident, stuck in a rut, following his daily routine. People often revealed more to a passing acquaintance than to a relative or close friend. So we hoped also to report as two, not inexperienced 'candides'.

In anticipation of a September start, we collected addresses, wrote to friends, and made contact with the British representatives in every country on the continent, and wrote to the cultural ministries of each government there.

We planned to travel light and to rely mostly on buses, river boats and trains. But with just a month left to our departure date, Feliks became ill, and his doctors advised against the journey. Malfunction of his right leg and possible complications made a trip of such magnitude extremely hazardous. Feliks felt distraught, and I felt jilted. But treatment appeared to ease the problems, and with a week to go, it seemed still possible that he could join me in Chile within a month. There was nothing else we could do but hope his recovery continued.

To add to our problems, while returning from a two-day trip abroad, my bag was stolen from Victoria station, with all our addresses, research papers, passports and visas. After constant warnings about the dangers of theft in South America, this was a cruel twist of fate. In twenty years of travelling, such a thing had never happened to me before. I had been so proud of my record, and suddenly I felt vulnerable, emotionally unprepared for the venture, almost a novice.

I had prepared far more meticulously for this trip than I had for my African and Hindu Kush journeys, and I had tied myself to a far tighter schedule with film dates, publishing contracts, magazine commissions, travelling companion, contacts alerted and waiting, and a long slow build up to the departure date. All this was just not my style and I found myself becoming a reluctant traveller. I felt a great weight of responsibility and a lack of spontaneity, whereas in Africa I had been free to move when, how, and where I wished. Then I had had no ties; I had been alone, and no one was expecting anything of me; it had been an adventure. But this was beginning to seem like hard bloody graft. The added weight of a film camera foisted upon me by our enthusiastic film director, provided yet further responsibilities.

In order to give a little more substance to the journalistic side of the endeavour, I committed us to the laborious, and as it turned out, futile, task of interviewing and making portraits of the presidents of each country we visited. We wrote ahead to all of them through their respective London embassies, and fortuitously secured letters of recommendation from the various ambassadors. But for the most part the presidents proved to be a pretty shy and retiring bunch of characters, and in the case of the first one, my pursuit of him nearly led to my early demise in Paraguay.

On the plane, after a frantic week recouping and replacing the most vital stolen items, I had a moment to reflect on the coming journey. I had sensed a hesitation on Feliks' part over the whole project, a lessening of commitment which undermined my own enthusiasm, and I found myself partly blaming him for my reluctant start. I imagined that his illness was a convenient excuse, but I suspected too that I might be conferring on him my own uncertainties. I was leaving behind a busy London life and close friends and while eight years previously I had gone happily to Africa and India for a year, without a second thought, I now felt a sense of loss. (Why does London always become so much more interesting and fun just as I'm about to depart on a long trip?). Perhaps I had changed more than I realised; perhaps I was no longer the free independent rover I imagined myself to be. I was more worried now about security, about robbery and attack, about arrest and murder than I had ever been in the past. The tales of South America's unpredictability were legion, yet in Africa, where the stories were no less lurid, I had rarely felt threatened, and then only for obvious on-the-spot reasons, and never from ordinary citizens. On this trip, we were paying far closer attention to locks, and the search for secure bags served to heighten an encroaching siege mentality. In Africa I had had no wish for lock up facilities.

There was no doubt about it. I was definitely getting older and more cautious. I had become soft and lazy. If that was so, then six months roughing it in South America would soon sort me out again.

It was with these somewhat negative musings and pre-trip nerves that I faced South America, and I was glad that there was no one to witness my confidence crisis. I comforted myself with 'action replays' and memories of other long journeys in China, Africa, India and America.

After transiting through Lima, the 'plane headed south-east towards Paraguay. Below, the Andes stretched for hundreds of miles, north and south, a daunting snow-capped barrier between the steamy sensuality of Brazil and the haughty severity of the western mountain states. Trapped in a circle of barren mountains lay Lake Titicaca, and tucked to one end of it La Paz, splendid in its isolation, defying all, with its tenuous but obstinate grip on survival. Because I was on Paraguayan Airlines, the cheapest ticket I could find, I intended to stop briefly in the capital Asuncion, to visit the Iguaçu Falls, to see if President Alfredo Stroessner was willing to be profiled, and then to move on to Buenos Aires and Tierra del Fuego. Things were beginning to look rosier already, and I determined to put all doubts and fears behind me.

CHAPTER 1   Prison in Paraguay

Asuncion, Paraguay's capital city, a down-at-heel, low-lying town, was showing signs of progress as the revenue from the world's biggest hydro-electric project at Itaipu, financed by Brazil, began to accumulate. Paraguay's rich neighbour was paying large sums of money for the right to develop the project on her territory. But Asuncion still retained what I imagined to be the character of turn-of-the-century South America, with dusty streets, and old men playing chess in the shady squares, and bright yellow antique trams rolling through the town centre. You could almost scent the sleazy corruption too, which was intensified for me by my contacts with various government officials. There was an 'all things are possible if you know the right people' feel as you walked the streets.

The main squares were neatly laid out in Spanish style, for the 'paseo' – the cruising, showing-off parade – enacted throughout the Latin world, towards the end of every day all the year round. Flirtatious groups of giggling girls – students, shopgirls, secretaries looked you straight in the eye with unexpected bravado. The macho men, lounging suggestively on street corners, watched them through narrowed, smouldering eyes, and passed challenging comments. And the ever-present prostitutes, very much an integral part of South America's social pageantry, patrolled their patch, dressed in the style of the moment, big bottoms squeezed into brightly-coloured, cord slacks, tottering along on very high heels, some young and brash, but most older, weary and less shapely. Many had the broad features of the Guarani Indian, and they contrasted strongly with the dozens of chattering, uniformed schoolgirls who ambled by on their way home, without so much as a second glance in the direction of their older and less fortunate sisters.

Shoeshine boys fought for customers, played tricks on the more simple of their colleagues, or lit up discarded fag ends and sat about taking the air in the peace of the late afternoon. These were scenes precisely repeated in almost every town, village and city all over the continent, every day. Old-fashioned photographers, with their ancient box cameras on stilts, took group shots and developed the pictures while you waited, in a time honoured process, involving dishes and mirrors and liquids, and a magic touch all carried out with the panache and flourish of a conjurer.

Above the main square, opposite the luxury Hotel Guarani, a neon sign blinked on and off: STROESSNER: PAZ, TRABAJO AMISTAD, IGUALIDAD (Peace, Work, Friendship, Equality). At the far end of the square, the only other sign read 'C—— Cola'.

Ancient buses careered down the streets, barely pausing to let their passengers on and off. The conductors, modern young cowboys, romantic extrovert figures, risked life and limb as they swung in and out of the windows of the tightly-packed vehicles, clambering over the passengers, collecting fares, shouting out the stops and running between the back and front doors trying to speed up the dismounting and boarding travellers.

One played a game of chance, to see how long he could delay his daring leap back on to the departing bus: the polished entertainer acutely conscious of his appreciative audience.

Below the Government Palace, along the mosquito-infested shorelines of the river Paraguay, lay the tumbling shanty town, a constant reminder to the authorities above, that despite the huge injections of revenue into the national coffers, there was little change to the depressing view across the river. But Asuncion is a free port without import restrictions, and the shops were full of luxury consumer goods like quartz watches, fashionable clothes and cameras. Unofficial moneychangers thronged the main street Palma.

People seemed relaxed and friendly, and the lifestyle, though poor, was easygoing, producing an atmosphere that belied Stroessner's gruesome reputation. His favourite method for disposing of those he did not like was simple and horrific. They were taken up in a helicopter and pushed out over the Chaco. But then what are the signs of repression? How does it show itself on the streets? The fact that twenty-five per cent of Paraguay's four million people chose to live abroad was one indicator, even though the government tried to encourage foreign investment by freely permitting the purchase of land to allcomers, and levying no tax on new business ventures. Another indicator was that all political parties, save the ruling Colorado Party, were illegal, although in a recent relaxation of the law, Stroessner had begun to tolerate some muted opposition.

Out walking one evening, I passed a hall where a meeting was in progress. The Revolutionary Party resistance group had attracted an audience of five. The speaker later told me that he had been in jail thirty times, for three years on the last occasion, but that now they were permitted a certain freedom to hold meetings, although they were not free to organise on a national basis. 'But we are ready to go out electioneering the moment we are allowed to do so,' he said. Any communist presence was stamped out however, so I was surprised to hear that the president was about to depart on a visit to China. Then I realised they meant Taiwan of course; they did not recognise mainland China.

There had been a little immigration all the same, but most of it had been in the period before Stroessner came to power twenty-five years previously. A large Japanese community now farmed the inhospitable Chaco region, and many Koreans had set up in commerce. A group of German mennonites had also settled in the Chaco between the wars, but they kept themselves very much apart. These newcomers had helped, a little, to swell the home-grown population that had been horribly depleted in 1850 when Lopez II led Paraguay into a series of disastrous wars against his neighbours, which left only 28,000 men alive from a population of over four million. It was only now, over 120 years later, that Paraguay had grown back to that original figure, and most of these were still of Guarani stock. The physical characteristics of the native Guarani, broad features, squat and thickset, were strongly reflected in the looks of the largely 'mestizo' (or mixed Spanish and Indian blood) population, although as everywhere, the higher you went up the social scale, the whiter and more European the people became.

I spent two days in this easy small-town atmosphere, paying occasional visits to government offices for interviews with unappetising, oily ministers who were supposed to help me to secure a meeting with the president. They posed and postured and smiled a lot, and tried to look grand, and ordered endless coffees from quaking minions, but they failed to set up the meeting. Letters that

I had sent on in advance from England had not, of course, produced any action. 'Perhaps we can arrange this for you next week, or at the end of next month when the president returns from China,' offered Senor Caballero of the ministry for external relations. 'If you could drop me a line in Santiago, I shall return,' I replied, 'because I have to leave this week.' Needless to say I never heard from them again. I booked on to the Buenos Aires flight for the next day. Two days of waiting and wasting reminded me of the frustrations inherent in this sort of loosely-prepared travel. Eight years in London had dimmed my recollection of the tedious side of travelling, and my lack of acceptable Spanish heightened a sense of aloneness.

Wednesday mid morning. I caught the local bus through the suburbs to the airport. The traffic was being diverted from the normal route and there were long delays. Down one street, I saw the reason for the diversion. The wreckage of a smashed car was smouldering away in the middle of the road, and only the burnt shell remained. People were milling about in the confusion and I was glad I had started out early for the airport. But on arrival, I found that the flight had been cancelled. Ex-President Anastosia Somoza of Nicaragua had just been assassinated and the airport was now closed. That blazing car I had seen on the road had been bazookad as it was carrying Somoza to town for a meeting.

While we waited to hear what the airline planned to do with us, I fell into conversation with a pair of businessmen. Jo was a loud American, selling light shows for casinos. He was in his early sixties, and an ex-green beret, a go-in-and-blast-the-bastards-to-hell type. Somoza, Trujillo, they had all been his friends. His stories of Vietnam and his views on how to carry out interrogations were lurid and inhuman, his assessment of the 'world stage' horrifying. The second man, Eduardo, was an Argentine, very British looking, middle-aged and was at pains to ally himself fully with Jo's views, even to outdo him, calling upon recent Argentine experience for support. Jo liked and expected to be the centre of attention. He explained how all opposition to authority had to be eliminated quickly and without mercy, including any relatives and friends, no matter how tenuous the links, otherwise the disease would spread like a cancer. Any means necessary were justified, so he reckoned, to extract information, a statement which he followed up with a series of illuminating descriptions of techniques.

Jo: 'The Nicaragua thing is just like Cuba. I was there then. I could have got that motherfucker Castro. I know the whole story. Somoza might have played a hard ball game, but he did a lot for the

country. I was working with Trujillo when they got him. Yeah, I
was a big shot in the US Navy in Korea. Jesus that guy Carter; a
peanut-growing, half-assed fag. He'd wear whatever suited to get
elected. No balls. Anyone else would be better than him.'

Then followed a long monologue about the most effective
interrogation methods. Not to be outdone, Eduardo chipped in.
'We deal very hard with the Argentine terrorists. They use a good
technique here, too. They call it the "bomb". You take them up in
a plane and push them out at 300 metres. The Europeans are all
soft, but they'll learn. Now they've got our terrorists who escaped
to Spain, Italy and France and they've got trouble. Now they have
it on their doorsteps, they'll be less critical of us.'

Jo talked about 'broads' and 'fags' and Vietnam and how we
should bomb the hell out of the lot of them. 'I've been a hired gun,
been all over. The Koreans I worked with had a good method for
getting information. We had to preserve our mine sweepers; two
had been blown up, so morally we had to protect the men on those
boats. An old fisherman knew where the mines were, so the Korean
soldiers asked him if he wanted a cup of coffee. You could tell by
the look on his face that he knew what they meant. They tied him
across a table and filled his nose and mouth with hot coffee and at
the same time they banged on his balls with a little hammer. He
talked. One guy I knew used to sit a fella down on a steel chair
filled with hot coals and just fan the fire.'

Eduardo: 'They do it to you and they don't care who gets hurt in
the process. So its best to get them first. The montenero pushed
letters through our doors telling us not to send our children to
school because of the bombs. This way they tried to destroy the
fabric of our society. We call everyone who lives to the north of
Argentina a bunch of Indians. They just aren't ready for democracy here in South America. Ah! the Germans. How I admire them.
The way they go to war is fantastic.

'Those Europeans and American liberal attitudes will never
change. I see in one paper, on the front page, "terrible terrorist
attack-outrage" etc, then inside outrage about Argentina "disappearing" a girl who was involved with a guerrilla. They just don't
understand. Here Stroessner has produced a stable country. He's
probably glad that Somoza is gone now. He had hoped that
Paraguay would benefit from the investment of the Somoza
millions but it never happened. Somoza just lived off the State.'
They spoke with voices of such reasonableness but distorting
known facts and basing their theses on false premises.

Jo: 'That mess with the helicopters in Iran. They were meant not
to work. Now McArthur: there's a brilliant strategist, but too

intelligent. His trouble was he wanted everyone to know it.' Eduardo: 'What the Americans should have done was drop one nuclear bomb in the right place in Vietnam and it would have been all over in seconds.' At the same time, Eduardo worried about how innocent people got hurt in Argentinian crossfire.

The sensible conversational tone of their voices belied their extreme views and made my blood run cold. They made me feel irrationally naive, and innocent, a child in a mad world. I was a namby-pamby, wishy-washy liberal, in a world where men were men and stood up, John Wayne like, to each other and cut each other's balls off. I remember that I had planned in London to interview Somoza in South America, but because my notes were stolen in London I had forgotten that he was based in Paraguay. It occurred to me that I could have been with him when he was attacked, or worse, been heavily implicated. But what a story it would have made.

Eduardo: 'Most dictators go too far when they take power. But not Stroessner, not Pinochet. They allow people their freedoms; they know when to stop. They just concentrate on the communists, the common enemy, the terrorists. Europe and the United States just don't seem to know who the enemy is.' Jo: 'When did you last hear of a commie leader being assassinated? Protection. We're not too good at it; all that shaking hands and cavalcading in open cars. Now Castro, that's a different story. He has twelve cars and three dozen guys all dress like him, and they all get out of the cars together. You could never get him. But our guys?!!' Eduardo: 'You'll like Argentina. It's very European, very clean and people behave. Not like the rest of South America.' Argentina turned out to be the country I enjoyed the least.

The passengers of flight PZ202 were taken, at the airline's expense, to Asuncion's best hotel, the Casino on the far side of the city, near the Argentine border. On the streets people were studying the twelve-page photo report of the assassination in the latest editions. We were assured that our flight would be leaving the next day.

After a dinner which I chose to share with the two businessmen out of a perverse desire to hear more of their contentious dialogue, we decided to go into town for a drink and see how the capital was taking the news. The bar that the taxi-driver took us to was more of a brothel-disco, and soon my companions disappeared to a nearby hotel with their pickings.

I finished my drink, left the bar, and set off down the street in search of a taxi. It was nearly midnight on a quiet street 880 metres from the city centre. As I paused to cross a road, a police car pulled up alongside me and three armed men leapt out. After a cursory look at my passport, they bundled me into the back seat and drove four blocks to the police station. A pleasant captain questioned me, and with my halting Spanish and his scant English, we established that I was a simple innocent tourist. No problems; and with lots of smiling all round, I prepared to go. But he thought I should just go down to the main station for a few moments to clear up a couple of points. 'Are you coming with me?' I asked naively. 'No,' he replied, 'but these gentlemen will accompany you,' and he pointed to two steel-helmeted thugs with submachine guns. The situation was beginning to look nasty but my protests were useless. They handled me with increasing roughness as we drove downtown to the central station, close to the presidential buildings, just two blocks from the British embassy. I was marched inside past lounging, smoking security men, who looked me up and down sardonically. Mounting anxiety.

I was led into a room which contained eight or nine others who looked distinctly nervous and guilty (of what?). I tried to keep myself separate from the group, in a forlorn attempt to make it clear that I was a foreigner, and that I had nothing to do with the others or with anything that might now be going on. It occurred to me that I must have looked equally shifty.

My passport disappeared and I studied my companions. No one dared look anyone else in the eye. Clearly we were all scared of being thought collaborators in some unspecified crime. Up to this point, I had not been told why I was being arrested.

There was a man in his thirties, a Chilean I discovered later, with his thirteen-year-old son; a tall, unshaven Argentine, thin-faced with a long drooping mustache, wearing a jeans suit; an old nervous Greek; another Argentine with his wife, both in their early thirties; and a couple of youngish, clean-shaven men, one a Uruguayan. An elderly Spanish couple were brought in during the hour we stood there waiting. Then abruptly a plain clothed officer appeared holding a pile of our passports and identification documents, handed them to a soldier, and ordered us to follow. I tried to speak to him, demonstrating my poor Spanish, realising that the deeper into the mess I fell the less likely it was that I would find a sympathetic ear. By now I had had time to get scared. I tried to explain that I was an English tourist still expecting them to realise their mistake. But everyone there was a foreigner and they were not interested in me. It was all too easy to see how events took over and no matter how rational, polite or on the ball you might be, you were doomed, caught in a rushing tide of chance, unless you could catch the attention of somebody in high authority. And at that moment, no one was listening to the bleating of Daniel Topolski, British citizen, who really had no business to be in the situation he now was. And of course my new guardians had no idea how I had been arrested or why. I was there, so as far as they were concerned, I was guilty. For them, I may have been a hardened murderer, a political activist, or a drunk. They didn't know, nor did they care. I was a detainee, looking no different from the other foreigners they were holding, just a bit noisier than most. But they would soon see to that.

We were led out of the room, along a narrow corridor to the back of the building, through a small door, across a dimly-lit street, and through another doorway. Inside, in the hallway, stood a thickset man in a leather uniform and boots, slapping a long, three-thonged, metal-tipped bull whip against his thigh. Now and again he would jerk the whip towards one of us, in a sudden movement as if he were going to strike us. He laughed as we shied away. Again I tried to speak up, but was quickly silenced by the whip. Our passports were thrown into a bottom drawer of the desk at the foot of the stairs. Now my legs were shaking uncontrollably and I cursed my lack of courage. The worst was not knowing where, why, what and how. 'I'm being disappeared,' I thought in panic. From now on no one knew where I was, and with my poor Spanish and these thugs to contend with, I was getting less and less confident about my ability to keep control of my own fate. Our whip-happy friend led us single file through to the back of the building, and arranged us around the perimeter of a small courtyard, backs to the centre, leaning forward with our hands against the wall. There we remained for forty-five minutes, struck with a stick if we moved. I had the dubious luck to be alongside the latrine, and was pushed aside whenever any of our gaolers wanted to relieve themselves; but at least I could move. I had the pleasure too, of observing them in there and of course had the first and fullest benefit of the foul stench.

Behind me, across the courtyard was a cage where the women were kept. We men were taken up to the cage on the first floor, a seven by seven metre cell, open, but barred along the side facing out on to the courtyard, with two lavatory-cum-shower cubicles, shielded by a dirty, red, torn curtain that hid nothing, in one corner opposite the cage entrance. Only one lavatory worked. It was gloomy, but I could make out four or five huddled shapes on the floor arranged around the edge of the cage. We newcomers settled near the door, standing, squatting or sitting on the floor, each of us hopeful that our stay would only be a matter of an hour or two.

A little later there was shouting from below which caused the huddled figures to stir. Two men rose and kicked a third awake. 'Hey Chino, te quierer stravez: espero que no sea ton malo como la ultima vez.' (They want you again; hope it's not as bad as the last time.) Slowly the figure began to move and painfully a mop-haired, Chinese youth struggled to his feet. The two men laughed and prodded him. Outside the cage the guards were impatient. Chino reached for a broom handle for support, limped through the open door, and stumbled downstairs. We watched fearfully. Few of my cell mates had any illusions about interrogation methods here, but for me it was a shock. While Chino was away, two more men were thrown in protesting. A wave of relief swept over me when I detected German voices and realised that now, at least, I had a little European companionship. It made it easier to face the unexpected. They were young, well-dressed, effete, on a two-week South American holiday with a German woman who, at the age of sixty-six, was unlikely to have been guilty of any misdemeanour that could justify her incarceration. But that made no difference: she was locked into the cage below with a feeding Argentine mother and the other women. Holga, the younger of the two men, was highly strung and outraged by their treatment. 'We went to see the place where Somoza was killed,' he wailed, 'but we left our passports in the hotel. These people are mad; they will not listen.' He and his friend were shocked into silence when Chino crawled back into the cage and curled up in a corner on an old blanket.

'Pongensen de pie.' (On your feet); 'Pasar la Lista.' (Roll call). 'Pronto!' A little tin dictator in a hard hat, mustache, fawn uniform and shining boots, barked orders at us from outside the cage. 'Pongensen de pie; sientensen; levantensen; sientensen.' Stand up, sit down; stand up, down, up, down, two dozen times until at last dazed and trembling we stood waiting. It was still dark outside. As our names were called out, we answered 'Presente', and when he had run through us all, we were called forward to the front of the cage, one by one, to supply our age, nationality, job, whether we were single or married – 'Casada soltero?' I had to guess at the meaning of some of the questions from the answers of the other prisoners.

Holga refused to answer when they called his name and immediately, out of the blue, he was hit hard across the shoulders. We were all stunned. It was the first time that we had been aware that five of the original prisoners locked in with us were on 'their side' and not on ours. Holga was terrified and stood clutching his shoulder. His friend James was furious but was prevented from going to him. The five 'delinquents', who were all Guarani, giggled moronically. I quickly realised that they were long-term prisoners, normal felons, who had been detailed to keep us, the political detainees, in line. They had been given sticks to help them perform their newly acquired responsibilities, and they carried out their work with relish. Anyone who fumbled an answer, or failed to reply promptly, or who stepped where he was not supposed to step, received a sharp thwack across the back of the head, the shoulders, a hand, or across the buttocks.

They were to continue to harrass us with these roll calls every four hours or so, day and night, as an excuse to beat us. They served no other purpose because there was nowhere for us to go, no means of escape.

We still did not know why we were there. There had been no charges, and no interrogation, but it was obviously something to do with the assassination. We were being held incommunicado. I tried to ask for the head of the prison, or my ambassador, just down the street, but was met with threats. The South American prisoners whispered to me to be patient, not to anger the guards. They were used to this sort of treatment; they had been cowed by years and years of irrational, unexplained random brutality and arrest. This was South America and you had no rights, so why make things worse for yourself by arguing and resisting.

Day came grudgingly and bit by bit we were able to examine our surroundings and our fellow inmates in more detail. The walls were of dark brown/red plaster, scarred and chipped with the scratchings of countless earlier prisoners, trying it seemed to claw their way out. The floor was made up of red tiling.

One small bundle of ragged blankets turned out to be a young, curly-haired, gentle Argentine boy, who had been arrested a few days earlier on a drugs charge. He quietly went about the cage at the bidding of the five, sweeping and mopping the floor.

Stolen, secretive conversations, cut short by the stick-wielding thugs, supplied me with information about my companions and our situation. Poor Chino for instance, had come three months earlier from Brazil on a motor cycle and had crossed the frontier without papers, an easy mistake to make, since there was no check on some of the border posts at Iguaçu, where people crossed back and forth daily to work and to shop at the tax free markets on the Paraguayan side, and to see the massive water falls. I had done the same three days before. Chino had been involved in an accident in which he was severely injured. He was jailed without medical attention, and had barely survived. Now he was permanently crippled. Since there was no Mainland Chinese diplomatic representation in Asuncion, he foresaw little hope of ever getting out alive. I promised to contact his embassy in Buenos Aires if I was released.

Our conversation was interrupted continuously because they did not like Chino talking to me in English: they couldn't understand.

All day Chino moved around muttering to himself. 'Fuck them! Yes I fuck them these motherfuckers.' Guards, police cadets, youngsters, even families of the security police, came by to peer in at us. We watched servants scurrying about, carrying platefuls of food to officers in the rooms on the floor above. We could also glimpse the sky. We watched some of our goalers shaving and washing at the upstairs basins. Others swaggered past smirking at our discomfort. They loved to play the roll call game. Stand up sit down, up, down, on and on, with the ever ready delinquents on hand to help those with slow reactions. Chino did not fare too well at times like these. Our tormentors changed continually. All the while I expected to be freed at any moment. But self-imposed deadlines passed: morning; my plane leaving for Buenos Aires; lunch time (the British embassy must be closed) – after lunch then. Hope faded as the deadlines receded.

Breakfast for us was maté (tea) and a tiny rock-hard, foul-tasting bun. We all smiled ruefully at each other. I wrote a note in Spanish to the chief of the prison naming the minister Saujeir that I had seen the previous day and handed it through the bars. The guard disappeared downstairs for a moment and then reappeared with a furious superior who tore the note up and demanded that everyone hand over all pens and pencils!

My protestations and my requests to speak to someone caused amusement at first, then anger. I soon became fearful and hesitant, even when I saw an opportunity to catch the attention of someone who seemed to be in command. The threat of retribution was a great dissuader. The word went round that we were all under suspicion for assassinating Somoza. Opposite our cage, in a solitary lock up with a tiny barred window, a man watched us; just his eyes were visible at first, then his teeth as he pressed his crazed face to the bar to shout abuse at us. Sometimes he would brandish his arm and fist in our direction. 'He's loco,' confided the young curly-haired Argentine. 'He's been in for a month for sexually assaulting a fifteen-year-old girl.'

Holga went to use the lavatory half way through the morning. A moment after he had come out, one of the 'delinquents' followed him over and dragged him back. We were held off by the other four 'capos'. A minute later, Holga emerged sobbing and shaking. He had failed to obey a cardinal rule. You do not drop paper into the lavatory bowl. They had made him scoop everything out – 'with my hands,' he cried. His holiday wasn't turning out quite as expected.

We were being continually intimidated, kept on edge. The beatings were rare but effective in keeping us cowed. The chief 'delinquent' – spy too, since they reported all to the outside guards – was a jack-booted Guarani Indian in a dark blue cape. Brutal and stupid. Another was a slimy, scrawny fellow of about fifty, in a grubby brown suit. The third was wiry, tough, about forty-five, wearing a bright yellow jacket with 'Honda' emblazoned in red across the back. I thought of my Honda car in safe London. They all spoke Guarani to each other and lulled our fears with friendly chatter before turning suddenly into hectoring brutal pigs, lecturing us to behave correctly and lashing out at us.

At midday, forty more detainees were brought in; twenty others followed an hour later, but ten were quickly released when they were identified as Paraguayan house painters known to one of the police officers. The newcomers swelled our number to over sixty. Carlos, a pugnacious, crew-cutted, blond Brazilian was confident, unbowed and friendly. He and his Argentinian friends took me under their wing, assuring me that a telephone call which had been arranged for five o'clock would secure the release of one of his colleagues and he would then ensure that the rest of us were also set free. I was doubtful.

A young Finn, a long time traveller in South America, joined us too. This was not his first time in jail. 'They will free us before long; this is normal.' He sounded confident. My original companions, the tall unshaven Argentine in particular, were equally hopeful. 'A day at the most. They arrested me a few months ago and it lasted no more than a few hours.' By the second day his confidence was draining fast.

The nicest people I'd met so far were my cell mates. We shared everything and the atmosphere was warm and 'sympatico'. And when at one time we were eighty, packed shoulder to shoulder, all that prevented a panic was the uniting camaraderie – the shared danger. Yet I was surprised by the way they all took this with such unresisting calm. Simply, they were used to it – their lack of rights; they were philosophical. It would end soon – one way or the other.

The optimism of my Brazilian friend Carlos raised my spirits for a while, but as five o'clock came and went we all fell into a deep depression. At lunchtime the delinquents collected the daily meal. It came in a huge urn; hot water in which floated some maize. This was dished out to us in bowls and jugs and passed from one to the other as empty bowls became available. At the bottom of the urn lay the chunks of meat which had gone into the preparation of what we could now see was a stew. These were piled high on to the plates of our five tormentors who proceeded to consume what had been meant for over sixty people.

Some of my cell mates had been arrested while with their families or friends. Now one or two food packages and flasks of coffee began to trickle in from the outside. Senor Julio Carbone, the bearded, eccentric Argentine architect whose car had been hijacked by the death squad for their assassination bid, and who had identified them as Argentines to the police by their distinctive accents, received a flask and sandwiches three times a day. He spent most of his time stretched out asleep on the floor, seemingly oblivious to all that was going on around him. He was respectfully referred to by our guards as Don Arquitecto but was still under suspicion. His sprawling position created not a little friction, since our living space had been reduced by a third when the delinquents decided to divide the cage in to Paraguay and 'abroad'. The five of them resided in the Paraguay third of the cell, complete with lavatories, while the rest of us were to stay 'abroad', crushed together in the remaining space. We had to request permission to cross the imaginary 'border' whenever we wished to use the latrine. Whether they granted the request depended on their whim. The head thug commandeered one of the lavatory cubicles as his own private room. The time dragged slowly. On the floor above a girl in a calf-length skirt would occasionally walk to the officers' lavatory. We could see her legs. Once she came down and passed outside our cage. She was long and graceful. Any attempt to stand up in order to peer down through the bars to the floor below, to search for a friendly or intelligent face, met with sharp and swift retribution. At other times surveillance was slack and conversation would be permitted. Then suddenly we would be silenced. Some prisoners chatted to the delinquents, offered them cigarettes, tried to prise a little common humanity from them. They enjoyed this hugely, particularly when they could turn, without warning, to hit out viciously at someone.

The roll calls continued throughout the day. One particularly cruel guard, small, tin-helmeted, in high boots, found, during one count, that he was short of two prisoners. We were beaten to the far side of the cage with sticks. Then we had to run past him, one at a time, calling out a number as we went, and line up on the opposite side of the cell. Twice someone was slow in calling out his number and was summoned to the front of the cage to be beaten across the shoulders with a broom handle. As the count built up and my moment approached, I tried to rehearse my number, to prepare myself. Thankfully, I got it right. The next man did not. He was bent over and hit across the arse. Again the figures did not match, and one man was picked out for arbitrary punishment. The process

was repeated. Again the figures did not tally. More beatings. The
guard referred back to his list, and realised he had miscounted in
the first place. End of session.

The worst thing of all was that no one would question us and
give us a chance to say who we were. We were being held
'incommunicado' and they were not interested in checking us out.
They were putting us under very heavy mental pressure. 'What
about the second law?' I asked one of the Argentines. (The
equivalent of Habeus Corpus which states that a person can only
be held for a certain time before he must be told his crime and
contact allowed.) A large sad grin was my reply. 'Yes it exists; but
the "certain time" is very long – indefinitivo.' Sometimes someone
would be called forward and the rest of us would try to pass
messages to him in case he was about to be released. 'Call this
number, it's my mother.' 'My brother works for the state bank – his
name is Ortiz.' 'Can you call the British embassy!' But it was
always a false alarm. In time we all made agreements with each
other to make contacts should anyone escape. 'My son is only
thirteen. He should not be here,' said the nice Chilean man. 'Please
contact my embassy.' When I did so on my release, his embassy
said that he was not their concern. They did not wish to damage
diplomatic relations with Paraguay, and were sure that the
authorities would release them soon if they were innocent. The
Argentine response was similar. Only Brazil, Britain, West Germany and Finland showed any interest in the fate of their nationals.
How I wished that my American and Argentine acquaintances
from the airport could see how it felt to be on the receiving end of
all that they were glorifying. I remembered too what they had told
me at my embassy. 'Paraguayan police brutality is probably the
worst anywhere in the world. Cruelty for cruelty's sake.'

Midway through the afternoon, a tall struggling gaunt, goatee-
bearded travelling bum was thrown in with us. He crouched there
with his fists up, torn jeans, long hair, eyes staring wildly. He
looked ready to take on the entire Paraguayan police force. His
sleeping bag was thrown in after him. One of the delinquents
shoved him towards the foreigners' end, and he whirled round and
punched out at him, knocking over a bowl of water which had just
been used to mop the floor. 'Wipe it up' he was told roughly. He
refused, daring anyone to approach him. I called out to him to take
it easy. My English voice surprised him, but still he stood his
ground. So they hit him with their sticks and called an outside
guard, who encouraged them to hit him again. Finally, slowly, but
with a deliberate insolence, he mopped up the puddle with one
cursory stroke. Then he threw down the rag, turned, and joined me

on the floor. He was an Australian and had no entry documents and no money. He had been living by his wits for two-and-a-half years and his aim was to get to Argentina and find work; I thought it unlikely that they would let him in. 'Then I'll go back to Bolivia and Peru,' he said. 'That's if I get out of here.'

Every beating would unnerve us all, creating a feeling of near panic because we were so helpless, and because often the beatings were so arbitrary. Already we were developing the captive's mentality. I wanted at all costs to avoid a beating – because I had not yet been hit. As far as the guards were concerned I was just another political prisoner, probably an Argentine pretending not to speak Spanish, or someone from another part of South America. Whatever it was, my European/Britishness was of little protection here. In Asia, China, India, Africa, the racial and colour differences were so obvious that one was automatically treated differently, although not necessarily for the better. But at least one was recognisably a foreigner. There was less possibility for mistakes to be made. Here in South America, there was no such obvious difference in pigmentation. To all intents and purposes I was a local – no obvious distinguishing characteristics – and I became increasingly aware of this fact and the danger it represented for my continued survival. I now appreciated what an unconscious protection my whiteness had always been in most parts of the world. It was a realisation that served to instil even greater panic into my already unhappy state of mind. Elsewhere, outrage and self-righteous indignation could open doors, but here it was considered comic at best and punishable at worst.

I thought of the thousands who had disappeared in Argentina, Paraguay, Chile, Uruguay, Bolivia – all over South America. And I marvelled at the courage of those who still dared to resist and to stand in opposition to the established power – not only the guerillas who knew the score and fought the war, but also those dissident academics, politicians, priests, intellectuals, and those Bolivian miners who stood up and declared themselves. And here was I, detained as a suspect, completely innocent, yet shaking in fear every time the stick was raised in anger. I was not even guilty of saying that I disagreed with the present policies of the government – a crime punishable in this world by imprisonment, torture and exile.

My mood changed constantly from deep deep depression to flashes of hope; from boredom to irritation to acceptance. Sometimes I felt completely calm – *tranquilo*, that much used Spanish expression telling you to stay cool – and then suddenly, I would be overcome with a terrible foreboding, a throbbing nerve-wracking fear. I would become claustrophobic, pacing about in the tiny space, faster and faster, winding myself up into a shaking bundle of nerves. Then I would be angry, irrationally incensed at what they were putting us through, and demand to see the head of the prison. Sometimes I responded to the camaraderie, and at others I was silent and moody. One moment I would be calming the German boys, while the next I was being soothed by the Argentines, and later by my Brazilian friend Carlos.

Paraguay's well-documented record for 'disappearing' people was discussed amongst us. Stroessner's helicopter technique was particularly mind-boggling. I remember a US Marine in Hong Kong in the late sixties telling me that he had done the same thing in Vietnam with children. It was the only way to get the villagers to talk he said.

My imagination played vivid scenarios: 'Oh get rid of them,' Stroessner would say distractedly. His minions would misinterpret the order and would suppose the 'usual'. 'No you idiots, I meant release them...' Oh well, too late. Or perhaps one of Somoza's assassins was indeed in the cell with us, and his comrades would arrive to break him out. BRITISH TRAVELLER KILLED IN CROSSFIRE would run the headline. Every look from a guard, every flurry of activity or shouting below was enough to set my heart pumping in panic.

Throughout the day there was movement up and down the stairs outside, peering faces, shouted instructions, and occasional flurries of violence inside, to keep us on edge. We lay crushed together, spoon fashion, trying to close our minds to it all, to block out everything; some talked in whispers, planning or discussing our predicament, trying to think of some rational course of action we could take. Only two days ago I'd been feeling a certain empathy for Paraguay – Guarani people – peaceful people, calm, stable. I even felt a moment of sympathy for Stroessner, trying vainly to rid himself of his past dirty reputation. But now, here, all was revealed. A chance incident and the superficial exterior of gentility had been stripped away. Police reaction was swift: 'Round 'em up, doesn't matter who, put them inside: – build up the numbers – we must be seen to be doing our job.' Three days after the attack on Somoza, they hunted down and killed an Argentine – ex-montenero (revolutionary) – who had been living in exile in Asuncion. Conveniently, he was named as the ringleader of the assassins. It was doubtful he knew anything at all about it, but scapegoats were necessary to preserve the status quo. Dead men can't protest their innocence.

Dusk fell. I dreaded facing another night here. Stupidly, I

remembered my bags which were sitting in a $50-a-day room (only the first night was paid) while I was stuck in jail. All day I had half expected release but somehow, with nightfall, came despair. Offices were now shut, and tomorrow, Friday, meant that unless something happened quickly, we would be detained through the weekend, with little chance of reaching someone in authority before Monday. Our living area was terribly cramped and it was hard to remain in the half sitting half kneeling or standing position for great stretches of time. We compromised and arranged a rota. While some stood, others could lie down; then we would change positions.

Finally, the tension snapped. Holga, the young German, started to tremble and cry out. He was going into a fit and began to retch. We helped him to the lavatory where he vomited and began shitting. Feverish and sweating, he screamed and gasped and then collapsed. James begged for a doctor but the guards only watched with amusement. The other prisoners looked sympathetic. 'Muy sensitivo,' they said, 'Muy delicado,' 'Poor boy,' and of course they were all thinking that he was exaggerating a bit. No one was moved to do anything. A couple of us fussed about a bit, trying to make him comfortable, but James was scared. 'He went completely rigid just now; his hands were like stiff claws. I'm so worried he's ill, perhaps it's cholera.' Someone produced an aspirin, someone else a valium and he dozed off, but he still looked grey and drawn. A little later they transferred him downstairs. James went too. I thought they were going to be released, but discovered later that Holga had been seen by a doctor and they had spent the night on the ground floor with the women.

There was calm for an hour or so while we pondered the reaction to Holga's fit. Then there was more commotion as a small group of senior guards arrived. Everyone fell silent and stood back to make way for the prison chief. He was a large, grey-haired man in his fifties and he seemed to be concerned. He asked a few questions and looked around. After a bit I approached him to ask if I could have a word with him. 'I looking to see you all comfortable.' He smiled. 'Enough blankets?' he said, looking at the half-dozen thin, ragged covers in one corner. 'Yes? Good.' 'I'm an English tourist,' I said hurriedly. 'I would like to know why I'm here.' He studied me carefully for a moment and then said: 'I shall call for you to come to my office in a while and we shall talk,' and out he went. When two hours later there was still no news I realised I had been duped and that he had had no intention of interviewing me. Surely, I thought, the hotel would have reported my disappearance by now; or the airline. But of course they would have told the police, and since I was with the police, there was little hope of any progress from that quarter. (In fact the hotel manager hadn't said a thing. He told me later they thought I'd gone off to the Chaco for a few days to do a spot of hunting.)

News filtered in about the assassination. Somoza had been ambushed in a street near his home and bazookad by six attackers in a well-planned assault. Three people had been killed.

I paced about and all it did was heighten my tension. I felt myself building up to a big scene – a screaming fit, banging my head against the wall; but I forced calm, and lay down. Carlos noticed and advised control. The Australian tried making an utter nuisance of himself, calling to every one who walked by, banging on the bars. But it was no use.

Another night. We tried to sleep, head to toe, some crouched against the wall. More roll calls. In the morning, still with no change, we tried to devise a way of getting messages out. There were two or three coffee flasks going in and out, but we knew everything was carefully searched. The Chilean was scared, but the architect agreed to help after a little Brazilian persuasion. One of the more recent arrivals had a pencil, and with Carlos shielding me from view, I wrote a note – 'contact the British embassy, telephone 49146, name: Topolski' – and carefully wrapped it around the inside of the screw cap of the flask. A short time later it was passed out. Tension mounted; we expected detection at any moment. It was midday Friday.

Shouting downstairs brought a murmur of anxiety from my cell mates, and then a cheer went up, and everyone was shaking my hand, whispering their messages, pressing scribbled notes with telephone numbers into my hand. I was called to the cage door and to ringing applause and back-slapping and hugging, I was led out, down the stairs and past a line of other prisoners, amongst whom were Holga and James. 'We should be getting out too,' said James. I assured him I would check with his embassy.

Released with me were the elderly Spanish couple. The police tried to bundle me off without my passport, but after an argument they returned it and out I went, blinking into the bright sunlight. Stumbling slightly, on weakened legs, I made my way directly to the British embassy. The ambassador had just set off for the prison to meet me and while I waited for him to return, I began to telephone the embassies of all the other prisoners and the relatives and friends of those whose numbers I still clutched in my hand.

It transpired that Holga had managed to persuade the doctor to contact the German and British embassies and to let them know we were in jail. Now the British embassy encouraged me, with an officially stamped embassy letter, to book on to the next flight out of

Asuncion. James phoned me later to say that they'd been freed four hours after me and that their embassy had insisted that they should remain in their hotel for a week longer. Their passports had been taken away by their ambassador. They were also told that there would be no planes leaving Asuncion for many days. I never discovered why they were kept behind.

I was astonished to find that Asuncion was calm and unruffled as I walked across the main square to find a bus to the hotel. It was hard to imagine that life was carrying on as normal in the city, but there were the schoolgirls walking home and the shoeshine boys still hard at work.

I caught a bus, delighting in the feeling of freedom – unaware that I was being taken far out of my way. When the bus finally let me off, I was some distance from the hotel but I could see it above the shanty huts and I began to walk towards it. As I approached the hotel drive, two soldiers leapt forward, bayonets at the ready. With mounting anger, I showed them my passport and the letter, but they weren't interested and started to push me towards a hut. This time I resisted, screaming at them, forcing them to look again at my passport, insisting that I was going to continue on to the hotel. Fearful visions of the terrible cage loomed large with yet more days under lock and key, and my fury increased. While one soldier guarded me the other disappeared with my passport supposedly to make a phone call. It did not occur to me that neither of them could read. When he returned, he was still determined to take me in, but as I shouted louder, and a crowd gathered, he began to lose his nerve. Sensing his hesitation, I seized my chance and stalked off towards the hotel. I expected a shot or a blow at any moment, but I did not look round until I reached the front steps.

I stayed in the hotel not daring to put a foot outside until the following morning when a taxi took me directly to the airport. The hotel management sent their messenger to book me on to the flight and insisted that I pay nothing for the room, apologising for the inconvenience I must have suffered. Not until Paraguayan Airlines Flight No PZ202 landed at Buenos Aires airport was I able to breathe freely again.

I kept track of my fellow prisoners through the Argentine press, and it was five more days before they were released. They were taken by boat at night upriver to the state of Formosa and turned loose like animals into Argentina. On his release from Asuncion, an Argentine lawyer who had been with me in the jail, complained in a public letter to his government about our treatment, and demanded that they extract some satisfaction from the Paraguayans. I doubt if he ever received a reply.

CHAPTER 2 ARGENTINA: a nation in search of a future

Buenos Aires was the antithesis of Asuncion. A huge, plush, handsome city, nearly seventy kilometres from edge to edge; hectic, sprawling and home for nearly nine million people, a third of Argentina's total population; spacious plazas, dominated by extravagant heroic statues, broad avenues and soaring skyscrapers; impressive and grandiose colonial architecture and a myriad of criss-crossing narrow streets at the heart of the city, streaming with buses and taxis, day and night; a city full of character, combining zip-fast modernity with traditional elegance. Here the population was all white, determinedly European in appearance, outlook and style of dress. What was new in Europe was immediately adopted by everyone in BA. There was little room for the individualist or the eccentric. Although jeans – high fashion, pressed and labelled – were common, the emphasis was on suits and ties, all very smart, all very middle class; conservative in dress and, as I discovered, conservative by nature.

The girls, handsome, stylish and identically outfitted, stalked by, haughty and unapproachable, and lacking any hint of vulnerability. Immaculately coiffured, they were, for the most part, dressed in the currently favoured tight-ankled, broad-bottomed 'baggy' jeans and high heels. A touch slavishly, they affected the cultivated French/Italian look. They seemed scared to relax, as if constantly on show, playing a part. Even some of the local boys I met complained bitterly about the 'shallow, conservative, vacuous' women of Buenos Aires. Yet I found later, when I travelled outside Buenos Aires, that these same girls, particularly the youngsters, shed their inhibitions when they were away from home, and displayed an unexpected vitality and sense of adventure.

I joined the Saturday evening travellers on the suburban train to Tigre on the outskirts of BA to stay for a couple of days with a friend from London. It felt good to be out of Paraguay. I noticed the headlines in the evening papers: ASESINATO DE SOMOZA: MAS DE 60 DETENIDOS. 'Well here's one murder suspect less,' I thought and reminded myself to call the Chinese embassy for Chino, first thing on Monday morning. I felt a nagging guilt. Had I done all I could to help my caged colleagues in Asuncion?

I spent the first few days getting accustomed to Buenos Aires. I met an articulate and widely travelled student called Felipo on my second day and we became firm friends. He was keen to show me his town. We dealt quickly with the sumptuous public buildings and the palaces and the abundant statuary and moved beyond the thrusting modern city and the centre-of-town attractions to the historic plazas of the older residential quarters like San Telmo, which had clearly seen better days. Run down, un-cared for perhaps, yet there was still ample evidence of colonial style and harmonious Spanish architecture. There were elegant courtyards aglow with colour and greenery, glimpsed fleetingly through archways. Lovely sculptured wooden and ironworked balconies hung out over the narrow streets. San Telmo had been the luxury barrio of nineteenth century BA, its elegant homes serviced by black slaves, until a fatal plague decimated the population. Slaves perished en masse and the rich moved out, leaving San Telmo to become the broken, colourful relic that it is today. But there were signs that it was winning back the affections of the chic bohemians and the young newly-weds, searching for cheaper, eccentric surroundings.

Close by was Parc Lezamé, the most attractive square in the city. It was a true people's park, with cool poplar trees, children splashing in the fountains, old men playing chess and draughts, mother prambulating their babies, and ice-cream vendors charging eighty-five pence for a cone.

Here, Buenos Aires took on a relaxed and less frantic air. In one corner of the park, the stylish, Historical Museum traced Argentina's colonial life story, highlighting its heroes like San Martin in the minutest detail, with careful reproductions of his living quarters and his trinkets and possessions, lovingly preserved. Felipo took great delight in reminding me how the British were twice thrown out of Argentina, the second time after they had broken the peace treaty agreed following their first eviction.

The Italian quarter, La Boca, down by the port, was alive with music and street paintings, coloured houses and cobbled streets. Half the Argentines are of Italian descent and La Boca was their focal point. At night the sleezy nightclubs and restaurants took over and rough, bouncy, La Boca become a suitably irreverent antidote to the prim puritanism of modern Argentina. Presiding over the scene was the La Boca Juniors' football stadium, and the roars of the crowd provided the surrounding district with a fulsome commentary on the game throughout the afternoon.

Back in the chic part of town, a coffee at the trendy Cafe de la Paix cost £2.50. Young girls paraded in their finery, while sporty smarties cruised round the block in dazzling sleek mobiles. The traffic jammed solid as people strained to see and be seen. There was a lot of meaningful eye contact, many noses in the air, many sly and hopeful comments. Down the street at another bar, we bumped into three young student girls, friends of Felipo. They proclaimed a charming prudery and were scornful of the show of flirtation being enacted outside. Yet one of them jokingly tried to match me with her friend: 'Touch her cheek, she is beautiful, no?' Later though they hotly defended the case for premarital virtue. However, they conceded that love could overcome, but only after many faithful years, and very secretly; only then might a girl make love with her boyfriend. I was quizzed about jealousy, cheap girls and infidelity in the northern hemisphere. 'Those sort of girls,' said one disparagingly, pointing to a big smiling girl in a tight, bursting, red sweater, 'they may do it, they don't care.' The eternal theme of good girls don't, bad girls do, was alive and well and resident in Argentina.

Nearly all conversation in 1980 got round to prices sooner or later. Just spending an easy day bussing around town was prohibitively expensive. With inflation running at over a hundred per cent, Buenos Aires had to rank as the most expensive city in the world. My first purchase, a sandwich and a coca cola, standing at the snack counter on the platform of the central Retiro station, cost over £2 and left me breathless in disbelief. Everywhere else in South America the cheapest hotels could cost as little as £1, while here nothing existed under £5 and for that one shared a bare, dirty room with two or three others. These high prices held true throughout the country. Inter-city buses cost £15 to £20 for an eight-hour journey, compared to £4 everywhere else on the continent. In the first three weeks of the trip, I spent nearly $700, about twice what I spent in seven months of African travel. How ordinary Argentines, on $30 or $40 a week, managed to pay the prices was a mystery.

Life was hard for the middle and working classes and most people depended on having two jobs to earn an adequate income. Unmarried youngsters could not afford to leave the family home. In conservative Argentina, some girls preferred this. 'You're considered odd if you don't live at home, and anyway you can't afford it. But we like it, because it preserves the family, which is important to us. Not like in Europe, where your family life has collapsed.'

Yet, paradoxically, Buenos Aires seemed to live nearly twenty-four hours a day, driven, perhaps, by a need to forget their difficulties. The luxurious shopping streets – Lavalle, Florida, Santa Fé, Corrientes and Maipu were always packed, mostly with window-shoppers, and there were cinemas galore, two airports, three railway stations and five television stations.

My friend Felipo was one of those who had to have two jobs in order to pay his way through college. Ultimately, he wanted to go and live in Europe. He complained of the lack of freedom, the rocketing prices, (more justified here, although the same complaint was angrily expressed in every country I visited in South America – as if the inflationary experiences of each were unique), the savage loss of friends and relatives during and after the troubles of the seventies. 'They still disappear, even now,' he said. He gave me a brief sketch of the turbulent events. At one stage, he told me, the rebel monteneros were so confident, they marched fully armed down the streets of central BA in a celebration of their power. Their bombing targets were usually the police, who have only just now dared to return to point duty on the streets. You can still see the concrete bomb shelters outside the police stations. But the monteneros miscalculated their strength and tried to set up a country within a country. They tried to take the army head on and they were defeated. The retribution that followed was perhaps more terrible than the excesses of the rebels, because it was institutionalised revenge and of the most arbitrary and brutal sort. 'Anyone who had shown the slightest sympathy for the movement, even privately, or who had attended any meetings, or who had known someone during his schooldays who had since become a montenero, or was related to one, simply disappeared. Thousands of them. And people are still now trying to find out what happened to them.'

The wilful harassment was still part of everyday life. Felipo told me of one occasion when he was arrested, along with many others in the audience, at the screening of *Woodstock*, on a fabricated drugs charge. The liberal youthful theme of the film gave the authorities

an excuse to frighten young Argentines. 'We were held incommunicado for forty-eight hours,' he said.

The uncompromising English language *Herald*, though not a
radical paper by any means, bravely kept a close watch on the
government's performance and did not hesitate to criticise its civil
rights record. The previous editor was forced to leave the country
when the lives of his children were threatened. His outspoken line
had been considered unacceptable by a regime that continued to
conceal the whereabouts of over 7,000 'desaparecidas' (disappeared ones) and which held a further 1,500 political prisoners in
Rawson and other jails around the country. He was replaced by
another fearless journalist who was attempting to continue the role
of watchdog with excellent editorial essays on the economic state of
the nation. Through its reports, I was able to keep track of the fate
of my fellow detainees in Paraguay and their eventual release up
river in the state of Formosa.

A very different view from that of Felipo, was expressed by
Martin a member of the long-established, notoriously conservative,
Anglo-Argentine community. 'Peron brought the country to ruin,'
he said. 'He was very corrupt and she was no better. No one in
Europe understands our problems here. Amnesty and the rest are
all too soft and stupid. Those kids were armed and trained by Cuba
and Russia. But our people fought back dirtily too, and boy did
those little revolutionaries complain. We had to be ruthless,' said
Martin coldly. 'Of course, there were mistakes and innocent people
died, but that was a price we were prepared to pay. The military
government is now trying to clear up nine years of mismanagement
and, of course, it hurts. But we'll make it, because we're rich. Our
problem is that we have too small a population, and prospective
immigrants and investors from Europe are frightened off Argentina
by bad publicity and all the twisted foreign press reports.'

'If the population of twenty-seven million is too small, why don't
you encourage immigration from outside Europe,' I suggested. 'In
Britain, we have small hard-working immigrant groups from Asia,
who are an integral part of our work-force...'

'Niggers,' spluttered Martin, 'niggers here in Argentina? Good
Lord no, you can't be serious. We spent a century getting rid of all
our Indians. No, what we need here are highly-qualified white
Europeans.'

Recent reports of Jewish persecution in Argentina, suggested
that one particular group of whites would not be encouraged to
make for Argentina for a long time to come. It was hardly
surprising, that with her fascist view of the world, Argentina was
developing a close affinity with South Africa.

The divergence of opinion and the uncertainty about the country's future was perfectly encapsulated in a discussion with two journalists at a reception given for visiting British agricultural minister, Peter Walker. The two British newsmen, both well versed in the ways of the country, had arrived at two completely opposing points of view on what was to become of Argentina. One, the editor of an English language paper in Buenos Aires, believed that Argentina was about to take off economically. He expressed his views loudly for the benefit of the government ministers and military men present in a most unattractively ingratiating manner. At one point he railed against the 'traitor' Doctor Sheila Cassidy who had been tortured in Chile. 'She deserved everything she got and more. They should have shot her. Do you know she was treating the terrorists in Chile?' The generals smiled in appreciative approval. And to preserve his reputation as a spiky, independent journalist, he joked to the generals: 'Your methods would have seen her off,' and gave them a sly, knowing wink. 'Cheeky fellow,' they thought, daring, outrageous, but liked him all the same – proving to themselves how tolerant they were. I'd seen the same type in Iran, during the Shah's reign, keeping on the right side, but pretending an irreverently independent line. Making sure he had the full attention of those around us, he took a sidelong swipe at me, saying that when he had been arrested he hadn't gone crying to the embassy to get him out. 'I sorted it out myself.' On closer enquiry, he had to confess that he had been drunk and disorderly at the time. To show his confidence in Argentina's future, he told us that he had just invested in some land and fully intended to remain.

One man who had listened quietly to all this was the London *Times* correspondent. 'I've lived here for twenty years working as a journalist,' he said, 'and I couldn't disagree more. I've just sold up my farm because I believe the country is heading for collapse.' He did not want his children to grow up in the prevailing atmosphere and he was going back to England.

Someone very much on the Argentine' mind at that time was Martinez de Hoz, the economic 'monetarist' wizard who had adopted for Argentina a Friedman/Thatcher line, and was thought to be the real power in the land. He had opened up Argentina's economy, dropped import tariffs and had left the home economy to fend for itself in the face of cheap imported goods and foodstuffs. Argentina's sky-high prices were unable to compete on the open market and many small businesses had gone bankrupt. Smaller landowners were having to sell off portions of their estancias to pay off their debts and these lands were being bought up by government agencies or wealthy neighbours. De Hoz's supporters, the large companies and the profiting landowners, who included many Anglo-Argentines, that distinct, aloof and often resented little band, said that the weak, the inefficient and the lazy would and should collapse and the strong would take over. In the end the economy would be in a far healthier state. It was accepted that there would be casualties, but one had to be ruthless. Others said he was meticulously destroying the small businesses and farmers in order to fill the coffers of the establishment. 'It's got to pinch,' said others, 'to solve our terrible problems.' Inflation was running at over 600 per cent – now it's down to a hundred per cent. 'You're following the same policies in Britain,' they said. 'Yes,' I replied, 'but in Britain we have a welfare state to cushion the blow a little for out of work millions.' 'Ah! here you can always find work if you want it,' was the rich man's glib response.

But not all the establishment agreed with this cynical policy. During visits to various government ministeries, seeking permission to profile President Videla, I encountered officials who were quietly very critical of the regime, the rising prices and the brutal policing methods.

Here, in South America, it was important to keep your nose clean and to steer clear of anything that smacked of opposition. The slightest link with dissenting groups, however tenuous, could be enough to bring about your 'disappearance'. The establishment, the Anglo-Argentine community, the comfortable middle class spoke callously and easily about those who 'went away', the suggestion being that since they had disappeared they must have done something to deserve it. There was little sense of outrage or doubt, scant anxiety or pity for friends and even relatives who had unwittingly been caught up in the daily tragedies. No pity, no rights, no appeal and no trial.

But many people had had enough. One elderly British couple I met, for instance, after fifty years in Argentina, were in the process of selling their beautiful house in Tigre to return to England. 'Apart from the fearful prices, we simply don't feel happy here anymore. There is a lack of character in people now, a lack of joy. There is no room for warmth in Argentina any longer. The uncertainty of life,' they said, 'now makes each day a trial of nerves.'

Yet, down the road, the banks of the river Tigre were swarming with sunning weekend picknickers and, on the water, the expensive La Marina Country Club was celebrating the first day of spring with a massive row past of oarsmen and women in Edwardian dress, reminiscent of Britain's Henley Royal Regatta. The club had 10,000 members, squash and tennis courts, a huge well-stocked boathouse, swimming pool, camping area, bowling alleys, luxurious ballroom and dining rooms, and served as the headquarters of the national rowing team, which was very hospitable to me. The San Fernando Club across town was bigger, with 15,000 members, and had football and rugby pitches too. There were a number of other similarly well-endowed clubs in and around the city. So, clearly, not everyone was finding life in Buenos Aires so difficult. The peaceful scene beside the Tigre river, seemed to lend a lie to the criticisms and fears that were being expressed by so many of the people I met.

Yet nevertheless a lack of confidence and an insecurity pervaded Argentine society. I was continuously asked questions like: 'How do you like Argentina? Isn't it the most wonderful country in the world?' – daring you to disagree – 'Don't you love it here?' An inability to laugh at themselves gave them a lack of ease and a sense of paranoia. When a visiting British rugby team toured the country earlier in the year, one of the team members was arrested and imprisoned for running off with an Argentine flag. The humiliation, the insult, was too much for such a nationalistic country to bear and the reaction of the police, the courts and the newspapers was out of all proportion to the incident. A drunken, post-match folly became a national outrage, and where a fine and a public rebuke would have sufficed in most countries, the unfortunate culprit spent weeks in jail and months under house arrest.

Brazil gave ultra-conservative Argentines many sleepless nights. They regarded their large neighbour with mixed feelings. In their arrogance, they sneered at the multi-racial character of Brazilians, their 'lack of discipline' and proudly expressed their sense of racial superiority. But at the same time, Brazil's sheer size and hundred-million-strong population intimidated them. Brazil's wealth and recent economic success made Argentina nervous. 'We're just building our second nuclear power station. Brazil is building eight,' said one government man. And to cap it all they seemed to have so much more 'fun' north of the border. Argentines flooded into Brazil in their millions, much to the Brazilians' disgust, to take advantage of the lower prices and the exuberant lifestyle.

However new attitudes were beginning to emerge and this was evident when I went to have dinner with a divorcee who worked for a British company in Buenos Aires. We were joined by two of her closest friends who were also divorced; all three were in their late thirties, tall, stylish blondes who were proud of their Scandinavian ancestry and who supported themselves and their children without social security help and without maintenance from ex-husbands. They were fiercely self-sufficient and were determined to stay single and independent, a feat not remarkable by European standards perhaps, but rare in the world in which they lived. They derived moral support from each other and were not interested in choosing the easy 'marriage' option, since that would mean dependence on a man. Rita had never allowed her boyfriend of six months to visit her at the apartment where she lived with her three teenage sons, and he was outraged that she was prepared to entertain an unknown English man there with her friends. 'He doesn't see that I have to think of my sons when I have boyfriends,' she said. 'It will never last with him; he won't allow me any life of my own. Argentine men only understand ownership in relationships. My needs must always come second to his ego.'

I went with Rita's friend, Sonjya, to a traditional tango club. A large, musty, fin-de-siecle style hall, a little out-of-step with modern BA, where the customers were encouraged to perform. It was an island of spontaneity and abandon, with a honky-tonk atmosphere of days long gone, when Buenos Aires was indeed the Queen of South American cities. Here was a display of blatant nostalgia, with the majority of the people well into their fifties, and where the cigarette smoke hung heavily in the air. The regulars discussed the world over interminable cups of coffee, and the amateur performers took us back to the twenties with traditional tango songs and dances. Some performers were comical poseurs, laboriously costumed for the part and affecting coquettish mannerisms. They never lasted long, booed from the stage. But others sang soulfully, with few frills and were warmly received. 'You could come here and spend a dollar for a night of entertainment, with dinner and good company included,' remembered one old-timer. 'Now we pay $25 for a coffee and a cheese sandwich.'

The charm of the old tea rooms of central BA were fast giving way to the quick counter service style of North American hamburger joints. Back at the cheap hotel I had moved to, the thoughtful night porter took up the refrain. 'This street, Maipu, was the heart of the city's night life. There were brothels everywhere, the girls were magnificent, and you spent a couple of pesos for a wonderful night. Now everything is too frenetic, too expensive and not very good when you finally get it.' Buenos Aires was becoming middle Americana at its tackiest, and the cool disinterest of the big city dwellers was all pervasive.

I went back to the room I shared with an electronics engineer called Jorge. He had been there a year and the smell of his socks was overpowering. He promised daily to take me out on the town, but somehow we never made it.

While I was on the continent's east coast, I decided to spend a couple of days visiting Montevideo, across the river Plate, in

Uruguay. I took the half-hour flight across the muddy Plate estuary, as large as a sea. This was followed by a gentle drive along the brown wave-lashed coast from the airport to the city, past the elegant but run-down villas on the ocean front. There was a nice feeling of relexation after the big city rush of Buenos Aires. I had been told by smart Argentines to forget about Montevideo; it was a broken down hole, they said, and they advised me to make straight for Punte del Este, the best holiday beach resort in South America. The first secretary at the British embassy confirmed my suspicion that Punte was a Miami Beach look-a-like, with wall-to-wall bodies all summer long, so I rejected the Argentinian advice and stayed in Montevideo.

Cold gusts of wind whistled down the tree-lined side streets, but the main road, 18 Julio, was crowded with people preparing for a festival to mark 'International Education' fortnight; Uruguay was proud of its reputation for a high literacy rate and rich cultural life, despite the repressive tactics of its current rulers. Small girls shivered in bathing suits as they prepared to run through their carefully-rehearsed gymnastic display. The president had promised to attend the celebrations, but failed to appear. There were speeches, however, and bands and parades and hot dog stalls and a lot of flag waving. But compared to BA, it was a hick town, down at heel, with gypsy girls selling cigarettes and beggars skulking in doorways. Old veteran cars – Fords, Morrises and station wagons – all beautiful collector's pieces, pottered along the streets, charming evidence that Uruguay's economy was on the rocks. The squares were gracious and peaceful with the familiar old men playing chess, sitting, smoking, talking and having their shoes shined. But the pavements were crumbling and the markets were decrepit.

The country was preparing to vote on a referendum to legitimise a new constitution drawn up by the military dictators. But the day before I arrived, a local magazine had published an article criticising the government, and this had broken the superficial calm of Montevideo and the pretence by the government that all was well in Uruguay. In a country considered by international watch committees to be the worst violator of human rights in South America, the publication of such an article was a courageous act of resistance. Although people seemed, on the face of it, to be cheerful, if poor, the illusion was rudely shattered a couple of months later when an English journalist, following up the earlier story, was arrested for preparing a report attacking the regime's record and anticipating a surprise result on the referendum vote. The subsequent poll confirmed his findings, as the military government was humiliatingly defeated by an angry population which firmly rejected the new constitution. 'It's a likeable place; easygoing people, good food,' an embassy representative told me diplomatically during my visit, providing me with a very limited and misleading view of the country!

In my usual pursuit of a local rowing club, I invoked to everyone I met the name of an old boat race oarsman and one of Britain's early twentieth century River Plate representatives, Eugene Millington Drake. His heroic deeds on the river Thames for Oxford as he himself related to my 1967 Boat Race crew, a year before he died, were matched only by his South American exploits in bringing about an improvement in the quality of life in the River Plate region. He was lovingly remembered in Uruguay and, quite by chance, I found myself in the back of a speeding car with a high school headmaster in his thirties, who had been taught and encouraged by the great man himself. Millington Drake's influence was enormous, said his former pupil, and he was a great motivator. He left a deep impression on Uruguay and on Argentina. But I never found the rowing club he founded, and flew back to Buenos Aires unfulfilled.

I had seen too many cities in the first three weeks of the journey. From London, I had travelled via New York and Philadelphia to Asuncion, Buenos Aires and Montevideo; and so I decided to give myself a treat and head south to Argentina's tip – Tierra del Fuego. It was time for a little space and a horizon or two.

As I prepared to leave Buenos Aires, suggestions and advice for onward travel varied enormously. Some said the west of the country was beautiful, while others insisted that the southern lakes were a must. I was told by many that the weather would be impossibly cold in the extreme south, but more said it would be warm and springlike; still more said it would be wet. In short, no one really knew. Everything was based on hearsay and, as always, it was better simply to go and see for myself. Despite the negative advice, I was determined to go to the southern shore of Tierra del Fuego, some 2,400 kilometres away. Cape Horn, Magellan, the Beagle Channel – how could anyone contemplate missing out on such romantic history-steeped outposts. Besides, I had to satisfy my preoccupation with extremes and extremities, with exploring the outer limits and pursuing impossibly uncomfortable tasks. Everyone shook their heads knowingly at my reckless obstinacy. 'Won't take our advice, eh? Wrong time of year. You'll find out, you'll see.' Since time was short and I did not want to be late for my rendezvous with Feliks in Santiago in Chile I decided to fly down to Patagonia, and then carry on by bus and boat to Tierra del Fuego. Consequently some of my impressions were a little fragmentary.

CHAPTER 3   TIERRA DEL FUEGO: to the edge of the world

Southern Patagonia was flat, barren and dappled with small, shallow, lakes. Scattered across the grey landscape were thin bushy clumps of scrub and grazing sheep. As always, one is trapped by preconceptions. Here, in the deep south of Argentina and Chile, in September, the days were balmy and clear, the nights sharply cool. Dire warnings in BA of arctic conditions proved groundless; and expectations of a raw wildness akin to the great open spaces of Africa and Brazil were soundly dashed. Parts of Wales or Scotland gave just as great a sense of desolation and remoteness.

Riding a bus along the straits of Magellan, I crossed from Argentina into Chile. Punta Arenas, the main town, was a bustling Chilean settlement, neatly laid out on a grid system, like most new towns in South America. New Honda Accords and Ford Mustangs raced through tidy streets, and space invader machines lined the far wall of the local bowling alley, the main teenage gathering place in the evenings. Torso-less legs scuttled back and forth at the end of the bowling causeway, replacing the downed skittles, while preening youngsters sported the latest European fashions in the restaurant bar. One girl had just returned from six months' schooling in Oxford. Even in this far-flung outpost, contacts with the rest of the world remained close.

Further north, however, the coast of Chile was barely inhabited and impossible to travel, save by boat along the broken coastline – a four-day journey, zig-zagging through the treacherous waters of a thousand tiny islands. But, here at the continent's tip, the energy, vitality and awareness of the people belied their isolation from the international community. Across the water, across the Magellan straits, a short two-and-a-half-hour's ride away, was Tierra del Fuego, standing guard to the mystery ridden and ferocious southern route around the world. History had recorded the feats of the great ocean explorers and Cape Horn, just a few miles south of Tierra del Fuego had always been regarded as the ultimate challenge. This was a magical place, a special moment and I felt uplifted and positive. After a shaky start in prison and then in unhappy Buenos Aires, a rekindled enthusiasm for the whole project began to flow through my veins. At last, I felt that the adventure was beginning.

Just off the central square of Punta Arenas was the British Club, on the second floor of a handsome white building which housed the Banco de Chile on the ground floor. Orlando Verra Villarroel, the steward, led a lonely life, since only a handful of members remained and even those that were still there rarely came. The Club was established in 1899 and in its heyday between 1910 and 1940, over 2,000 members thronged the library, restaurant, billiards room and bar. The guest book proudly displayed the signatures of most of the great explorers of the period and in those days 150 new visitors a year was normal, even in this remote haven. But my name was only the eighth for 1980. Looking back through the lists, I recognised the names of one or two friends. British television producer, Brian Moser had passed by while preparing a film on the concentration camp on Dawson Island, where the remnants of Allende's ill-fated government were incarcerated. And two years earlier, the Beagle II had come into port to film the Darwin series for the BBC. 'All the local army chaps dressed up as Indians for the landing sequence,' recalled the current president of the Club, Denley King, who was honorary consul in Punta Arenas and had been there for fifty years. 'We were busy then; there were forty or fifty of them on that film and they came to visit us on two occasions. There was another crew here as well making a wild life documentary. But it's all over for the Club now. There are only fifty members left and I can't afford to run it any more. The bank will take it over at the end of next year.' The war killed off some of the members and the old pioneers were all gone. There used to be a thriving British community, but nearly all of them have left, mostly for the Falkland Islands. 'Sheep farmers, bankers and the employees of British firms based out here made up the membership,' King told me. 'The Anglo/Chileans who owned the big farms with up to 120,000 head of sheep, faded away for political reasons, under President Frei when he decided to subdivide the properties, some of which were bigger than an English county. Immigrants from Scotland and the Falklands had come and squatted on the land and they got it very cheaply. They were shepherds who brought their own dogs. We used to have an annual Caledonian Ball at the Club, you know, complete with bagpipes and country dancing.'

The Club now languished and crumbled, eerie in its solitude, yet still lushly furnished with the best Victorian leather-covered armchairs and settees and grand tables. The billiard room with four silent tables, yearned to be used, but the dust gathered and the cues remained in the racks.

The library was a proud affair, stocked with books provided by arrangement with Hatchards in London, who agreed at the turn of the century to supply the Club with all first editions published in England. The agreement ended in 1920, but the library still contained a thousand or so books from that period.

The bar was handsome and Orlando maintained it beautifully. Next door was the committee room and ranged along one wall were the portraits of all the past presidents of the Club, who had also been British consuls. 'Until 1935 they were career diplomats,' said King, 'but since then, apart from a small period during the war, the post has become an honorary one. I've been president five times and treasurer too, which is an awful headache; and now I seem fated to be the last.' At the end of the row of portraits, on the far wall, between the two windows, hung a print of a drawing of Churchill, legs akimbo, done during the war by Feliks Topolski. The same print hangs in my bedroom in London.

I felt a foolish sense of personal identity with this barren, heroic corner of the world. This was the most famous of all the British clubs that once peppered the west coast of the continent. Now it seemed that even this dilapidated relic of Britain's early presence in nineteenth century South America was to disappear.

King recalled the great names which had graced the Club in the early years: Shackleton, First Sea Lord Sir Valerie Begg, Admiral Harwood, just before the Battle of the River Plate, and Eugene Millington Drake. 'I helped Millington Drake a lot when he was here,' said King. 'We got on very well. I told him I lived in Putney and he immediately adopted me as if I had a boat race connection. He left me a book with a dedication in the front referring to me as if I had rowed in the race. He was a curious old boy; worked very hard for Uruguay and Argentina.'

The Club ran a school for 250 Chilean children with a headmaster whose salary used to be subsidised from Britain; but now the local Anglo/Chileans paid his salary. There was an Anglican church too, but the new methodist minister spoke very little Spanish and managed just one service a month. He faced competition too. Fresh-faced mormon missionaries in smart blue suits and brief cases preached the gospel for their 150-year-old church of Jesus. Elders Foster and Williams were on a two-year tour and claimed 2,000 mormon converts a month. They worked for nothing, travelling all over Chile before returning to Salt Lake City and normal mainstream life. 'What will you do?' I asked. 'I'm a law person,' said Williams. 'A lawyer?' 'Yeah, gee that's it, a lawyer.'

I boarded the ferry to Porvenir, the docking point on Tierra del Fuego, across the Magellan Straits from Punta Arenas. The passengers were hardy, wind-worn people, heavily wrapped in thick woollens, their features rough and reddened by the extreme climate. They were tough, cheerful pioneers, working the most challenging of frontiers, confident in their abilities and proud of their achievements. Survival in the harshness of this land seemed to create a contentment and satisfaction that showed on every face. Opposite me, a warm smiling Figueran worried that she had no documents for her journey to Rio Grande on the Argentine side of the island. Behind her, an elderly couple, fat, happy and demonstrably in love, cuddled and touched like teenagers. He was dark, heavily mustachioed and constantly stroked the rosy cheek of his huge, ugly wife, who clearly adored him. They may have been locally born Figuerans, but could also have been Yugoslavs returning to the large Yugoslav settlement at Porvenir.

As the ferry approached the low-lying northern coast of Tierra del Fuego, backed by a range of hills in the distance, a young Chilean, Jorge, whose Yugoslav parents owned one of 300 private estancias on the island, offered me a lift in his truck out of Porvenir, which was just a scattering of multi-coloured bungalows, all the way to the Argentine border. I was filled with elation as we sped, bumping and bouncing on the dirt track, through the rolling windswept countryside, past flocks of hardy sheep and scattering huge white 'caicenes v tarda' which flapped away from the road side like great clumsy helicopters. Across the Straits and Bay Inutil, the white peaks of the Andes rose majestically behind Punta Arenas; and, between us, lay the notorious Dawson Island prison. Jorge had recently returned from France and Italy and since he had not been able to speak either language there, he was patient and helpful with my hesitant Spanish. He was returning one of his father's employees to their estancia. But first he had to take supplies to one of the herders out in the bush, who was working a stretch of land rented by Jorge's father from his grandfather. The man saw us approaching his shack from on top of a hill across the valley, and we watched him ride down to join us, picking his way through the stunted brush and the grazing sheep. His home was sparse and cold and very lonely. He welcomed our visit and pressed us to stay. Talk was about the weather, the animals, some of them sick or injured, some dead; and he spoke enviously of the high-life in tiny Porvenir as if it were a large city.

We passed many estancias and their appearance bore little resemblance to the great ranches of the wealthy cattle barons to the north. These were spartan affairs, a few corrugated prefabs, huddled in the lee of small hills, seeking protection from the blinding blizzards and stabbing cold winds. The owners were, for the most part, absentee, living the city life of Santiago and schooling their children in Europe. Here, on Tierra del Fuego, four or five farm hands ran the show, living lonely and meagre lives.

Jorge's spread was no different. As we approached the tightly-grouped bungalows, the cook was already preparing a hot mutton stew and tea. The hands were out with the flocks and wouldn't be back for a few hours. The rooms were bare, save for a couple of pin-ups on the wall above a table in the kitchen, and three stools. This was the main living room, because it was the warmest one on the estancia. The cook fussed busily about replenishing empty bowls, pleased to have guests. He had the rust brown hands and face and the broad Indian features of the southern Chilean.

Jorge drove me on to the border to wait for the bus through to Rio Grande, from where I could travel on south to Ushuaia on the south coast of the island. In between lay tall, forbidding, snow-covered peaks and driving blizzards.

Because of the growing tension between Chile and Argentina over the disputed ownership of three small islands in the Beagle Channel off the south coast, the border formalities were unnecessarily protracted, as both sides sought to intimidate the nationals of the other. The unsuspecting traveller got caught up, willy-nilly, in the game playing. Five men questioned each passenger, filling in identical forms in triplicate, asking the same questions and all painfully scrawling the answers in slow capital letters. Women were particularly harassed by the guards, who were eager to steal a cheap thrill at the expense of a frightened and humiliated young traveller.

At the best of times border crossings in South America were

hazardous and insistent greasy palms were a constant irritation. Of course, constant travelling produced endless confrontations with officialdom which could sometimes dominate the journey's character and produce a slightly unbalanced picture of a country. But here, as in Africa, the greatest danger to life, limb and property came from the men in uniform. Whether soldiers or policemen, the guardians of peace and order were the worst perpetrators of the crimes they were employed to combat. Once in uniform, a man seemed destined to succumb to his worst instincts and to set himself firmly above the law.

The reason for the delays on this occasion it transpired was that Argentina had recently stolen a Chilean fishing boat and in retaliation Chile had stolen two Argentine border officials. The game continued and the Pope had been asked to mediate on the 'Islands' problem.

Caught with me in the five-hour grapple with authority were an American couple – he, a professor, gaunt, russet-haired and bearded, aged about forty-five, she, gamine and hippy, pale and enthusiastic as a teenager. Although they had been turned back from the border on the mainland a few days earlier, they had made no attempt to re-adjust their appearance and presentation into something more acceptable to ultra-conservative Argentina. They were at the end of their second travelling year and waxed lyrical about Central America, which they had visited at the beginning of their trip – Mexico, Belize and particularly Guatamala. 'If you want a taste of Latin American life, you need go no further than those three countries,' suggested the professor. 'Down here its so depressing. People are humourless and cowed. They've so little sensitivity, so little feel for the quality of life. The cost, the hunger for power. We saw the military parades of goosestepping soldiers on 19 September, celebrating Chilean independence. It was horrifying.' Peru and Bolivia they said were at least more relaxed than here and half the cost – 'but so poor!'

Rio Grande was a desolate collection of bungalows on the Atlantic ocean, facing the Falkland Islands. The wind drove you mad and you sought out buildings, fences, posts, anything, to shelter behind for a moment's respite. From across the plain it whistled and gusted and howled overhead as I crouched in the lee of a beachside hut, like an old tramp, digging into my bag for a cheese roll. When the sun went in the air became icy. The ominous grey sea was flattened by the gusts some 300 metres back from the black gravel shore until the crashing waves became too strong to be held back any further.

The town was stark and barrack-like, laid out in the now familiar dull grid pattern for 7,000 oil drillers and refinery employees and their families. But there were few signs of entertainment and people spent most of their time inside in overheated sauna-like bungalows. My hotel was mainly inhabited by television-obsessed young workers who paid £7 a night for the dubious privilege of occupying tiny, sweltering cubicles where the heat could not be regulated.

Registering with the police was a comic performance. The officers had difficulty reading and writing, so to camouflage these embarrassing deficiencies they sent people with simple requests away for a day or two suggesting that the petitioner was the one at fault. They were at a loss with my papers though and took the tourist card and border clearance telling me to go away and return next day. I refused, saying I had to travel immediately. After a long delay, the border clearance was returned and I could leave, but they would not relinquish the tourist card, without which I was not supposed to leave the country. A dozen people waited patiently behind me in the queue. This was nothing new to them. I gave up and left.

The bus south was an hour and a half late leaving and the passengers were given no explanation as we sat in the cold booking hall. It transpired we were waiting for a smart-suited, middle-aged gentleman and a fey young man with a camera. Imperiously they swept up in a taxi, and without a word of apology, demanded the seats in the front already occupied. We were all shuffled around to accommodate the ill-mannered official and his boyfriend.

The land of southern Tierra del Fuego was stark and beautiful. After crossing flat scrubland and occasional petrified forests of bare whitely-knarled trees, and fording shallow river beds, the bus straining all the while in first gear to cut down speed because the brakes did not work, we skirted icy lake Fagnano, set at the foot of snow-capped mountains. Clouds were forming as, brakeless, we began the ascent of the Garibaldi pass high above the snow line, sliding and slipping along the narrow dirt track. The raw craggy peaks towered over us, and a silent grey lake, Escondido, glistened far below, nestling in a crescent of sheer cliffs. The passengers were silenced, partly by anxiety, partly by awe. In the gathering dusk a gusting blizzard made conditions even more hazardous. The descent was utterly nerve-wracking.

It was late when we broke out of the clouds and down on to the narrow coastal strip overlooking the Beagle Channel. Ahead lay Ushuaia its lights blinking hazily through the falling snow and opposite, across the water, the dim shape of Chile's Navarino island was just visible. Beyond were Cape Horn, Drake Straits and Antarctica. To the east were the three disputed islands.

*Ushuaia had a vitality and messiness which was very different to the corrugated drabness of the towns further north. Here was a warm vibrant outpost displaying a stoic confidence born from its long-established and historically important presence as the world's southernmost town. The next stop was the South Pole. Ushuaia's steep, narrow, muddy streets ran back up Mount Martial from the deep green Beagle Channel, and its solid buildings gave off a sense of permanence, very different from the temporary feel of Rio Grande, Rio Gallegos and those other bungalow settlements. Six thousand people earned their living here, raising sheep, fishing, timber cutting, trapping or servicing the rest; they were subsidised by local tax exemptions, which made life a little more comfortable in this antipodean corner.

The cinema on the main St Martin street was showing *10* and a Kung Fu movie and the shops were full of the latest electronic equipment, Hi-fis, televisions and Mary Quant cosmetics. I ate king crab at Don Pipo's for dinner, while watching a soggy but theatrical Mohammed Ali flail despairingly on television against a super-fit, sleek, prowling Larry Holmes, who bided his time, impassive before the antics and the tauntings of the 'greatest'. The end came quickly, when Ali failed to come out for the tenth round. Sad and broken. So was my hotel room, which I shared with someone who was already asleep when I got back and again when I left next morning.

Although there was little time to reflect on my safe arrival on the shores of the Beagle Channel, I could not help noticing that despite the remoteness of Ushuaia, tourism played an important part in local life. There were national parks, flights over Cape Horn, fishing and hunting safaris for up to 30,000 visitors a year. Rugged overland trips were always destined to be shadowed by the quick airborne tourist with money in his pocket and limited time, but with a certain adventurousness in his spirit. I had to resign myself to the fact that throughout South America, I would not find that sense of 'exploring' that I had done in Africa, unless I took off for a few months into the Amazon jungle. South America was already well advanced along the road to the 'American way of life' and a carefully-cultivated nonchalant play at cool sophistication prevailed. There could be no harbouring of romantic notions about breaking new ground, or enjoying unprejudiced encounters.

Leaving Ushuaia posed a problem. The thrice-weekly flights were heavily oversubscribed and even an advance booking guaranteed nothing. A fast-approaching rendezvous with my father in Santiago dictated my travel plans, but a still skimpy command of Spanish did my cause little good when it came to the cut and thrust battle for a seat. I was left protesting at the gate as the passengers were herded out to the plane which stood on the runway in the still, blue-tinged whiteness of the approaching dawn. But help was at hand. The only calm and thoughtful face I had seen that morning decided to listen to my plaintive story. He spoke English, he was the pilot of the plane and, why, of course, I could ride at the back of the plane on the jump seat.

Ushuaia, a little snow-clad spot amid a confusion of mountains and islands, fell away astern into the murk as a snowstorm enveloped the surrounding countryside. After a twenty-minute flight and a brief pause in windswept Rio Grande, the captain invited me to the flight deck to share his view of the curving southern tip of the coastline of South America, laid out below, as if on a map. Tiny specks in the Magellan Straits marked the sites of drilling oil rigs, which were the real cause of the dispute over the three islands. My host explained that, apart from the oil beneath the islands in which Argentina claimed a share, the course of the frontier which ran west to east in a line to the north of the islands meant that Argentina was excluded from any rights to the vast territories of Antarctica far to the south. Argentina's early rulers had stupidly relinquished these massive territories without being aware of their later significance. Now she was trying to reclaim her rights by disputing the way in which the frontier between Chile and Argentina had been drawn up in this region. Everything rested on whether the channel ended before or after the three islands. The British Crown had been asked to intervene and had decided in favour of Chile; but this was rejected by Argentina, since she was in the midst of a dispute with Britain over the Falklands and mistrusted everything the British said. So, after many skirmishes and threats of war, the problem had been laid at the door of the Pope.

The captain was convinced of the justice of their cause, but he was less sure about Argentina's economic future. He was a likeable man, with a big sad face. 'No one wants to come to Argentina,' he complained, 'at least, no educated people. It's too politically unstable here, and those that do come only want to settle in Buenos Aires, because everywhere else is so unsophisticated. There is no development in the provinces. But no one can make any money at the moment, anyway, because the present economic policies are simply killing off the small businesses.' His co-pilot had just returned from the British Farnborough air show and they were on their once-a-month taxi service duty flight to keep their hand in. They were mainly employed in administration in Buenos Aires.

My plans to visit Lago Argentino, site of the only glacier in the world which is still growing, fell apart on arrival in Rio Gallegos. Between the time, four days ago, when I bought the ticket on the way south, and my return, the schedules had changed and my flight had now ceased to exist. Refund? Not a chance. Once again, my pilot friends came to the rescue. May I say, friends and readers, that the best way to see the famous Ventisquero Moreno Glacier, is to befriend your airline captain.

It took little to persuade him to 'take some time off', as he put it, and to fly beyond his destination on an eighty-mile diversion to the western corner of the glittering blue Patagonian lake, where the relentlessly moving ice river stretched back up a narrow valley into the Andes. It was a huge, living mass of deeply-ridged pack ice, trapped between two mountains, and it drove inexorably down to the lake shore. At its head, it was forty-five metres high and nearly 1.6 kilometres wide, and it ran out across the lake and up against the rocky shore of a small island opposite, effectively cutting the lake in two. Over a period of ten months every year, the waters built up on the inflow side and when the pressure became too great, they burst through in a deafening monumental explosion to join the waters beyond. All in their path was swept away, including any foolhardy sightseers who strayed too close to the waters' edge. Throughout the year, small icebergs broke off and floated away down the lake, dotting the surface with what, from 3,000 metres, looked like white flecks of foam.

'Back to work,' said the captain, after two circuits of the glacier fields, carrying his confused but delighted passengers back to their destination at Calafate, three quarters of an hour late. In a typical burst of patriotic fervour, one of the passengers, à propos nothing, insisted on passing on to me some vital information. The air at Lago Argentino, I was reliably and proudly informed, was considered by the UN health authorities to be the cleanest in the world! It rated zero impurities and was the air against which all other airs must measure themselves.

The flight continued northwards, hopping from small settlement to small settlement, with twenty-minute stops at each, via Gregores and Perito Moreno, until, with only eight passengers left, we landed at Comodoro Rivadavia. It was a good way to see the Patagonian countryside – a vast expanse of undulating tundra, dotted with small ponds, reflecting the sun, like huge puddles after a heavy rain storm. And all along the western side, was the massive line of snow-clad mountains and glistening blue lakes. Occasional gravel strips of track crossed the landscape from horizon to horizon. At each stop I chatted to the co-pilot. 'Here is nothing but wind and desert,' he said of Gregores, 'and some Welsh sheep farmers.

No one wants to come here.' Then he added accusingly, 'The mountains and Chile steal all the humidity from us.' If all of my intended journey had been to Patagonia, I would have enjoyed the isolation and the chance meetings along the way. But people were so few and far between, that I felt little frustration at the speed with which I was covering ground.

The landscape in and around dusty Comodoro was dotted with preying mantis look-alikes, heads dipping up and down, bent over rectangular troughs filled with water. This was oil country and the pumps were ruthless in their quest for black gold. Nowhere was sacred. In public squares, private front gardens, on islands in the middle of the road, day and night, silently they plunged on. And around them life bustled by in the biggest town of Patagonia, a boom town on the eastern seaboard. Clinging to the steep cliffs, overlooking the town, were the inevitable shanty homes of the underprivileged workers, watching over the shops, bright with consumer wealth, the cruising jean-clad boys and girls, the bowling alleys, gymnasiums, cinemas, and bars, all blossoming below under the protective shadow of the oil boom. Its benefits spread only so far, however, and a walk to the top of the cliff provided an intimate view of life's less glamorous realities among the rudimentary boxes the people there called home. And as always, despite the crushing hardship and poverty in which so many people exist, there were laughing, teasing children flying kites, playing football, asking questions, risking contact. 'Are we nice?' 'Yes,' I said. 'Am I?' 'Yes,' they said. Somehow, man's remarkable capacity to enjoy life always breaks through, which indeed it must if he is to survive with any dignity; yet in some ways, that resilience camouflages the hurt and the oppression and reduces the impact of that poverty. Would our obsessively acquisitive societies feel guiltier if the 'poor' went round with hunched shoulders and miserable defeated faces? Would they do more to ease the burden? Would greater social equality or justice ensue? Doubtful. Thus the often-heard cry 'but just look at the people – they are so happy' comes easily to the lips of the oppressors. But it depends on where, how and when you look. Whether in crushed Bolivia, wretched Sahel, suffering Calcutta, tightly-controlled Kiev or violence-round-the-corner Belfast, the laughter and the joy in the simple things will still burst out. But it makes the suffering no less hard to bear, the misery no less stark.

A group of boisterous young girls playing football on the cliff top were delighted to be photographed. The prettiest was very shy and hid behind her friends, while the youngest one cheekily insisted on the full treatment. 'Photo me, me, me.' They giggled at my halting

Spanish, but they brightened up the day. Batman kites, and even plastic bags on strings fluttered overhead. It was free and light-hearted, but I was still anxious and secretive with my camera, expecting at any moment to feel a military hand on my shoulder. Whatever I did, wherever I went, I felt oddly guilty, that in some way I was transgressing the rules, that I was witnessing something the rulers wished to keep hidden. Military dictatorships have that effect.

Still, here was contact up amongst the shanties. Below it was harder. In the evenings as the 'paseo' took on a more serious beat, it became increasingly obvious that while I was separated by solitariness and lack of language, the young of Comodoro, were just as separated by sex. Sitting in bars, in groups, alone, cruising, walking, the boys passed the girls and the girls passed the boys, watching each other longingly. Cars streamed by, often containing groups of scouting girls. It was common for girls to go out with chaperones, or at best in pairs. Eva and Gladys were parked in their father's pick-up, watching the world walk past, and we fell into a conversation which developed because, like me, they had a Polish father. I was allowed to sit in the cabin with them. Eighteen-year-old Gladys was due to marry her boyfriend who was away skiing. She would, she said, be shot if she were to go out with anyone else. Eva liked a boy but couldn't find a way of letting him know.

There was not a lot to do, they said. The night clubs were too expensive. Most boys worked in oil, and the few girls who worked were usually secretaries. 'Will we be in your book?' asked Gladys. 'If you say something nice!' I said. 'How old are you?' asked Eva. 'Thirty-five,' I said. Shock. 'We thought you were twenty-five.' 'You'll be in my book,' I said. 'Let's go and have a coffee.' But they couldn't go to the smart places because they didn't feel well enough dressed, and they wouldn't be seen dead in the cafe across the road, because it wasn't nice enough. So we just stayed in the van.

Next day, I flew west to the lake district in the Andean foothills, from where I wanted to make a land crossing into Chile.

Bariloche, centre of Argentina's favourite skiing resorts, was a replica of a Swiss mountain village, complete with wooden chalets. It was crowded with teenagers, mostly girls, celebrating the end of school with their classmates on class outings, supervised by indulgent teachers, and financed by doting parents. They were delightful and friendly and very different on holiday from their home-town personas. They insisted on taking me in hand. One day I visited the nature reserves on the Isla Victoria, the largest island in lake Nahuel Huapi, with its unique Arrayan forests, in the

company of thirty, sixteen-year-old girls from Cordoba, all of them
outfitted in the statutory baggy jeans, sun glasses perched atop
perfect coiffures, high heels and dizzy fashionable manners. That
evening I was taken by another class of fifteen girls from Buenos
Aires to the luxury discotheques of Bariloche.

Another day, a third group decided that I must go with them to
ski on Cerro Catedral, overlooking the azur Nahuel Huapi and the
surrounding forests. Although none could ski, they hired or bought
all the latest and most expensive boots and ski suits, simply to go
up to the top on the ski lifts, where they tumbled and slid on their
bottoms gleefully in the snow all afternoon. There was never a
suggestion of them actually skiing; but they did persuade a kindly
Uruguayan boy to lend me his skis for half an hour. Who could
refuse twenty fetching, imploring young girls? And what alert,
thoughtful, lively girls they were. They came from mixed schools,
but as a rule, only two or three of their male classmates would
accompany them on such outings. They overflowed with noisy
curiosity. For hours they would crowd around me to discuss
Britain's attitude to the Falkland Islands, and were horrified when
I suggested that very few Britons even knew where the islands
were, let alone that there was an argument in progress between
Britain and Argentina over sovereignty*. They wanted to discuss
world politics, European attitudes to sex and morality and religion.
They were appalled at what they had read of European behaviour
and they demanded my first-hand accounts and experiences. Those
that were bi-lingual translated for those who couldn't understand.
The scenic wonders of Isla Victoria floated by, irrelevant to our
stimulating conversations. The boys at the beginning showed signs
of interest, hoping to discuss Liverpool FC and the wonders of the
Argentine players Ardiles and Villa, and their heroic contribution
to the British footballing scene. 'What is your name?' they asked.
Then, indicating towards one of the girls, 'You like her, yes?',
nudge, wink. The girls ignored them, and they soon drifted away.
They spoke only Spanish and their interests were limited. But the
interests of their sisters were endless.

Throughout the south, I had been struck by how few boys I saw
making their way to school every morning, and how the streets
thronged with smart uniformed girls of all ages. It seemed that
South America's men were losing out on the educational battle of
the sexes by default. After my early unhappy experiences, I began
to see hope for South America's future; and that future lay in the
hands of her women. At present a girl's career ambitions and
dreams of an independent lifestyle foundered in the face of family
pressure to marry and settle, and were drowned by a male-

dominated society which frowned on too much female freedom and initiative. But the mood was changing as more and more girls began to pursue careers with greater vigour, increasingly confident that they were not alone. They were eager to hear of the European experience, which they recognised as valuable, although they still could not reconcile themselves to its concepts of sexual liberation. This side of women's lib was hard to understand for conventional, catholic seventeen-year-olds. Romantic love, fidelity and virginity before marriage were the bedrock of their lives, but they still questioned and listened with an urge to know everything.

The stiff neo-conservatism of Argentina, the impression of a country at odds with itself and out of step with the world, was sharply contrasted by the beauty, wit and intelligence of these schoolgirls. It was heartening to find that our conversations had made as much of an impression on them as they had on me. A profusion of letters from my newly acquired pen-friends awaited me in London when I arrived home six months later.

Our last night together was undermined by the hitherto unobtrusive head teacher, who issued the instruction that the girls should stay in the hotel for the evening, because she considered that three discotheque outings in a row was enough for any young girl. The boys, however, were given permission to go gambling at the casino.

I caught the early morning bus around the northern shore of the lake, through the wild shadowy forests, up over the mountains and across the border into Chile. I was late for my rendezvous with Feliks, so I had time only to spend an hour photographing in Puerto Montt, the southern terminal point for Chile's land communications, before catching a luxurious pullman bus, complete with uniformed hostesses, for the overnight 1700 kilometre run up to Santiago.

* Britain's failure to recognise the strength of feeling amongst Argentines over the Falkland/Malvinas Islands and to take more seriously the pursuit of an acceptable political solution was a major cause of the South Pacific debacle a year and a half later.

CHAPTER 4   CHILE: under the junta

LONDON–SANTIAGO

Sorrowfully, more, funereally, I am without curiosity whipped along, because already off the Gatwick train some tendon (in my good leg) cracks and, in pain, I follow routines.

The fearsome flight (chopped into hate closeups: Germanic blond giant hems me in with his soft-porn reading matter, bare belly emerges, an unbuttoned robustness) of more hours than bearable to think; but the grand sunrise, countered though by the straining at the port-hole on Rio touch-down for the multi-advertised, unparalleled beauties of the bay – of which no trace; only cloudy drizzle.

I move seats, for the last lap, next to a girl – truly a Miss Latin America lovely – wishing for the elating aura of my descent on Chile to have this demi-goddess as a motto; but she (eighteen-year-old classical singer, half orphan, five languages, Austro-Belgian – and South America only adopted to start new life with torn bag and plaster on her bare foot) departs, also into rain, at Sao Paulo.

I remain almost alone, eye-to-eye with darkly animalistic, tight-knitted (as I imagined those pitiless machos) youngster, who has earlier been trying to pick her up (without any smile) with a coca cola bottle temptation, and who now saw, from a further seat, her and my farewell embrace. I seek comfort therefore within my three-seat lair and, furtively drawing him, ponder the possibilities of vengeance by my first Latin enemy – I presume, the appropriate mood for entering South America.

At the port-hole: we are surely closing on Chile, yet all still flatly polite, agriculture patched and, equal politeness, sown with cottonwool cumulus bundles; but on comes the captain's voice about the Andes. I roll over to the other side and – bizarre magnitudes, convulsing alieness: tightly, defensively, in endlessly gnarled ramparts, stands the rock army – multi-ranked in black depths, unbroken and invincible, topped by white helmeted horizontals under azureness of indifference. Slowly, meaningfully this battling line presses forward (the wide-winged machine static) and mounts upward, the threat, ever closer; then, hard to bear, the massive attack opens its chasms, lifts its cragginess above us – engorges us. But we, the plane as if waking up, leap forth and down and miraculously enter and then slowly, over improbable calm flatness, circle Santiago airport (the Andes retreat and hide in greyness): peopled balconies and randomly spread carpet, redly meagre, rolled out and brush-dusted by busy dots – not for us, but for the president of Brazil. Just the same, some youth greets me, extricates me from commotion and causes, amazingly, my luggage to be passed from hand to hand without (but only just) searchings; I ride into the town through reasonable suburbs along a reasonable roadway, reasonably punctuated by universal hoardings (BIENVENIDO SANTIAGO DE CHILE) and tele-poles – as anywhere else; but to fly to it over half the world . . .

In time of civil calm, oppression does not walk the streets announcing its existence, and the streets of Santiago showed little outward sign of the tragedy of the last seven years. Arriving by bus in Chile, the change in temperament and attitude after Argentina was striking. The warmth of the people contrasted sharply with the edgy insecurity of their neighbours. The horrors of the past decade had not destroyed the ordinary Chileans' commitment to moderate European-style liberalism. Only their heavy-handed, brutal military rulers lacked the Chilean sense of intellectual freedom and debate. Physically, Chileans tended to be smaller, darker and swarthier than their fine-featured, paler, good-looking Argentine cousins. But they were also earthier and more sure of themselves.

The landscape around Santiago also showed a softness, with the green rolling fields of the central valley backed by the snow-covered peaks bordering Argentina and separating it from the dry Patagonian wastes beyond. Most Chileans lived in this predominantly agricultural central section of Chile, while less than one per cent braved the ocean-lashed, inaccessible southern third of the country. Not many more chose to live in the northern desert of Atacama. Chile's resources were inadequate and the country was not self-sufficient, relying heavily on imports. The military government, like the one in Argentina, was following a rigid monetarist policy, which had left thousands of small Chilean businesses destitute. But the policy had produced a consumer boom in the smart shopping centres of Santiago, so that the upper middle class stood behind the military dictator, Pinochet. However, even his supporters resented the restrictions being placed on Chilean freedoms, and the wording of the 1980 referendum seeking a mandate from the people, was regarded as an insult. 'Many of us voted "No", because we are an educated and sophisticated people, and we felt we were being treated like children,' said one society woman. 'We were given two choices only. We were invited to vote for him or against him, which meant, in his terminology, a vote for military rule or for chaos.' But he still drew sixty-five per cent of the vote.

Feliks had been in Santiago a bare day when I arrived and he had not been idle. Already he was caught up in meetings and receptions. We booked a double room at the traditional Foresta hotel. Chilean friends in London had directed us to a variety of interesting people, from artists and intellectuals to a member of the four-man ruling Junta. We were assigned an official from the foreign office, Bernardo. He was a cultured Europhile, who had spent many years in European diplomatic missions, and he became a good friend, leading us to the most unexpected and intimate corners of Chilean life, taking to heart our professed desire to avoid the normal tourist attractions.

Another Chilean friend, Carlos, also anxious to show us the full range of Santiago life, guided me one evening to the seamiest side of town. He complained bitterly about how the puritanical militarists had dampened the natural Chilean zest for life, how curfews, car bans after two in the morning, and harassment in the red light districts had had an inhibiting effect. 'People are scared to express themselves.' He pretended coyly not to know exactly where the disapproved of places were, saying, 'It's so long since I came.' But he always went directly to the spot.

La Carlina, particularly, was an off-limits transvestite club in the roughest part of downtown Santiago, the only bright light in a dingy winding road through an industrial area. La Carlina, herself, was reputed to have retired to the South of France, having established her renowned venue. A small group stood outside the entrance, and a slim blonde in a blue catsuit broke away, came over and led us inside. She was quite spectacular, the star performer, with thick hair falling over her shoulders and a lovely face, with only a subtle touch of make-up, which was unusual, since thick, exaggerated layers of cosmetic paint were an integral part of the business. She appraised me with a cool haughty stare, decided I was not a normal punter and left me to her more voluptuous, jolly friend. Inside, other less attractive transvestites waited for customers, but it was a quiet night. Both our friends were utterly convincing as women and seemed keen to involve us in their favourite pas-de-deux. We had hardly the time to order a drink, before they ushered us into a room off the main corridor. While Carlos discussed prices with the icy blonde, her seductive partner adopted more direct means of persuasion with me. They offered a show in which they would perform for us, describing graphically what they proposed to do. At no small extra cost we could also take part. Carlos declined but we accepted their invitation to return the next night with Feliks for a party to celebrate the birthday of one of the 'girls'. On our way, we got a colourful 'alternative' guided tour from Carlos.

Santiago enjoyed a rich variety of red light districts. In one street of brothels, the girls sat in the open ground-floor windows of the multi-coloured houses. Potential customers prowled up and down while taxis waited for them, and young boys noisily dispensed hot coffee from large portable urns. The girls, old and young, all sizes and shapes, some with strong Indian features, some very European, held shouted conversations from window to window and across the street. They were a cheerful, good-humoured lot, that is until I produced my camera. Then, as proved often to be the case, thay began cursing and protesting loudly, until I put the thing away. At the same time, they struck funny, outrageous poses for Feliks, delighted and flattered by his interest. They clamoured round to see the drawings. I envied Feliks his chosen medium.

Although photography was my work, there were times when I disliked the process intensely. My camera appeared as a rude intrusive weapon, and separated me from the scene I was trying to record, when what I really wanted was to get closer to it. The camera caused consternation and resentment. People adopted stiff, unnatural postures or covered themselves with their hands, or in some cases, threw things at me. Felik's drawings on the other hand, won their hearts and their interest. His was an observable, creative activity with which people could identify and which they could share. They could admire the way the picture took shape and marvel at the artist's dexterity. But taking a photograph meant exactly what it was; it took something away. Often I tried to keep the hated instrument concealed, bringing it out only when I thought a situation had mellowed enough for it to be accepted. At other times, while wandering the streets, I would try, while on the move, to tear off quick shots, from the hip so to speak, without people noticing, hoping to capture the spontaneity of a scene. Then

"La Carlina" SANTIAGO

Transvestites' club, Santiago

I would ask permission, often refused, to photograph, in order to repeat the shot with the correct exposure and focus, in case the first attempt had failed. Invariably these second shots were artificial and awkwardly posed. But Feliks coveted my photography for its immediacy, the swiftness of its action and the accuracy of the image.

In another street of slum houses, old, slovenly matrons and wasted transvestites vied with each other for customers, opening car doors to pleasure their customers there and then, while feeling all the time for bulging pockets to pick.

The well-born Chileans affected distaste towards all these girls but used them constantly. They were after all a brash exuberant lot and most of the streets of the red light districts of South America, and there were many, were unpretentious and full of atmosphere. They lacked the cynical sophistication of the Europeans and North Americans, and having committed themselves to a life on the street, seemed determined to try and get some fun out of it.

The La Carlina birthday party was memorable. The marvellous blonde had swapped her blue catsuit for a flowing black gown and smouldered ravishingly across the room. At intervals throughout the evening she disappeared with customers to a back room, reappearing a few minutes later unruffled. The place was packed with gays and straights, old and young, in costume and out, and the mood was warm and happy. One huge, broad-shouldered, fierce transvestite, stunningly ugly with her hair severely swept back in a bun, became enamoured of Feliks; but her glowering threatening stance was pure show and she proved to be a sweet and attentive friend. And how we all danced, and ate, and drank pisco until we could barely stand. And when we thought we could take no more, the lights went down and the show began. For openers, our ugly friend put on an act that throbbed with energy. The master of ceremonies introduced each act with a well-studied imitation of the clipped, measured, precise voices of the best known television and radio announcers. She was enthusiastically received. The girls wore shimmering, revealing outfits and their dancing was sweaty and sexy. Each performer dared to outdo the previous act and as a finale, the son of the manageress, in full drag, did a comic turn that brought the house down. Even to the non-Spanish speakers, his mannerisms and delivery were superb. Here was uninhibited South American flair obstinately surviving under the most restricting and stifling circumstances, which provided one of the most spontaneous and uplifting moments of our trip.

On another occasion, at one of the two burlesque shows in town, again on the outer fringes of respectable society, the strippers were gloriously inept, the choreography a joy of mis-timing and inelegance, and the girls homely and friendly, rather than provocative and alluring. The small audiences were loyally supportive, urging the ill-assorted performers to even greater feats of unimaginable incompetence. The leading singing star, however, was a buxom, impressive old trouper. But the highlight at both venues were the outrageous comic sketches, crude, enthusiastic and politically irreverent. One comic, in a take-off of Pinochet's oft-repeated television 'call to the people', pulled out the waistband of his trousers, looked down and mimicked encouragingly the overexposed slogan 'VAMOS BIEN, MANANA MEJOR' (It's going well, tomorrow it'll be better). The sight of my camera served to bring the very best out of them.

In front of our old-fashioned but graceful hotel in the centre of Santiago, rose the steep, shapely hill of Santa Lucia, thickly wooded and brimful day and night with courting couples. From the watch tower of Hidalgo Castle at the top, you could see the city below, spreading east to the rich neighbourhood of Providencia along the Mapocho river and west past the commercial centre to the poorer districts. On a terrace in front of the castle gate, the 'Libertad' flame burned continually, where only a few weeks before a duty policeman had been assassinated. In the early evenings, young children played amongst the self-absorbed lovers, and single men salaciously pursued their solitary, voyeuristic prowling. Across the valley, on top of San Cristobal hill, stood a huge statue of the Virgin, keeping a catholic eye on her unruly adherents. The white peaks of the Andes to the east sometimes provided an imposing backdrop to the city, but the bowl in which Santiago rests was generally muggy with pollution and smog and the full splendour of the view was a rare treat.

General Pinochet, Chile's president, was revelling in his first diplomatic coup since he took power. The Brazilian president, João Baptista Figueiredo had accepted an invitation for a state visit, the first to little Chile by a foreign head of state since the coup, and Pinochet was making the most of it. It was very important to him. He was still smarting from the humiliation he received at the hand of President Marcos of the Philippines, when at Marcos' invitation he had gone to Manila. But at the last moment, Marcos had changed his mind, and Pinochet had to sit in the plane while the two sides negotiated the next step. He was not allowed to disembark and in shame flew back to Easter Island off the coast of Chile, where he spent a long week brooding over this public snub. Back at home strenuous efforts were made by his supporters to prepare a triumphant national welcome. The kids were given a school holiday to attend the procession and the foreign minister, who had set up the visit, lost his job. When the delicate egos of Latin dictators were bruised, heads had to roll. I heard that the Paraguayan chief of police, who had been responsible for my internment in Asuncion, had had his face publicly slapped by Stroessner, and had been subsequently 'disappeared', for failing to track down Somoza's killers. After all Stroessner's prestige was at stake so someone had to pay.

At the handsome Musée de Bellas Artes, Santiago's gathered illuminati, well-heeled and fur-draped, awaited the arrival of the two presidential wives. They came late, and after meeting one or two dignataries, stood stiffly and glassy-eyed, with fixed plastic smiles on their heavily made-up faces, while speeches of welcome were read out. They gave the appearance of two painted wax effigies and to compound the impression, neither replied to the greetings. Afterwards everyone trouped upstairs for pisco sours and fruit cocktails. The talk was of the cocktail party variety, but even so, people were prepared still to discuss politics, albeit in a muted fashion. Middle-class people seemed to agree that living standards were better than they had been under Allende, and that at least you could now walk the streets safely at night, as long as you were on the right political side. But the reasons given for Allende's failure varied enormously. Some said that he tried to do too much too quickly, without a proper mandate from the country. It was not that his policies were so bad, said others, but he frightened the United States into withdrawing all economic support and persuading the international agencies, the IMF and the World Bank, to pull the rug from under him by withdrawing their grants. There was little he could do in the face of such a united campaign. Why Russia did not come to his aid with economic assistance was not clear, but it was likely that the Kremlin regarded the United States as unchallengeable in the area, and Allende as a lost cause. I was even told in all seriousness that Allende and Castro had been in the throes of a passionate homosexual affair. There were pictures, I was told; he simply had to go. The character assassinators had a field day.

A completely different view was expressed to me by a middle-aged teacher who stopped me in the street the next day as I was photographing the prettiest colonial district in Santiago and he engaged me in a discussion ostensibly about photography. But few Chileans could avoid talking politics for long. Checking that no one could overhear us, he urged me not to ignore the true situation in Chile. 'There is terrible poverty and hardship here. You should know that there is cruel oppression.' He said that the repression and brutality suffered by Chileans since 1973 was the military's response to the first democratically elected marxist government in a country which had established the first Latin American communist party on the continent in 1918, whose people had always been more liberal and better educated than elsewhere in South America, and who had been irrevocably politicised by the recent governments of social reform led first by Frei and later by Allende. 'They both gave Chileans a sense of identity and pride,' he believed. 'Until Allende, I had never questioned the privileges of my class. We treated our servants like slaves; we thought that if people were poor it was because they were lazy or drunkards. Under Allende, Chile was beginning to grow up.'

In the basement of the museum was an exhibition of paintings by two of Chile's leading artists, Rodolpho Opazo and Ricardo Irrarazival, and when they heard that Feliks was in Santiago, they arranged a small dinner at Rodolpho's studio. They both complained about Chile's isolation from the mainstream of European art, and spoke enviously of the 'great museums' of the northern hemisphere. Feliks gently scolded them for assuming their inferiority and needing European inspiration, instead of concentrating their attention on developing their own individual talents.

A CONTINENT OF STATUES

Is it right for me not to know anything about this – possibly the grandest statuary-folly ever (Rome's Victor Emmanuel memorial? But does it not fall into the mausoleum category?): its viewing contains the harshness of the Andes as the background, the vast city-bred neon announcement 'SIEMENS', whatever it may mean, the diminishing perspectives of bronze horsemen interrupted by a shapeless modern 'form' and closed by some obelisk or other – fossils of past commemorations. And the immense IT: sprawling, in the manner of the untrammelled Santa Lucia hill, this, albeit many-symbolled monument, washed all over by mini-waterfalls fought by the upward-reaching vegetational vigour. It has an onward intention, stated by a vessel's prow somewhat led by water-stamping superbeings (perhaps female) some winged yet part-submerged, and out of the mid-deck of this near-craft there rises a rock surmounted by the handsomest naked immense male (though unfairly G-string-equipped) shouldering a banner and Roman-saluting distances of planted greenery and blue-tinted mountains – accompanied by another, smaller (but well-muscled) one, rather outshone; and more, after the bare length of obedient waterfall activity (yet there are also at far edges the counter-demonstrations impossible to interpret – the dolphins rising from the floods and spouting BACK at the hero-in-the-centre strong protest streams of water), a surprise – a calm, seated male, nude again (but covered in places), not pensive, but rather a reserve player waiting his turn on the plinth. After this, rounding off the

scene of extravagancies, an ornithoid ending: either a symbol of deserved glory
or memento mori, or both, as they most often pair off: a perched eagle (or
vulture?), wings spread, threatening (the reserve player?) or doing the job of
an emblem rounding up this colossal, one guesses, allegory – of Chile? of South
America? of the past, the future?

Would some meaning come out of obscurity, if I added that I shared the
bench at the foot of this enstoned eloquence (and, no mistake, an impressive
creation) with a young mother and child. They appeared to be taking all this
(and presumably the political present) for granted; this was their daily walk
and rest; the mother's face was finely boned in the mestizo handsomeness,
neither melancholy nor resigned, its mood, the gravity of sheer living.

General Matthei, commander of the airforce, was considered by
Chileans to be the most intelligent member of the four-man ruling
junta. We had an introduction to him from London, and he invited
us to tea at the central government offices in Diego Portales. This
building was in temporary use, while the official Moneda, bomb
damaged during the coup, was being repaired, and it housed all
three representatives of the ruling armed forces. It resembled far
more a heavily-defended fortress than a seat of government, and
security checks were very strict. While we waited in an ante room
for our meeting, a stern Germanic-looking, middle-aged man,
straight backed, in a white polo-necked sweater, paced up and
down. 'Definitely a military man; probably a gun runner or a
mercenary from the nazi era,' we thought, as we sized him up. He
went in first, but his meeting was short. Ours took longer. 'Who,'
asked Feliks, 'was the gentleman you saw just now?' 'He is the
leader of a ballet company due to tour Chile soon,' replied Matthei.

Matthei was formal and polite; a thin, pale man in his fifties, he
was every inch a military figure in full uniform. We talked about
our journey and he began to show interest when we mentioned the
BBC film. At first he declared his deep distrust of the BBC, but he
thought it was still a pity that they had not seen fit to include a
Chile sequence. We explained that it had not been possible because
the crew were dividing their timetable between two films. 'Very
well then,' he said suddenly, 'I shall give you all the facilities you
need for filming. My assistant here, Colonel Jahn will supply you
with aeroplanes, helicopters and a film crew.'

His offer took us very much by surprise. We had no desire to
involve ourselves in a public relations exercise on behalf of the
Chilean government, and we insisted that we prepare a memor-
andum establishing our freedom to film where and what we
wanted, listing the locations and subjects we would wish to cover.
We explained too, that we had no control over the final cut of the

film, nor could we guarantee that any of the material would definitely be used. A telephone call to our director in London confirmed that we could give no guarantees, and would film on an ad hoc basis only. We were surprised when the shooting outline we produced was accepted. Although we were not planning a 'hard' news film about Chilean repression, we were still determined to record our personal view of Chile and no one else's. But we hadn't reckoned with Colonel Jahn. Even though he was present throughout the discussion, he proved to be a hindrance from start to finish.

Ultimately, although we did film and travel extensively for a week, we spent half the time sitting waiting and trying to reorganise the mess that Jahn left us with every day. When we had finished in Chile the material was sent back to London for us by their foreign office while we continued our journey. But they failed to include the small amount of sound we had managed to get the one time we had a recordist and despite repeated requests, it was never sent, thus making the Chilean footage virtually unusable. One of the first days filming went something like this and the rest were little different.

Thursday: eight in the morning: meet to start filming in Santiago. Eight-thirty: cameraman, our third in three days, arrives without equipment; while our liaison man, Lieutenant Pabst, goes to fetch it, I explain to new cameraman what we are trying to do; Bernardo arrives distraught, he is being taken off the assignment. While we try to persuade Bernardo's boss to change his mind, Pabst returns with five rolls of film to last us for six days and begins to phone for more, and to arrange the interview with Pinochet that had supposedly been set up by Matthei the day before. (It never happened.) Feliks must go to the ministry with Bernardo to placate the troublesome boss, so we decide I will film while they are away to save time. They leave. Then Pabst says, 'Oh dear, I forgot; all the equipment is in their car.' We try to locate the car and get the driver to return with the equipment. Another hour lost. It is now one o'clock and the morning has gone. As the car returns, the cameraman remembers that he has forgotten his light meter. 'Take a cab and hurry,' I plead. At one-thirty all is ready. At three we are due to record an interview with two artists at the museum. 'Sound?' says the cameraman. 'You want sound?' The good colonel is exasperated that we want sound as well, and is slow to respond to my suggestion that film without sound, particularly for an interview, is like a car without petrol. 'Why?' says Bernardo. 'Why do they offer so much and then make it so difficult. It gives such a bad impression.' The foreign office comes to the rescue and provides a sound man, who will meet us at the museum at three. So at two o'clock, six hours after our scheduled start, we hit the road, without syncronised sound, without camera assistant. The sound man speaks no English. And he in fact is the last sound man we have for the rest of the week, despite daily frustrated telephone calls to Jahn. Thus the pattern was set and continued in varying degrees of intensity throughout the week.

Another problem was communication within the team. At first I was unaware of how little information was getting through to the various members of our little troupe. Part of the difficulty was that we would forget to translate for the cameraman or the driver and this led to utter chaos, some hilarious moments, but more often, loss of tempers all round. As time went on, I found myself pushed more and more into directing the operation and was spending most of the time making sure that everyone knew what was happening at any given moment, having to insist, to the annoyance of all, that everything be repeated in both languages ad-infinitum. Yet, constantly, someone would mis-hear the simplest instructions, suggestions or bits of information, which would lead to the inevitable farrago. On reflection, all the ingredients were there for epic scenes of high farce and we should have turned the cameras on ourselves. But at the time we were driven to distraction.

Bernardo, sweet, friendly, vague man that he was, was the worst offender. There he was, our main interpreter, with the frustrating habit of not listening, of wafting away into daydreams, never translating simple but vital instructions for the non-English speaking members of our group, or for the various people we had picked up on the way and were trying to film.

Feliks and I were going through a few teething problems too, in these first days of our journey together. I felt that he often reacted as if he had heard everything but then showed by his subsequent actions that he had not. 'It's very frustrating,' I pointed out, 'when even we, who speak the same language, seem to misunderstand each other.' 'I prefer to leave all the organising to you,' he replied; 'but I've also grown into the habit of focusing only on what attracts me for my drawing, and I shut out the rest. So I purposely don't listen to a lot of what's going on. It's distracting for me.' That, of course, though understandable, didn't help matters much. 'I've got things I would rather be doing too,' I pointed out. 'I don't see for instance why I have to waste time providing you with detailed travel arrangements, bookings and confirmations of reservations. We don't need them and besides, nothing we plan ahead for, here in South America, can ever be relied on.' 'But these anxieties of mine are only slight,' chided Feliks. 'I'm still remembering how you took me a few months ago to Heathrow Airport instead of Gatwick for a flight to Paris, and how you had all our notes stolen at Victoria Station. I'm just being cautious.'

The general tensions created by all these problems, put considerable strain on the first few days of our journey together. I had to reconcile myself to the growing realisation that this journey could never reproduce the informal drifting of my earlier overland journey through Africa. That uninhibited, spontaneous and solitary trek up the Nile had been pure adventure with something new and unexpected every day. But this time I was tied to filming responsibilities, a travelling companion, book contracts and travel schedules and I was beginning to bridle at the loss of freedom. I found myself bowing to other people's plans, staying in costly hotels, getting involved in tetchy arguments that distracted us from the passing world outside. We spent too much time planning and discussing, and too little time doing. Our travelling routines seemed to be proving more different than I had imagined.

Feliks felt these frustrations too. 'I also have travelled all my life on my own,' he told me, 'preferring the outward looking of the loner, to the face to face dialoguing with a companion, backs turned to the passing scene. But South America, hanging over me as a continent unexplored, has perhaps come too late. Hence this journey could only materialise engineered by you, with me, which never happened before, playing second fiddle. I probably feel quite sore about that.'

Nevertheless, Feliks still liked to provoke things. He also preferred to descend on specific places, on incidents, recording the action on the spot, and then move on, filling his sketchbooks at speed and using the time in between those events to transfer the essence of the drawings into large scale paintings back in his studio. I, on the other hand, enjoyed the journeys in between the events, the long twisting roads over changing landscapes, the miles in between when usually very little happened, but during which I made friends, stayed, unobtrusively, in curious places, and had adventures on a small day-to-day basis. Feliks chose to be driven by well-briefed locals, so that he could concentrate on drawing even while on the move. He wanted to have the uninteresting mechanics of moving done for him, and this, I thought, tied us too much to the whims and desires of a host. Thus, because the general offered the world, flying us hither and thither, we relinquished some of the control over our freedom of movement and decision-making, and became victim to the vagaries of unreliable or capricious third parties.

THE FATHER-SON WATERSHED

This voyage, extra-difficult, framed-in by prescribed footsteps of 'received ideas';
yes, Daniel finds his explorations through hardships and human encounters,
which instantly grow as events into his life. I always pursued/participated in
history-in-the making; my travels were questing conflicts, changes, restlessness of
the global map (to the inclusion of border-line 'ceremonials', marking decline/
collapse), not its static or archaeological geography. Hence this time, I battle
ceaselessly against being subjected to the predictable.

A contributary and significant factor to the initial mood was Feliks'
health. He had slipped getting off the train at Gatwick Airport,
loaded down with bags carefully designed for easy carrying, and
that combined with the uncomfortable twenty-hour flight from
London, produced severe pain in both his leg and his neck and a
general feeling of below-form weakness. Instead of realising these
as passing aches, I became anxious about the advisability of setting
out on the immense project at all. But I dared not share these
thoughts with Feliks. Simply driving around Santiago's bumpy
streets caused him excruciating pain and I had to hold him firmly
in his seat from behind. 'I am not an invalid,' protested Feliks. We
both maintained a charade of false chirpiness, neither wanting the
other to sense our worries. Later, back in London, he told me that
he had been determined not to be a burden, and he confided that,
prior to his departure, friends had tried to dissuade him from
embarking on the trip altogether. 'Daniel is pursuing his own
selfish purpose,' they said. 'He will kill you.'

I too had had dire warnings from similar prophets of doom,
whenever I had mentioned the project, all trying to undermine our
resolve to go ahead. We only compared notes about this when we
were safely ensconced back in England.

After a few days however when the effects of the flight had worn
off, interest in the project took the place of worry and we warmed to
our task. Nothing deterred Feliks from producing a mass of
exceptional drawings.

Wherever he goes, Feliks makes things happen around him, and
South America was no exception. Although he was not widely
known there, it soon became apparent that his arrival had caused
quite a stir, and doors opened as the word spread, and the trip was
made against a backcloth of admiring enthusiasm.

We had to face the problem of being father and son, established
older statesman and pushy new boy. I bristled whenever I thought
I was being downgraded and treated like a companion/helper,
playing second fiddle to the master, and I reacted over-sensitively.
I felt that he unwittingly expected me to defer to his wishes and

service his needs, which in the circumstances was not unreasonable, since we were alone in an alien world and dependent on each other. However, over and above the necessary, I reckoned that he liked to have his own way. But then so did I. We were not yet collaborating equals.

Eager for us to cover everything, he would press me to photograph this, check out that, listen to a conversation there, write notes for him, regardless of the possibility that I might already be photographing something else, or had considered and rejected a particular shot. I argued that I, too, was involved in serious exchanges and that what he was doing was not necessarily always more important. On one occasion, at a party, he wanted me to write some notes for him in his book and he called me insistently away from a conversation I was having with the leader of the outlawed Christian Democratic Party, who had just returned from a prison term in the north and who was the first overtly dissident person we had met. I expressed my irritation later. 'That was a valuable conversation I was having.' 'I think there was a misunderstanding,' he answered. 'I sometimes get anxious that you may go too far. I feel too that you may be missing something of importance. I get trapped into offering shallow, father-child advice, because I don't know you so well and I see occasional childishnesses which automate dormant reactions. You dispense your energies in "charming", which eats up large portions of attentiveness and time, leaving too little for reflection and taking in experiences. You over-use the telephone.'

'I'm trying to live this journey fully,' I countered. 'That's the way I am. I'm not here to "study" South America as an academic exercise; it doesn't matter to me if I "miss" something, because I'm involved in something else. I want to go out and do, not sit in the hotel making notes. There'll be time for that when we get home.'

We accused each other of sulking and of resorting to occasional temper outbursts, rather than discussing in considered and calm harmony. We were supposed, after all, to be discovering and reacting to each other, as well as to the world outside. But we were two headstrong individualists, both determinedly solo travellers, and initially we were reluctant to compromise.

However, sons should be attentive to their father's needs, and I sometimes failed in that filial duty. Besides, his demands were not malevolent, not frivolous, and it took me quite a long time to appreciate that. We had not spent a long period together for many years, and we were discovering each other anew. The birth pangs of establishing a different relationship were painful indeed.

Gradually, we began to stabilise and adapt to each other's

quirks, because we recognised over and above all the irritations, the enormous benefit and pleasure we could derive from the joint venture. What we lost as solitary travellers, we gained in the dual view of everything, in the exchange of ideas and the shared observations. I enjoyed watching him at work, proud at the way people crowded round, marvelling at his speed and accuracy. I valued the depth and perceptiveness of his view of human behaviour, and his unexpected theories, wholly original and thought-provoking; and his horror of the mundane and the cliché was invigorating, and exercised me to the full.

Daniel-watching is high-tension theatre; his is a heroic mould and purpose – his able-bodied ever-preparedness and his Homeric head-neck fit his ever-search, ever-taking challenges, against his inattentive impatience, often surfacing – naturally, within the limiting world around him.

He is in permanent haste, seeking out and running with equal dedication several parallel races: athletic – social justice – appetites of all kinds – camaraderie – heights and distances – hardships . . .

He presses towards fullness of life, infuriated by red light for him-green light for other traffics, selecting at speed – if the alternatives are the mountain peak or tasting the subtleties of the passage – the former.

Of course, I have been, and still am, susceptible to diversional appetites, and may search for and find similarities between us. But in contrast, I recognise that I tend to be pedestrian. And so, when with him, I consciously stand back in recognition of his top-form manhood, hold back my speech and my actions, do not stir my latent aggressiveness (in the earlier days of the journey with some peevishness); and I appreciate the attention directed at him mainly.

But, in consequence, he most often does not comprehend my intention, and takes over my territory, assuming my stepping-down a weakness, mere sybaritism, signs of old age . . .

Then, unavoidably, now and again, when I think I see a mistake or omission on his part, I break through with advice, which he then takes (having framed me into limitations imagined by him) as impositions.

And tied to this the last consequence of his commendably aggressive spirit: he has to be without doubts – chinks in his fighter's armour – so he tends to put blame in difficulties on others (mostly me). Thus it may be said, that he lacks detachment, that is a sense of humour (though plentiful in high spirits). But let's be clear: I say amen to all this, since these are the prerogatives of men of action.

At a dinner on our last night in Santiago, we were invited to a meeting of Cien, a society of intellectuals and friends who gathered twice monthly at the prosperous but 'civilised', modest but grand suburban villa of Hernan and Carmen Edwards, to discuss esoteric subjects about Chilean culture and history. They were academics, architects, musicians, artists, writers and poets, and they were determined to portray Chile to us as a culturally and artistically unique nation, superior in every way to her neighbours. The dean of the catholic university, who presided over the meeting, explained why he thought Chile was so special in the context of South America. 'Because we are cut off from the world by vast mountain chains, by desert and oceans, we have had to fend very much for ourselves. And it is partly due to this isolation that we have wanted to maintain close links with Europe. Furthermore, because we have only a very small Indian population, we are a very homogeneous people.'

Such chauvinism was universally expressed in every country we visited, but in Chile's case, I thought, with slightly more justification. Here, though, their intellectual conceit emerged most tellingly, when they discussed the merits of a new book on aristocratism in Chile, written by one of their women members. They took it for granted that they were all part of that aristocratic elite, displaying a snug self importance, which placed most of them almost unconsciously above the uncomfortable need to adopt any troublesome or unacceptable position on the political state of their beloved country. They eschewed both Allende and the junta regime. We filmed and recorded our meeting with them, but the non-arrival of the sound back in London rendered the sequence meaningless.

Unfortunately for us, their meetings concentrated somewhat pedantically upon vague historical references to Chile's past, architectural development in late eighteenth century Santiago for example, and studiously avoided controversial contemporary themes. A lady anthropologist sang to her own guitar accompaniment, her latest clutch of folklore songs, brought recently from a remote area of Chile.

When we asked their advice on the locations and subjects that we should pursue in our film, they responded with long dull lists of archaeological sites and touristic attractions. But one man urged us to visit Arica in the far north, which, in his view, had the most spectacular scenery in the country. 'I should know,' he added wryly, 'I've spent three, three-month periods of exile there in the last four years.'

We left them to their discussion and went to film the burlesque shows downtown, and later to Regines, where only Feliks was allowed to draw ('I have exclusive customers here,' said the manager; 'you cannot film. I do not wish to upset them.'). Three months later, I read that political activists had bombed the club into oblivion.

Our filming expedition took us all over Chile. The tumbling living hillsides of Valparaiso, facing out over the Pacific Ocean, were a multi-coloured patchwork quilt of decaying wooden shacks, corrugated shelters and fine colonial homes that had seen better days. Drying laundry fluttered from the windows. Valparaiso provided an evocative link between nineteenth century South America and the present. Five miles down the coast was modern Vina del Mar, the fashionable high rise, high cost resort of which Chileans were so proud, but which left us cold. It was the exuberant, tightly-packed port of Valparaiso, with its noisy sailor bars and teeming brothel life, its funicular railways, or Ascensores, and steep, winding, cobbled streets, its compact fishing community and the dramatic sweep of the bay which delighted us.

The squares were filled day and night with flirting teenagers, sailors on the prowl, children skating, balloons fluttering and families taking their daily stroll. A lay preacher stirred the crowds with his oratory, moving from street corner to street corner, shadowed by his faithful, guitar strumming congregation and a growing stream of converts. Opposite him, the yellow-fronted '7 Mirrors' brothel, its rude reputation legendary amongst the sailors who travelled the west coast of South America, was not yet open for business. The middle-aged proprietress, a cigarette hanging from her lower lip, promised girls and boys and rooms to rent by the hour, and floor shows and bacchanalian scenes – 'but you'll have to wait until we open at midnight.'

Our next foray was south by six-seater Piper Chieftain airforce plane to Temuco, centre of Chile's 20,000-strong pure-blooded Araucanian Indian population. Here, too, were the firmly-entrenched descendants of the early German settlers who had come to Valdivia, Osorno and Puerto Montt over a century before. The seething market, like markets all over the world, was a profusion of colour and noise and extrovert stall-holders. The local mestizo people demanded to be photographed and posed extravagantly. But in the square, on the other side of the road, there was a very different atmosphere. The Indians, who had come to town to sell their precious livestock, refused to be pictured.

Panting, terrified sheep, their feet tied together, lay on their sides in the hot noonday sun, while humourless dead-eyed Indian owners negotiated their fates with the town slicksters. Ducks and chickens too, their legs also bound, flapped sporadically, resigned to die. The crippling heat and squalor of their last hours seemed a cruel addition to their suffering, but the humiliation of their condition reflected the experience of their owners. Exploited by local merchants and despised by the mixed blood mestizo town dwellers, the Indians were still the focus of attention when visitors came to Temuco, much to the aggravation of the local smarties. Nevertheless, the Indians position in society was not an enviable one. 'Whenever Chile goes to war,' one local youth told me, 'the Indians are always pushed into the front line.'

'It's so ugly and smelly here,' complained Bernardo, covering his nose with a silk handkerchief. 'This is not interesting.'

Later in the day, a helicopter swept us out across the green rolling hills around Temuco, eastwards towards the snow-covered Cordilleras and the smoking volcanoes on the distant horizon. Below us, people scurried out of farmhouses to stare up at the thundering machine. As we swooped and circled and hovered, the flight crew whooped with delight, enjoying the exhilarating sense of their power. All this conjured up for me vivid images of US flying gunships devastating the Vietnamese countryside. That monstrous sensation of superhuman power was irresistible, dangerously seductive, and it was depressingly easy to see how men could become enflamed with an irrational urge to destroy.

Felik's reaction was different, and he recalled his Vietnam experience. 'For the officers particularly, it was like blood sport, and they performed like birdmen of prey, on a jungle safari hunt. They commanded a wide range of the luxurious gadgetry that men love, and a wide range of possible moves and encounters. Theirs was high level supremacy. When I dared to suggest that it was also low level hazard, they were hurt in their sporting fair-play hearts. On the ground, the VC is superior, they said defensively.'

People scattered as we came in to land and I felt positively shamefaced at the style of our arrival. It was not the most effective way of meeting people on their own terms, in an 'atmosphere of mutual trust and understanding'. The encounter was brief and uncomfortable. I was urged to 'go and mix with people, you're so good at it', so it could be filmed; and there was a lot of patronising talk about 'simple peasants' and 'lower class' and an overriding feeling of 'them' and 'us'. While my preferred way was to slip by unobtrusively, as much as possible on equal footing, (although, in truth, that could never be), without making value judgements, without pushing myself forward, without 'studying people' or summing up the encounters, our crass, disruptive crash-bang visit was boorish. But in Feliks' view, such a village, inaccessible as it was, had given us something, however polluted, so ultimately it was worth it.

The incident demonstrated perfectly why I like to travel alone, differently from the way Feliks travelled. Unaccompanied, you were responsible only for yourself, and your own behaviour, and you survived or fell by your own attitudes, your own perception of a situation, your own ability to read it right. I valued the encounters with the people I met for what they were – friendships, and did not regard them primarily as subject matter for my work. The journey for me was an accumulation of experiences.

This was a problem that most photographer/journalists encountered at some time in their careers and Feliks and I had discussed the dilemma before. Should the reporter intervene in an incident, try to prevent a summary execution for example, or should he record it? The journalist as maker, or recorder of history. Feliks did not see himself as a reporting journalist, but as an artist performing 'his grave duty as witness of his time, in his medium, bearing testimony within history'. Other journalists could be motivated either by ideological commitment or lucrative sensation seeking, into giving prominence to an event. But too often personal feelings dictated my reactions and I would usually miss out on a story altogether by getting involved. Either that or I made myself scarce.

Set in the heart of the Andean chain was Mount Villarica, a still active volcano, smoking amiably. At its summit, the crater rim was broken down on one side, and the snow around it was charred and darkened by recent outpourings. A plume of smoke drifted straight up into the calm air. Twice, we circled sixty metres above the threatening beast, peering down into the deep black hole. Then we turned north west, away from the snow, away from the lush green countryside of central Chile and headed towards the dry brown wastes of the Atacama desert.

La Serena stood trapped between the desert and the sea, a neat, pretty coastal town, made up of two-storey colonial wooden houses. There we rendezvoused with a taciturn old 'elquino', a native of the Elqui river valley, who took us up into the wild barren hills that rose out of the desert behind the town. He drove us in his swaying, battered truck, across grey-brown, dusty, scrub-covered terrain, along narrow, winding, gravel tracks to Andocollo, a tiny gold-mining mountain village, where once a year at Christmas, a special festival was performed. But on this October day, the whole village had been asked to replay their famous parade for special honoured guests. Us.

As the rehearsal was about to begin, a long funeral procession, led by grim-faced, black-clad village women holding bunches of flowers, wound its way silently into the square. They unloaded a coffin from a beautifully carved, wooden funeral trailer and filed into the huge church of the Virgen del Rosario de Andocollo, for the service. A few moments later, the square burst into life as crowds of young girls in salmon pink frocks, supposedly fashioned under Chinese influence, dancing to the sound of thumping drums and lilting flutes, paraded out of a side street, followed by flag-waving singers dressed in swirling white costumes. The service inside the church struggled stoically on, while the people in the back pews gazed back over their shoulders at the tumult outside.

Then as suddenly as it had begun, the parade abated, and as the little dancing figures moved off down the narrow streets, the funeral cortege, now feeling free to end their ceremony too, emerged from the church, loaded the coffin back on to the little cart, and set off in the wake of the retreating pink backs. As we filmed, children gathered round, fighting for attention before the lens.

The next day, another reconstructed festival in the desert town of La Tirana, complete with elaborate masks and ritual worship at the altar, proved to be far less spontaneous. It was performed theatrically and unemotionally by a troupe of professional entertainers within an empty plaza and church which would, on the occasion of the celebration itself, have been filled with thousands of pilgrims.

We had begun the day in Iquique, one of Chile's most colourful colonial ports, with a seven-mile national fun run, along the desert coast. Over 5,000 people took part, schoolchildren, invalids in wheelchairs, athletes, housewives and whole families, in an event that was being simultaneously staged in towns and villages all over the country. In a mad burst of athletic fervour, and mindful of my fast-dissolving fitness, I entered the race. Road running in the Atacama desert, with temperatures into the hundreds, is not quite the same as jogging in Hyde Park, but, thankfully, I was up against moderate competition. I managed a speedy first half which placed me, all eager and hopeful, amongst the leaders, but from there on, I slipped into a more pedestrian stride, and finished a disappointed thirty-ninth.

Families crossed the line hand in hand, fathers carried their toddlers on their shoulders, invalids raced their wheelchairs valiantly over the last hundred metres and a group of bouncy plump girls trotted and strolled in, loudly encouraged by their classmates, who were hanging from their school balcony, just short of the finish. Diplomas were liberally handed out to all the competitors, and free coca cola made the whole thing worthwhile. In the hubbub of celebrations a dilapidated giant cardboard coca cola bottle at the roadside, collapsed, symbolic victory, perhaps, to a cherished shaking off of US dependence.

Jogging, like roller-skating and skateboarding, was obviously becoming a worldwide fashion. True to form, what was good for

General Motors and the US of A was equally good for aspiring South America. Hand in hand with the virulent burgeoning of fashionable fads, came the fellow travellers of mediocrity and tackiness. Nowhere was safe, it seemed, from creeping ordinariness. Traditional ways were blandly being eschewed in favour of the garish, the disposable and the mundane. Drum majorettes in tennis skirts twirled batons at the head of every parade throughout South America. Quick service junk food was fast becoming the predominant way of eating at the stand-up counters of Hamburger Heavens across the world. A never-ending flood of 'police' films provided the normal television diet. Even the gay transvestite scene was stepping out into the open and on to the streets, daring to challenge the tough guy concepts of Latin machismo. If San Francisco could boast a twenty-five per cent gay community, then Santiago and the rest would do their level best to follow suit. South America was eager to become a consumer paradise; it was an ad-man's dream. All this was, of course, encouraged by governments anxious to provide simple distracting panaceas for their countrymen's problems; 'panem and circenses'. Ironically though, while relentlessly pursuing the 'American dream' way of life, Latin America despised 'the gringo', and hated the United States for her political role in their misery, and for their dependence on her.

The Iquique fun run quickly became the excuse for an impromptu carnival, and we joined in, forsaking filming for a little flirting. We took twin sisters, Andrea and Julia, to the decorative, demi-kitsch, turn-of-the-century Spanish club for lunchtime drinks. It was rich in ornaments, and alive with decorum and we drank surrounded by extravagantly painted panels depicting the story of Don Quixote. But the break was short lived. Another flight, this time in a small five-seater helicopter, had been arranged to take us to Humberstone, a ghost town out in the desert.

Humberstone had been a flourishing mining town until twenty years before and it stood, as if betrayed, surrounded by vast sheets of dry, caked and cracking salt flats. Now it was a graveyard of rusting machinery, twisted broken equipment and boarded-up, dilapidated, wooden bungalows. Clumps of tumble weed blew eerily down the dusty, deserted streets, and disintegrating windows, hanging from a single hinge, creaked to and fro in the stifling hot wind that whistled through the cracks in the planking. Stubbly brush sprouted obstinately amidst the rubble, but the place possessed an aura of quiet dignity, in consequence perhaps of its decaying isolation.

Failing light prevented us from helicoptering on to visit the old German hermit who lived in the hills east of Humberstone and instead we returned to Iquique for an unexpected formal dinner with the local base commander. Assignations made earlier in the day with local beauties had reluctantly to be set aside in favour of good diplomacy. However, the delightfully eccentric and irreverent wife of the commander relieved the potential stiffness of the occasion. It was a universally suburban scene.

Our hectic week-long jaunt was punctuated now and again with late night visits, led enthusiastically by Bernardo, to bars and brothels and dance halls to ensure that all our senses were fully nourished. More often than not, though, these little sorties, out in the provinces, never quite lived up to their promise, and we usually returned home unfulfilled.

Feliks and I had professed our intention to ride the ancient British-owned train which runs from Antofagasta on the Chilean coast over the mountains to the Bolivian capital, La Paz, and this caused everyone no end of amusement. Our travelling friends and everyone we met, including the railway owner himself, Lord Montgomery, whom I encountered in Santiago, advised us against the plan. I was a little unnerved by the unanimous hostility, but reasoned that if local people travelled on it every week, there was no reason why we couldn't do the same. The horror stories became more and more lurid as the time approached. The journey would take four days (it took thirty-six hours), there would be no seats (we had a sleeper compartment to ourselves), there were regular derailings, there would be no lavatories and conditions would be filthy (untrue), there would be close mingling with Indians (true), there would be long delays (untrue), and the change in altitude would be dangerous for Feliks (untrue). When, finally, in Antofagasta we were told that there was a strike, and the train would not leave for a week, our sceptical companions were delirious with joy. 'We told you, we told you,' chanted Bernardo, in shameless triumph. 'Now you can take the plane like we said you should.' But the strike threat was a false alarm, or maybe a devious ploy, and despite the tales of woe, Feliks and I remained loyal to the original plan to join the train at the desert town of Calama, two days later.

Our last exhausting day in Chile began with a visit to Chuquicamata, the world's largest open-cast mine, measuring three by two kilometres and half a kilometre deep and over three thousand metres above sea level. Previously this massive copper mine had belonged to a United States company, but it had been nationalised. Thirty thousand people lived in neat rows of bungalows, each sprouting a television aerial, each with a Ford parked outside, compensation for the inhospitable desert surroundings.

Then we took off by car across the blazing brown sand towards

San Pedro de Atacama, following for a while the tremulous green sliver that was the river Loa valley, the only stream that dared to challenge the parched Atacama, trickling bravely from its source in the Andes all the way to the Pacific Ocean. Huddled in the comforting embrace of this narrow fertile strip, small pockets of humanity eked out barely enough to survive, in much the same way as did their pre-Inca ancestors. The nearby archaeological ruins bore testimony to the historical validity of their struggle in the face of grim hardship.

Beyond the valley, the Andean foothills loomed through the shimmering haze. We drove through Chiu Chiu, site of the first church in Chile, a softly rounded, white-washed building. Peeking through the window of the schoolhouse across the road, I watched a class of children trying not to be caught by their teacher, as they stole surreptitious glances out at our curious filming group.

We carried on to the proudly guidebook-announced, but utterly mundane 'perfectly circular' lake, and across the misleadingly titled, but suitably desolate 'Valley of the Moon', and on to San Pedro. There, an old German priest, who had died only a few months earlier, had assembled a startling collection of magnificently preserved mummies, some dating back 2,300 years, which led Graham Greene to be quoted in one guidebook describing the collection as a 'display that puts the British Museum in the shade.'

The mummies apart, the enthusiasm of the Latin temperament often raised the inconsequential to the level of uniqueness, submerging the genuine article in a sea of scepticism. Every physical curiosity, the smallest historical site, took on preposterous dimensions and were recommended far beyond their value in outpourings of national pride. It was an ego-boosting exercise in self-discovery, designed to reassert national confidences, sparked off by the international focus on Inca culture. The almost breathless reverence in which infinitely dull 'sights' were held, was creating a wide credibility gap, and by the time we reached Toconao and Chile's beloved LONGEST SURVIVING CHURCH TOWER, both Feliks and I had had enough. We were showing signs of severe archaeological overkill.

We returned gratefully to Calama to catch the train. Our companions' chorus of ridicule reached its crescendo when the rickety train pulled into the station and the waiting horde of struggling overloaded Indian merchant women battled aboard, their uniquely Bolivian bowler hats askew and their plaits in a twist. The tumbling, billowing skirts they wore provided the only refuge for the tiny, wide-eyed tots that hung on to their mothers for dear life. But as we settled into the evident comfort of a leather-

Posed in London by torture victim

lined, albeit well-lived-in, sleeper compartment, Bernardo, the most vociferous of the doubters, began to look ruffled. Although the detractors were confounded, they were pleased that the journey might not turn out to be as wearisome as they had supposed.

The filming expedition, in spite of its frustrating shortcomings, had afforded us an opportunity to see a lot of Chile in a short space of time, covering its length and breadth in an unexpectedly VIP way, and our companions in the venture became our good friends. The failure of the limited sound recording to arrive in London with the film footage was unlikely to have been their fault; but it effectively put paid to the possibility of the film being considered for inclusion in the BBC documentary.

In retrospect we felt that our Chilean experience lacked a cutting edge. Without delving deeply into the intricacies of Chile's political opposition, the extent of the brutality and repression of Pinochet's regime was difficult to fathom, and we felt a sense of fraudulence in the impressions we drew of the country. It was not good enough to pass through and conclude glibly: 'We didn't see anything sinister.' That would be sheer irresponsibility and an insult to those who were disappearing, dying and resisting. In effect it would be collusion and the weak response 'I'm not interested in politics' that many give to excuse their silence, was unacceptable. In London, a Chilean detailed to us the horrors of the tortures that had been administered to her in the 'Palace of Laughter' over a one-year period in detention. On her first night she was stretched naked on a metal bed for five hours with electrodes attached to her mouth, ears, nipples, vagina, stomach, anus and between her toes. 'The electric shocks tore screams from me which I hardly recognised as my own. They drank coffee while they did it to me. My body is very supple and the violent convulsions produced by the shocks did not damage me as much as they did most people. Many could no longer walk. I am deaf in one ear and my back is permanently injured.' She described the broken, brutalised women in the prison with her, and explained how the torturers of DINA chose their methods according to what they determined would most humiliate and damage their victims. 'The prim women were raped, sometimes by dogs. Pregnant girls got electric shocks. They reckoned that after the first two days any information that they thought you might have, would have become out of date and useless, but they continued the tortures anyway because they took pleasure in destroying people; the smell of sweat and fear was awful. People are still disappearing, but now the new tactic is to kill those they don't like on the street and make it seem like a random assault or some act of inter-faction gangsterism. It causes them fewer problems that way.' She had finally been released because they could find nothing to charge her with. She was not 'disappeared' because her father was a high-up naval officer who had at first dismissed the reports of torture as 'anti-government propaganda'.

CHAPTER 5 BOLIVIA: in the aftermath of revolution

It was a relief to be able to sit back and relax. We now had a couple of days to reflect on our first two weeks and we realised that we had not yet brought each other up to date on the month and a half which followed my departure from England. Feliks wanted to know in detail about my prison experience in Paraguay and I wanted to know about his last weeks in London. Slowly, as we unwound, we began to feel more trustful of each other. We realised that there would have to be considerable compromise on both sides to accommodate the needs and wishes of the other, but that it should not necessarily entail any hardship for either of us. At the same time, as our confidence in each other returned, the journey began to take on a different flavour. Although we had been determined to face the journey without preconceptions or prejudice, I had to admit that so far, South America was not the South America I had anticipated. Physically the continent was stupendous, but the aspiring European-ness of the southern cone had disappointed me. Although I could not deny its existence, I was too familiar with the lifestyle, ambitions and customs of the people there to be enthralled by it. But I was glad to have seen it. Now, as we began the long ascent to the Bolivian altiplano, surrounded as we were by

Quechua and Aymara Indian fellow passengers, the way ahead looked more hopeful.

The antiquated little train trundled slowly towards the Cordillera, its sturdy wooden carriages creaking and groaning after more than eighty years of faithful service under the comforting patronage of the Montgomery family. I found a tenuous but exhilarating vantage point on the footplate between the carriages, from where I could photograph unobstructed. Dried white salt flats stretched like vast lakes away to the south and the train skirted round them, as it climbed closer towards the imposing volcanoes which lay ahead; it swayed ominously as it crept along the narrow, winding and often precarious tracks.

At sunset, we pulled into Ollague, 3,300 metres up, and encircled by twelve monstrous volcanoes, including smoking Santa Rosa, whose snowy flanks reflected the glow of the dying sun. We took our microen tablets to prevent nausea, although we were experiencing no ill effects. The attentive guard brought us maté-de-coca, tea made from coca leaves, which in their processed form became the cocaine which earned for Bolivia's military dictators over two billion dollars a year on the open market. Here it came in neatly packaged teabags and was considered the best way of combatting the effects of altitude. The Indians of the altiplano chewed the leaves to induce a high that numbed the senses and offset the debilitating consequences of cold and poverty. Coca was a distraction from the harsh realities of mountain life and served the useful function of making the chewer feel as if he had had something to eat. I tried the magic leaves, but after hours of fruitless munching, I gave up with an aching jaw. It was some while later that I was told that you had to add lime to the leaves to get the desired effect. Its use was so widespread in the Andes and the income from the sale of cocaine so high, that any efforts to curb its production by worried western governments would have to be accompanied by viable and lucrative alternative crops and a big influx of aid to improve the living conditions of the Andean campesinos.

On the platforms of the little lonely stations we passed, young children, and old Indian ladies dashed up and down, brandishing all manner of fruit, cheeses and delicacies for the passengers. Most of the travellers were traders returning home from one of their twice-monthly sales trips to Chile. But two young, long-haired Chilean hippies were heading for the mountain mines, where the higher wages would provide them with enough money to travel north to visit a brother in New Jersey.

In the eight first and second class carriages, the passengers had spread themselves out comfortably for the long trip. They shared out between them the ham, cheese, yoghurt and bread that each had brought from Chile.

We were now on the bleak, 4,000 metre high altiplano of the central Andean plateau, a flat, depressing, treeless expanse, freezing cold at night, windswept by day, dry and inhabited only by llamas, sheep and alpacas and hardy red-faced, round-cheeked campesinos. We learned quickly to refer to rural Indians as campesinos and not as Indios, which was regarded as a term of abuse and, since the population of Bolivia was three-quarters Indian, it was a lesson worth knowing. The women were more in evidence than the men, selling their wares at the stations, travelling the train, herding the llamas on the gruelling desolate plain, wrapped in multi-coloured woollens and layer upon layer of skirts and petticoats. Here in Bolivia they wore the now traditional brown or grey bowler hat. But as we travelled north to Colombia the style changed from bowler to a variety of stetsons, white toppers and trilbies.

Occasionally, the train passed little huddles of mud and wattle adobe huts, sitting vulnerably within a grey landscape, with only the distant eastern Cordillera to break the monotonous view. Thin bunch grass, or ichu, provided what scant vegetation there was to feed the herds of llamas and flocks of mangy sheep, which were invariably tended by women or tiny children adrift in utterly isolated and seemingly uninhabited spots. The llamas were mainly pack animals, but their wool was an important commodity in the inhospitable world of the Andean highlands. The campesinos also kept alpaca for their wool and they hunted the untamed and disappearing vicuna for its fine valuable silky wool.

One of the main settlements of the altiplano south of La Paz was the depressing tin mining town of Oruro. All round the edge of the town were vast rubbish dumps, spreading from the outlying houses into the plain, as far as the eye could see. Children and pitiful, old human wrecks picked their way across this grim landscape of stinking refuse, dead animals and rusting tin cans, sifting through the filth and competing with rats and scavenging dogs for salvageable tit-bits. There were few places in the world where the conditions of life were more tenuous.

We arrived in La Paz at night and were welcomed by the spectacular sight of a trillion lights filling the teeming bowl in which the city was set. The train circled the rim allowing us a variety of appealing perspectives, dropping lower with each circuit, until it rumbled to a halt in the heart of the bustling market area. It was the antithesis of Santiago and the whole southern cone, full of market life, delicious hilly streets, earthy and unpretentious.

Bolivian altiplano

The loftiest capital in the world at 3,600 metres, La Paz was cradled in a basin, protected from the bitter winds of the altiplano by a ring of stark, sharp-edged mountains, coloured blue, red and grey and dominated by snow-tipped Mount Illimani. The vitality of the city was invigorating. The physical breathlessness caused by the high altitude only served to accentuate the sense of excitement. At every turn there were tableaux of colour and unexpected moments. Here was unpredictability, because at last we were in a different world with unique reactions, a far cry from the familiar attitudes and lifestyles to the south. The scathing snobs in Chile and Argentina had assured us that we would hate Bolivia, with all her Indians. They told us that Bolivia was a country of unsophisticates and that a day in La Paz would suffice, because of the boredom. Within moments of arriving, we knew they were wrong.

We booked into the Hotel Sucre, which we discovered later was known as the drug traffickers hotel, where the big dealers stayed; but to our unpractised eyes, they all seemed like nice, wholesome, European visitors.

We tried to make contact with 'friends of friends', those experienced local observers of the prevailing scene, who were always so important for a better understanding of the things we were seeing as we travelled. We needed the views of those writers, politicians, journalists, taxi-drivers, students and diplomats as well as the market place to give us a balanced and more informed picture of 'our' South America. However one of these contacts had not appeared at his office for three months, and they gave me his home telephone number. The person who answered refused to talk and, after further enquiries, we were left with the suggestion that he had fled the country or had been 'disappeared'. Once again we were reminded of the uncertainty and insecurity of daily life.

Bolivia was a country in the throes of yet another military coup in its turbulent history of dictatorships, (more coups than years of independence), struggling to survive in a desolate land, where the majority of its people lived on the savage altiplano, while the potentially rich Yungas, down the slopes of the eastern mountains in the Amazon basin, remained relatively unpopulated. Nothing seemed to go right for Bolivia, yet her long-suffering people were kind and supportive. They had learnt to live with the violence, and coped with the constant political upheavals in a multitude of different ways. For the most part, the Indians – nearly eighty per cent of the total population – remained virtually outside the monetary system, operating an economy within an economy, trading in the markets in their own way and avoiding involvement with the authorities. What happened in Government House in the lower section of La Paz, well guarded by soldiers, was of little consequence to them high up on the edge of the city's rim and in the countryside, since their living standards and the quality of their lives hardly changed, no matter who was in power. The campesinos were destined always to lose out, even though, if politically mobilised, they had the numerical weight to enforce reforms. Opinions about why they did not, varied. Some said that the campesinos had no interest in politics; that they were illiterate and unintelligent; and that their passivity made them bystanders at election time. Others suggested that they chose to remain silent as a result of centuries of brutality and repression and that they had made a conscious decision to remain independent and outside the power game altogether.

To observe them in La Paz, enjoying the markets, going about their business coolly polite but separate and aloof, the second opinion seemed to carry the most weight. They had learned to leave the militant tin miners to fight the political battles, to form unions and to get killed by successive military regimes. As a result, the living standards of the miners were higher than for most Bolivians. There were signs, however, in the political slogans written on walls and in the voting patterns of recent elections that the campesinos were becoming politicised too.

An eleven o'clock curfew had been imposed on La Paz and anyone caught out after that time was shot or arrested. Soldiers piled into the backs of trucks patrolled the streets, shooting at random. At ten-thirty, every evening, the pavements were full of rushing, panicking stragglers, hitching lifts, cramming into the last buses. Up until that time, the town was alive with colour and noise and people walking, eating in restaurants, thronging the markets and leaving the cinemas. But at eleven o'clock, everything fell silent, save for the occasional shot echoing across the deserted city and the few official white cars or trucks that raced by flaunting their immunity. One telling feature of the Bolivian character was that, after eleven o'clock, householders routinely left their front doors unlocked, so that unfortunate stragglers could slip in off the street to safety, there to spend the night until the curfew was lifted next morning. The people of La Paz pulled together in troubled times. In other countries, under similar stress, it would be hard to find such an example of solidarity. A few days later, I read of the death in San Salvador of a journalist, shot by security soldiers after curfew, while he was trying to get into a locked house.

Bolivia's hectic political history was neatly encapsulated by the previous two years of activity. Hernan Siles Zuago, the sixty-eight-year-old veteran UDP socialist campaigner and an ex-president of the country, had emerged from a year of vigorous democratic electioneering with a total of thirty-eight per cent of the vote against eighteen per cent by his rival socialist, Victor Paz Estenssoro of MNR. The right winger, Hugo Banzer, fifty-five years old, a past military coup leader and also an ex-president, had polled fifteen per cent. But, since no one had polled the necessary fifty per cent, there had to be a congressional decision on the next stage. Congress dithered for months and, finally, Mrs Lidia Gueiler Tejada was elected interim president. In an utterly cynical move, the military intervened with a right wing coup, and the corrupt, unpopular and stupid Meza seized power, killing Marcello Quiroga Santa Cruz, the leftist leader of PSI, who had polled twelve per cent in the elections. Thus, against the express wishes of sixty-eight per cent of the electorate that voted for socialist reform, Bolivia had become, yet again, a right wing military dictatorship and Siles Zuago had to flee the country. Was it any wonder that the majority Indian population had turned their collective back on party politics.*

This and the example of Chile soured many to the whole concept of free democratic elections and socialist governments. Helped into power by Argentina, Meza failed to win international recognition for his government and his coup was seen by Bolivians as a blatantly opportunistic attempt to camouflage a thriving drug operation worth two billion dollars a year. And a year after his coup, he was still in power, despite weekly rumours of counter coups and assassination attempts. He tried, unsuccessfully, to induce Banzer into his government to give credibility to his faltering regime. When he toured the country, the people were ordered out on to the streets to greet him with banners which read 'Thank you to our father (Meza) for giving us our liberty' and 'Nationalism, yes – Communism – No'. Failure to turn out in support could mean losing their jobs. People were paid to vote a particular way and tended to vote for the man who promised to keep them in work. Thus you voted for who your boss told you to. But parties did exist that upheld their rights and there were signs and slogans everywhere, some on officially designated 'propaganda' walls, left over from the election, promoting the MITKA Party (leftist Indian) and a multitude of other revolutionary parties too. But money and threats were stronger than promises. And, anyway, they knew that whenever there was the chance of a democratic government of the centre or left being elected to institute social reforms, the militarists would inevitably step in to preserve the status quo.

A conversation with the Bolivian aide to a foreign diplomat

resulted in an outpouring of disillusionment and anger. With detailed precision, he spoke of the political detainees, of those who had disappeared, who had been killed and tortured. He pointed to the government's involvement in the cocaine trade, the collapse of the economy and the brutal eradication of the popular left. Here too, like Paraguay, Uruguay, Chile, Argentina and Brazil, the puritan military minds demanded strict obedience to the conservative concepts of uncritical discipline. They regarded the people of the country as an extension of the armies under their command, and expected to rule the lives of civilians as they did their soldiers.

One of my greatest pleasures was to stroll alone through the streets of an unfamiliar town. Usually I took my camera and tried to photograph unostentatiously, trying not to cause offence. But here in La Paz, the tough bowler-hatted ladies were wise to most of the ploys. They hid their faces, hurled abuse and generally expressed their displeasure; or they demanded large sums of money. To them, I was a tourist – ripe for the picking. The police too, tried to prevent me from taking pictures, and indeed up until a week or so before, they had been under orders to arrest journalists and photographers alike. But now it was quieter. I turned my camera towards the mountains above the city, which together with the myriad of perching Indian houses, formed the backcloth to every view of La Paz.

In the market, fat-faced, brown-cheeked saleswomen scurried or squatted everywhere. Most had the regulation, suckling infant, chewing on their large, sagging breasts, which they heaved out of blouses and sweaters and pushed into mewling mouths without a break in either stride or conversation. They continued their chores with what seemed to be a natural appendage or extension hanging down their front. These lovely, sturdy women appeared outsized because of the layers of underskirts and sweaters and shawls they wore whatever the temperature. The younger girls, often very pretty with long black plaits, but just as wide in girth as their mothers, imitated them in every detail from the earliest age. They were married at fourteen, had babies from fifteen on, chewed coca leaves and helped out in the market from the age of four. They too were swathed in colour and seemed to be bowler-hatted at birth. On the whole, the women appeared to dominate the scene, displaying greater character resourcefulness and willingness to work than their men. Indeed when there were any anti-government demonstrations, these tough, determined, vociferous women were usually well to the fore.

In the tumbling raucous market along the steep cobbled streets of Camacho, above Plaza San Francisco, I found the 'black magic' section, with exotic herbs, the foetuses of llamas, dried and stretched at tortuous and grotesque angles, trinkets and charms all designed for clandestine witchcraft activities. In a record shop nearby, luxurious, beautiful Marguerita in Bo Derek plaits, and peasant blouse and skirt, decided to take me in hand and talk me through the market. She was a popular girl and was hailed by all the locals we passed, which was a little disconcerting. But she insisted on buying me a silver charm and we agreed to meet later in the evening by the obelisk, the favourite local rendezvous on the Central Avenue, the Prado.

Needless to say I waited in vain; this was a normal social hazard in South America. At first I used to fume and rage, but in time the unreliability of Latins wore me down and I stopped expecting people ever to appear as agreed. These I decided were tests, trials of strength, and the purity of one's intentions was measured by one's perseverance in the face of rejection. At first my impatience and displays of irritation were very counterproductive and I learned the hard way how to play the game according to the rules. The direct European-style approach was fatal. For Latins the traditional manoeuvres still applied. Man chases girl, girl flees, man traps girl, girl struggles, and after winning concessions, gives in. Man reneges on concessions and leaves. Girl is determined to be wilier and less trusting the next time. I spent many fruitless hours, on different occasions propping up this monument, that clock-tower, or some obelisk, along with many patient hopeful locals, taxed with the same frustrating situation. By the time I met Juanita, I had learned to be patient. She was a student at the university, but the government had closed all colleges indefinitely because they were considered breeding grounds for revolutionaries; so she was on extended leave. At the third attempt to rendezvous in as many days, she arrived. I was astonished and delighted. We joined the milling couples strolling over the hill in the centre of town, where in the past, rebel guerrillas used to hide. Now it was thick with Sunday evening trippers watching the lengthening shadows creeping over the distant dappled peaks to the west of the city. Juanita led me through the popular twisting, turning, snakes-and-ladder game of catch but came to the conclusion that we were perhaps a good match and that it should be played out to its finale. The more liberal-minded attitude of Bolivian hotels was a welcome change from the rigid puritanism further south, and we were able to spend a few tumbling pre-curfew hours together.

Recklessly, with curfew fast approaching, but like a true English gent, I taxied with her to her home; on the way back, the taxi-driver decided that time was running out, and dropping me at

Murillo Square, headed for home. Racing through the streets I got back to the hotel with a minute to spare. I stood, panting at the entrance to the hotel, watching other stragglers rushing homewards. Some foolhardy young men played a dangerous game of 'chicken' ambling along nonchantly, challenging the authorities. One or two others, drunk and confused, staggered from doorway to doorway, searching for an opening in which to collapse for the night.

When it came to keeping appointments, the boys were no more reliable than the women. Two young men, one claiming to be the son of a military leader, had made a great show one evening of offering to drive me to the Bolivian version of the 'Valley of the Moon' the next morning; but they failed to appear. 'You promise to come,' I'd said firmly; 'I'm leaving La Paz tomorrow afternoon, so it will be my only chance. If you can't come I'll arrange to go on my own much earlier; so please don't say you will if you can't.' 'Have no fear,' they assured me. 'We shall come at eleven o'clock.' Perhaps they really had meant to come, but like Marguerita, and Maria and Bella and Antonio something else had cropped up. For someone like me with limited time, it was cause for considerable knashing of teeth and the kicking of innocent wooden newspaper stands.

However I did manage to get to the Valley by hitching and bussing out of La Paz on my own. Feliks had been there a few days earlier and had urged me to see it, and it proved to be well worth the effort. It was a dry, eerie, mud-grey landscape of jagged, sharp-edged ravines, and wind-sculpted shapes. No bush or cactus grew there and only scorpions and snakes survived in the broken forbidding terrain.

The minor frustrations of La Paz's social life were more than compensated for by the charm of the city itself. Murillo square was a constant source of delight, particularly in the late afternoon, at the height of the 'paseo'. Young men from the military and police academies, resplendent in their Germanic uniforms, walked their girlfriends, confident of the fine spectacle they presented. Women too were out cruising in the same police cadet attire. One walked with her identical twin sister, who wore a shocking pink frock and garish make-up. The generous fulsomeness of the cadet was constrained within her tight-fitting costume, while the other burst provocatively from hers.

A cool but insistent shoeshine boy, decided to take charge of my shoes. Throughout South America these street-wise kids ran the squares and ruled the roost. They were also mines of information, like taxi-drivers in London or New York. After a conversation about my journey, during which he showed great interest in the fact that I was travelling with my artist father, he set to work on a particularly stubborn white spot on my right shoe that had resisted some of the most talented shiners on the continent. After a moment he looked up and said: 'Some of your father's paintwork here I expect,' and moved on around the shoe, respectfully avoiding what he had decided was a work of art.

On one side of Murillo square were fine, balconied colonial buildings with cinemas and snack bars in their ground floors. Grouped round the opposite side, were the handsome cathedral, the presidential Quemado palace, recently gutted by fire and the Congreso National. I went one late evening to walk around it with a French journalist from *Le Matin,* who was convinced that another coup was imminent, and that all would be revealed by a visit to the Congreso building. But 'all' was peaceful. He had been covering South America for some years, and he was now travelling incognito around Bolivia preparing a feature story. He backed up the views of our other informants about the reign of terror, the drug scandal, the silencing of the miners and the expectations of a further coup. He was an intense and nervous man, in his forties. 'The problems of this continent are insoluble,' he said. 'It will never change; it is in their character. They make my work so difficult. It takes days to do anything here. I will retire soon, and buy a small farm, perhaps down here, but only as long as I have nothing urgent to do.'

I had a hunger for an early taste of tropical jungle and could not contain my impatience. Although Feliks too anticipated our crossing from mountain to steamy rain forest, he was determined to resist temptation, and not interrupt the continuity of the Andean world; he preferred to await the proper final descent into the Amazon at Leticia in Colombia. I had no such resolve and joined two English friends from the diplomatic mission in Chile, on a drive down to the Yungas.

Within a three-hour journey, we travelled out of La Paz, through the crumbling shanties above the city, up the steep slopes of the Eastern Cordillera, over the bleak 4,725 metre high La Cumbre pass, and then down the steep, winding, dirt track into the hot tropical greenery of the Alto Beni jungle. In the short space of eighty kilometres we dropped 3,200 metres, traversing the most extraordinary changes of vegetation and scenery. Crossing the swirling, dank, misty heights of the snowy La Cumbre, we passed fierce-looking solitary dogs standing like silent sentinels along the track. Wild scavengers, they existed on titbits thrown from passing trucks and whatever else they could find. They patrolled the barren landscape like mysterious werewolves. They held their ground

Presidential Palace, La Paz

beside the road, one every two or three hundred metres as if defending their patch, brooding and threatening. A monumental fifteen metre high coca cola bottle stood incongruously near the summit.

As we began the descent of the steep escarpment, herds of ragged llamas scattered away from the road. Cold stark crags gave way to scrub-covered gorges, with running streams fed by the melting glaciers above. The thin scrub in turn handed over to flowering bushes and then trees all of it becoming thicker and greener the further down we went. Anoraks came off, and soon sweaters too were discarded. Small villages, surrounded by precarious culti-vated plots of land, became more numerous. We stopped for a breakfast of eggs at a roadside snack bar, no different to thousands dotted along remote mountain roads in Africa, the Himalayas and the rest of South America. Coffee and coca plantations now lined the road, and waterfalls tumbled across it bursting out from green overhanging cliffs. Red tropical flowers blazed from the thick jungle and T shirts finally had to be removed as well. Ahead, on a forest-covered spur, stood the red-tiled, white-washed village of Coroico.

Our driver, while patiently stopping for us to photograph, professed his admiration for the new government. Taxi-drivers, owning their own cars and earning good money were invariably keen supporters of the military rightists and our friend was no exception. Talk of land reforms and tax and social services appalled him. 'If people don't like it here they should get out,' he argued. But wouldn't that pose a problem for Bolivians, with governments changing every year, and policies changing just as frequently? 'This government has got it right,' he insisted. 'Under the communists, if you have two cars, they'll take away one.' He refused to believe that there were legal communist parties in Italy and France and that in Britain there was a functioning social security and health service. He resented 'outsiders' coming to make revolution in his country and pointing proudly to the hills across the valley he said: 'We killed Che Guevara over there and that's what we'll do to others like him who disagree with our government.' Blacks from across the border in Brazil had, over the past centuries, settled in the hot plantations of the Yungas, ('leftovers from black American sol-diers,' said our bigoted driver), but they were spurned by mestizo and Indians alike. Prejudice flourished where insecurity prevailed. It was always comforting to look down on someone else, and a small black minority provided the perfect scapegoat. The Indians were themselves despised by the mestizos, who were in turn a class below the whiter-skinned mestizos of the cities.

A young English boy from Bath, who had settled in Coroico two years earlier, worked locally as a carpenter and ranch hand. He spoke the local dialect and got on well with the villagers. The old Indian mother of his delicate sixteen-year-old girlfriend was furious with him about something and kept thumping him in a good-natured way, laughing in mock anger. At a festival a few days earlier he had been seen in close company with a black girl from the same village. 'She was so beautiful,' he grinned apologetically, 'how could I resist.' Mother wanted no more to do with him and tried to set his long hair alight with a match. 'Don't be so racist,' he begged the old lady, 'she's a fine girl.' His girlfriend seemed unworried by his indiscretions, and as they continued their argument she made arrangements to try to meet me in La Paz at the weekend. Needless to say she failed to appear.

Narrow cobbled streets ran steeply up the lush hillside, over-looked by crooked, peeling, two-storey houses. Erect black women, in thickly-layered black skirts, swept haughtily by, with black bowlers perched at jaunty angles. Indian women, a foot shorter and bent under the weight of their loads, scurried and shuffled past at a trot.

The atmosphere down here was easygoing after the misery of the altiplano. Here life was enjoyed for its little daily pleasures. Up there life was played on a grand and tragic scale. Yet there was a great reluctance on the part of the campesinos to move down to the tropical valleys and settle in the Yungas. Those who did, lured by various government directives, met with mixed fortunes. The rapidity of the move left many defenceless against unfamiliar diseases and unable to cope with such different climatic conditions. Furthermore, not all the lands on to which they were transferred were as fertile as had been supposed. They found when they cleared away the thick forest vegetation, that the soil underneath was thin and stony. But the government just left them to it, and it was estimated that nearly sixty per cent of the new migrants died as a result of the experiment. Peru was in the process of adopting a similar project and appeared to be falling into the same terrible trap.

The drive back up over the pass left us short of breath and a little sick, but we had recovered by the time we got to La Paz.

I left my English friends and rejoined Feliks. We were due to meet the film crew in Lima and we had very little time left; but we were both determined to press on overland through Bolivia to Peru. The bus to Lake Titicaca was loading when we arrived at the depot, but for safety we kept all our four bags inside with us. We felt overloaded and decided, once we got to Lima, to cut down on our luggage, and get rid of one bag.

This was to be our first bus trip together and I was determined it should all go without a hitch. We stocked up with oranges, bread and bananas for the five-hour drive to Copacabana, close to the Peruvian border on the south eastern end of the lake. Titicaca, like Tierra del Fuego was another of my childhood ghosts, which since school days had held a special appeal.

Indian women, laden with blankets full of belongings, children and chickens tied at the feet, clambered aboard. In front of us sat two French girls, returning to Peru, delighted with their Bolivian experience. 'People are so much warmer and friendlier here than in Peru.'

The bus climbed out of the bowl and on to the altiplano, heading north west towards the lake, with the thin white ribbon of Andean peaks far away to our right. The landscape changed quickly from dust brown scrub to lusher pasture as we approached the shores of the great inland sea. Then abruptly it was there, a vast expanse, seeming to bulge up in the middle as it disappeared over the horizon.

The road ran above the marshy foreshore, where water buffalo and cattle grazed amid the tall reeds. The land was green and the earth dark brown, and it was the richest farming country we had seen since leaving central Chile. Trees and terraced fields brought a softness to the rugged Bolivian scenery. The sun glinted off the corrugated roofing of the farmhouses, a sure sign of comparative wealth in these parts. But further round the lake, where we crossed the straits of Tiquina, the shoreline became rugged and steep once more. Here were the headquarters of Bolivia's homely little landlocked navy, with a fleet of half-a-dozen motor launches moored below the port buildings. The hundred-strong naval force practised on Lake Titicaca for the time when they might one day win access to the ocean. But for the present they had to content themselves with being the world's most impotent armed force, carrying out manoeuvres nearly 4,300 meters above their potential enemy.

For the crossing of the straits, the passengers had to leave the bus, which was gingerly loaded empty on to a flimsy raft. Feliks went to look for a lavatory and I changed the film in my camera. We failed to notice that all the other passengers had boarded a small launch a hundred metres along the shore and had set off after the bus. We were stranded on the deserted shore. We watched as they all unloaded on the other side, and disappeared round the port buildings. Surely the French girls would have said something to the driver.

After a while a ferry arrived from the other side bearing two large military trucks. At first the ancient mariner was reluctant to take just two of us across, but he relented at the sight of a 10 Bolivar note and we reached the other side nearly forty minutes behind the others. Although the driver had been determined to leave without us, the other Bolivian passengers had persuaded him to hold on for the *loco gringos*. They dismissed our apologies with broad grins. As we climbed up the steep cliff away from the shore, the sun was setting over the lake, reflected redly against the white peaks in the far distance.

We pulled into Copacabana main square, in front of a huge, elaborate church, which looked like the Taj Mahal and seemed a little grandiose for such a small place. The town was in semi-darkness because the electricity was not due to be turned on until December, and the glow of hundreds of candles and butane lamps gave the interiors of the little, white-washed houses a magical, Rembrantesque quality. The lovely mood was not lost with the arival of daylight nor the drizzle that punctuated our short time there. We chose a cheap hotel on the main square, in the throes of renovation, with small rooms on two floors, ringing an open central courtyard. The family who ran it were miserable that they could not provide dinner but promised to make lunch next day.

The inside of the huge colonial church was splendid, more ornate and more rich, kitch and bloodthirsty than any we had seen so far. Dramatic sculptures of profusely bleeding Christs hung from crosses, or crawled on all fours weighed down by the cross, and the many Disneyland/Madame Tussaud-style statues of the Virgin looked suitably sad and wistful. The gore and the pain of the life-like figures were lovingly detailed down to the perfect flesh tones, realistic blood and hair; gold and silver adorned the walls, roof and altar, and meticulously carved wooden screens and heroic murals provided a sumptuous feast. Perhaps the exaggerated exuberance of the local Indian craftsmen who had added their own skilful styles, and the sense of Baroque overkill and graphic sensationalism might offend the purist, but to us it was an extravagant explosion of the extrovert Latin temperament.

In the square, in front of the church was a flamboyantly coloured naive statue of the Inca king Manca Kapac, whose children were commemorated in the names of the two islands, the Sun and the Moon, a few miles offshore.

Above the town, home of the miracle-working Dark Virgin of the Lake, or Virgen de Candelaria, patron saint of Bolivia, stood a steep conical hill with a row of crosses and stone alcoves at the summit which housed depictions of the miracles of Christ. Lining the precipitous path up were twelve more stone crosses, mounted

on small pyramids of rock, which represented the stages of Christ's ascent. I followed an elderly pair of campesino pilgrims as they struggled from one station to the next, praying and resting at each, before heaving themselves breathlessly on.

Every Saturday there was a fiesta, followed by a Sunday penance which involved a climb to the top of this hill. An energetic, enterprising little campesino girl, carrying two buckets of ice, coca cola and beer, and a pack with more bottles on her back, raced past the pilgrims and set up a makeshift stall at the top. Whenever she spotted anyone going up, she dropped whatever she was doing in the village, and took off after them. The climb at that altitude was exhausting enough carrying just a camera, but this hardy athlete barely paused for breath as she laid out her wares. She charged a peso above the normal price, earning half a penny per sale for her efforts.

Back down in the village, I joined Feliks in the market for a drink of hot api, the thick red local maize drink, before we set off for the Peruvian border.

* Siles Zuago was finally recalled from exile to take office at the end of 1982 when Meza was forced out by the military in favour of the democratically elected president.

CHAPTER 6 PERU: the tourist route across the roof of the world

By now, we were running into the tourist route through the Andes. Although the flow of overland travellers was still a relative trickle, the route between Lake Titicaca, the floating reed island homes of the Uros Indians at Puno, the 500-year-old Inca trail of ruins and roads to Cuzco and Macchu Picchu was part of Peru's well-established and comparatively efficient tourist industry. A constant stream of package tours arrived in Lima by plane from Europe and North America and from there the daring ones took off on their own, while the more wary flew in organised groups directly to Cuzco, Puno and La Paz. Hazardous journeys through the Peruvian mountains aboard overcrowded local buses, produced a unique sense of adventurousness and excitement, but the destinations – Cuzco, Arequipa, Macchu Picchu or Puno – were always swarming with the fast-moving arrivals from the morning flights, suffering altitude sickness, loud in their Bermudas, Nikons and Instamatics, and overwhelmingly intimidating as they moved, en-masse across the landscape. For them, there was little mingling, little merging with the surroundings, little subtlety or sensitivity in the face of new and alien cultures and languages. Lima was their starting-off point, and the reverberations radiated out from there in ever-increasing waves. Of course not all travelling groups followed the norm, and perhaps we travellers on the outer edges of these groups could pretend to be more serious or experienced overlanders, with more time at our disposal, and more concern about understanding where we were. But in the end all of us became inexorably absorbed into the general impression of an alien human flood, a second invasion on a scale much vaster than those early conquistadores. However much we tried to maintain a separate identity, in a pathetic attempt to set ourselves apart from the horde, because we believed we had a more 'noble' purpose, the truth was that we were no different. Like it or not we were swept along the route by Australian matrons, French school parties, Italian, German and English hippy back-packers and geriatric Japanese and North American tour parties. Although we spent most of our time off the beaten track, poking into less visited places, seeking the informalities of daily South American life, away from the bright brashness of the 'sights', we were trapped for these two weeks on the roof of the continent. So we rationalised our confusion by 'observing' the tourists at play and including them as part of our overall brief to explore the clashing diversities as encountered in this Latin world. We heard other travel snobs complaining about the 'tourists' and recognised the comic hypocrisy of our dilemma. But all the same we pressed on with our declared aim of attempting to observe with a fresh eye, trying to avoid the clichés, and picking out the unusual and the unexpected.

One of the hazards of the upsurge in the traffic of tourism was theft. The dangers were well-documented by other travellers and were detailed in all the travel books. Their experiences served as a warning signal. Train stations were considered to be a thieves' paradise, and crowds and markets were no better. Mercifully, Peruvian robbers were not particularly noted for their violence, unlike the notorious street bandits of Bogota in Colombia. But few people we met had escaped unscathed: cameras, suitcases, wrist-watches, money, glasses and, in the case of some people, everything. In Arequipa, the thieves followed a peculiar code of honour. Travel documents and personal items could be retrieved from the local radio station where they had been deposited with other non-valuables by the considerate felons.

But seen from another angle it was the price we interlopers paid for disrupting the peaceful life of the Andes. Feliks sympathised with the predicament of the campesinos and saw the thievery as an understandable reaction to a foreign invasion of new conquistadores. In the manner of their forefathers, these new victims of the White siege resisted with a nationwide guerrilla pocket-picking operation, sniping from behind, exacting their revenge under cover of darkness.

Their methods were described in breathless admiration. 'One moment my watch was on my wrist, the next it had gone.' 'They sliced open my bag from underneath while I was walking in the market; I never felt a thing.' 'How could they undo the zip so quickly?' Three boys, travelling together, one an Argentine, one a Swede and the third a Brazilian, none of them inexperienced or naive, suffered the same fate. While I changed some money for two of them, the Swede waited inside the station at Puno, guarding the luggage. He was engaged in conversation by a young boy and although he was sitting on top of their bags, a second older youth grabbed one and ran off. The unfortunate Swede was helpless, for to set off in pursuit would mean abandoning the rest of the luggage to the first boy.

Feliks and I took no chances. While we waited for the train, we settled in the back of the hall, so any prospective thief would have to escape through crowds of waiting passengers. We kept locks fastened at all times; we used body belts for money, passport and travellers cheques; and we sewed special lockable pockets inside the linings of our cases. Watches and cameras were never displayed without a firm grip being kept. The whole business made you feel you were constantly under attack. We were always looking over our shoulders and we came to distrust everyone; it seemed that all Peruvians were up to no good, and even the friendliest overture, was regarded with suspicion. Our travelling became inhibited by anxiety, and it became harder to mingle freely, harder to enjoy chance conversations, harder to linger and relax. Hotel rooms were regarded as unsafe, particularly in the more popular tourist centres, so we began to make for the more respectable establishments. And even then, in one of the smarter traditional hotels I had a $100 bill taken from a locked case in my room while I was in the bathroom.

Because of our imminent rendezvous with the BBC film crew in Lima, our travelling became a bit of a scamper. We bussed to Puno through the rain-sodden altiplano of Peru's lakeside farmland. We spent a day there so that I could boat out on to Lake Titicaca to see the floating reed homes of the Uros Indians. Then we caught the five am train to Cuzco, but the twelve-hour-long spectacle of Peru's eastern mountain ranges was leadened by the grey drizzle. At one point, while I was out on the platform photographing during a brief stop, the train began to move off. I jumped on to the footplate but my entry was barred by a locked door. The steward kept the doors bolted to deter thieves and I now had to hang to the outside of the train as it gathered speed. For fifteen minutes we skirted rocky ravines and crossed bridges over gorges hundreds of metres deep, until at last I was recognised as a bona fide passenger rather than a particularly persistent pickpocket. Reluctantly the steward opened the door to safety. Those locked doors effectively cut us off from the realities of Peruvian train life and we became armchair travellers, watching from the cocooned comfort of a sealed fish tank. No old ladies passed through selling their wares, no bare-footed kids came with baskets full of oranges and skewered meats. But at least for a brief while we were 'safe'. To the intense irritation of the steward I took every opportunity to unlock the door and get out on to the platforms to photograph, or to stand on the footplate to catch uncluttered shots of the passing scene.

Sitting opposite us was a friendly Swiss man called Bruno who had taken time off from a business visit to South America to do an overland trip from La Paz to Lima. His German friend Lena told us that she had just spent three months working in the jungles of Peru on an agricultural survey. She had first hand knowledge of the living conditions of the new settlers in the forest areas of the eastern lowlands and the devastating effect these newcomers were having on the local Indian populations, who were being forced off their lands. She confirmed what I had heard in Bolivia, that the soil under the forest was unsuitable for farming and what there was was quickly swept away by the violent rains, once the protective cover of the forest had been cut away. But the Peruvian President Belaunde, as part of his election campaign, had promoted the building of a road across the mountains to open up this region which he believed would solve all Peru's economic problems, and the project had become a symbol of his candidacy. So he was not prepared to countenance the findings of the various international surveys. Meanwhile the colonists, encouraged by government programmes and publicity campaigns, continued to arrive and were driving out the local inhabitants only to find that the promise of wealth and prosperity was a hollow one.

Lena and her colleagues on the project, were very concerned by the government failure to recognise the problem, but her tour of duty was finished and she had to return to Germany. For the time being she had just stolen a few days in Bolivia, and was returning to Lima via Macchu Picchu. Then she intended to spend two weeks on the Galapagos Islands before flying back to Europe.

It was night when we pulled into Cuzco. Hanging tightly on to our bags, we went in search of a hotel, conscious of the vulnerable fleeceable image we presented to the town's notorious thieves. Cuzco was cast very much in the same mould as Katmandu, Kabul before the Russian invasion, Bali and Istanbul. It was a town given over to the tourist industry, with streets of colourful 'ethnic' restaurants playing loud disco music and serving some local dishes with hamburgers and pizzas for the less adventurous or homesick diners.

Western hippies and easily recognisable and always appealing Brazilian hippies squatted alongside the local Indians, selling roughly-made crafts and trinkets to fund their continuing journeys. Dozens of shops and stalls offered sweaters and ponchos, artifacts, carvings, gourds, silver, jewellery and mock Inca relics. Like all such centres where the international travelling community gathers, a generous supply of coke, hash and pills was always on hand. Local sharks mixed easily with amateur foreign drug peddlers, supplying the needs and habits of the travellers. Sometimes they did deals with the police, shopping the unsuspecting and claiming a reward thus getting their money twice over. There were always enough naive, wide-eyed innocent or plain stupid foreigners for the local villains or the unscrupulous 'gringos' to make their easy money and of course the pickpockets had a field day with the planeloads of daily arrivals. The sad droning complaints of the victims with their stories of mischance, could be heard being miserably related in coffee bars all over Cuzco. Rumours flew around about arrests or raids, or super heists, but they just added to the general circus atmosphere.

Cuzco was also a great meeting place for fellow travellers. 'Didn't I see you in Asunción, or was it Santiago?' 'Are you going to Cajamarca from here or down the Amazon?' 'No, I haven't got time for that; I have to be back in Paris for the start of my job at the end of the month.' 'How was that river trip you were going to do into Brazil from Trinidad?' (the Bolivian one). 'What a coincidence, I stayed in Santiago with Fleming as well. He's nice isn't he?' Fresh-faced English girls managed to retain their clean-cut openess, their virginal look and their wonderful Englishness in the face of the most persistent onslaught of macho locals and equally pressing fellow travellers. Sally for instance detailed an assault typical of the kind she dealt with daily. A policeman had approached her in the street, grabbed her in the crotch and with a big grin suggested they go together to a hotel. 'If I'd screamed or yelled,' she assured me, 'I would have landed in jail out of spite. I wouldn't be able to prove anything.' Instead she had to smile and say that she didn't think her husband (imaginary), whom she was on her way to meet, would care too much for the idea. The policeman immediately let go. His ego was unharmed, since he was not being rejected. He'd simply met her too late. She was the property of someone else.

But generally these girls, like the imperious and unruffled Freya Starks of the post Victorian world, who passed through similarly hazardous landscapes, came through it all white as the driven snow. Even after months on the road, they gave the appearance of having emerged only days before from the safe confines of an English country village. They were strict and firm with hopeful suitors and had travelled everywhere. Whether they were riding with the gauchos in Argentina, sailing down the Amazon in Brazil, or living with an Indian family in the Andes, they had seen and done it all. But throughout they preserved that awe-inspiring air of innocence, and even the most evil-intentioned people they met, finally fell over themselves to help and guide them.

Of course there were many exceptions. Some fell by the wayside, laid low by illness or misfortune, while others succumbed to their natural lusts and desire for a good time; not all cared to cling to virtuous images. But these descendants of those dogged nineteenth century pioneers carried on the tradition fearlessly.

Laura, an Oxford graduate, was British through and through and had been nine months on the road. She scolded us for travelling too fast and doubted that we had sufficient grasp of Spanish to make any valid observations about South America. How could we possibly make judgements and write a book on such scant experience? I protested that we were recording experiences and conversations, things that happened to us as we travelled, and that those, with pictures too, would serve to tell our patchwork story. Our book was not intended to be an authoritative work. But she was not convinced. 'You came with preconceptions and they're bound to affect what you write,' she insisted. 'Who will you have conversations with? How will you know they aren't spinning you a yarn?'

The conversations and friendships made when lonely travellers came together in places like Cuzco after months on the road, were warm and comforting and bound many into a sort of international fellowship of adventurers. Even though we would go our separate ways in a few days, there was always the feeling that we would meet up again sometime in the future. One young French artist I met on my second day in Paraguay, turned up again in Rio six months later, drawing portraits on the beach at Ipanema. A girl I met in Santiago had grown up with my truck-driving farming friend Jorge, in Tierra del Fuego. Feliks ran into a Polish childhood friend on the streets of Rio, and a Polish pre-war diplomat in Quito.

Cuzco managed to remain an idyllic place despite the unconscious efforts of us messy travellers and tourists to spoil it. It was a beautifully-preserved colonial town with Inca traces at every corner. Two huge churches faced each other across the main square, which was encircled by arched walkways and stylish first floor wooden balconies. Radiating from the square, were narrow streets of white plastered houses, with quiet courtyards and reddish-orange tiled roofs, which when they were viewed from the surrounding hills, gave the appearance of an orange cobble-stoned valley between two green mountains. The town bustled day and night, and in the late evenings, the strong scent of hash hung on street corners where the sound of guitars and low European conversations floated from behind closed doors.

Talk in the cafes was about Reagan's victory in the US elections. Bellicose Israeli hippies were delighted; but opinions elsewhere were divided. 'O lagrimas, o peligro, o mundo triste' (Oh tears, oh danger, oh sad world) proclaimed the headlines of *El Diario*. 'Un golpe para los trabajadores y campesinos de Sud America; al ultra halcon cowboy conservativo esta in La Casa Blanca.' (A blow to the working people and peasants of South America; the ultra hawk, conservative cowboy is in the White House.) Others feared for the futures of Nicaragua and El Salvador, and expected early recognition of the Bolivian regime, and support for the governments in Chile, Argentina, Guatamala, Paraguay and Uruguay.

Many people we met had experience of arrest or harassment, of thievery and thuggery to tell, and all felt, like us, the insidious uncertainty of daily life in South America. The insecurity was so pervasive that one felt the mood of the people of the continent to be as volatile as the land itself, with the ever-present threat of volcanic eruptions and earthquakes. Unsettled. Unstable. Irrational. Irresponsible. Capricious. Erratic. Precarious. Although there might be occasional upheavals all over the world, for South America this state-of-affairs was permanent. The elections in North America seemed to herald a continuation of the unrest and repression, and the rejection of reformist policies and representative government.

In and around Cuzco, the Inca ruins lay in profusion, broken and symbolic, yet disappointing in many ways when we recalled that they were after all, only 500 to 800 years old. Were we not losing perspective? Even my university college was older than that, and it was still very much in use. And what of Karnak and the Pyramids, and Rome, India, China and Athens? Two thousand years old and more. Were we perhaps overloading the Inca and Aztec civilisations with greater importance than they deserved? The way in which the Inca had dealt with the impossible terrain, building roads and cities throughout the tortuous Andes, was indeed a superhuman feat. But the ruins themselves were less imposing. The terracing on the steep slopes, the water transport systems were certainly impressive, but the far older Himalayan civilisations were just as extraordinary.

South America needed its history, its antiquities, its heroes and legends. Each South American country had a need to place itself in the spectrum alongside India, China and Europe, to satisfy the desire for greatness, for world stature. The Latin need to be admired, respected, to be the best. So all historic references heavily supported by the modern upsurge of travel PR, were inflated with little selectivity, to create an exaggerated sense of grandeur.

Sacsahuaman, Kkenkko, Puka Pukara and Tambo Machay were all manifestations of Inca architecture and civilisation and lay on the luxuriant mountain route to Pisac, a small village on the Urubamba, the sacred Valley of the Incas, nestling at the foot of a steep cliff. On the flanks of the cliffs, were layer upon layer of immaculately-preserved farming terraces. A fortress and temple watched over the town from the top. Half way up, tucked against the cliff face at crazy angles, were the granaries, hanging as if in mid air. Once they had stored the winter food supplies for the whole Inca community, but now they were empty.

Feliks chose to return to the village by car to explore, while I made for the top, enjoying the physical effort in the thin air; my intention was to descend the sheer hillside in the manner of the old Inca fleetfoots. But the trouble was that their skilfully constructed, but tiny trail of steps, which ran straight down from the fortress, ended abruptly at the edge of a 200 metre drop, just below the granaries. I could see the central square below between the red-tiled roof tops, and what seemed to be a crowd of children, gathered in a circle. I realised from the car parked in the square, that Feliks must have settled to draw and had attracted the inevitable admirers. I dreaded to think that they might all be watching my unhappy and undignified descent as I slipped and scrambled, and slithered down the nerve-wracking mountain. But I found that although I could see them clearly they had not in fact noticed me at all. There I was imagining that my dicing-with-death drama was being played out under the anxious gaze of an audience of hundreds, when all along I was alone in my own private vertigenous hell! It transpired that I had missed the normal trail, which took a much gentler route round the side of the hill.

The medieval village itself was a delight, with farm animals wandering the cobbled streets at will, and school children doing handstands in the village square. Shopkeepers laid out their wares in front of their grubby shops with old oak doors overhung by drooping wooden balconies. Oil lamps and candles lit up the gloomy interiors.

Back in Cuzco we had a choice of trains to Macchu Picchu, pride of Peru's Inca heritage. The first class tourist train at seven am, was reliable and safe from thieves, while the local train was slower and crowded and left at five-thirty in the morning; and on that you were guaranteed to lose all but your underpants. We played safe and joined the jetting visitors on a spectacular train ride through the Urubamba river valley, the mountainsides becoming more abundant the further we went, the tumbling river below, more turbulent.

From the train terminal on the valley floor, the ruins of Macchu Picchu were hidden from view, which made anticipation all the greater as seven coachloads of middle-aged tourists with us in the lead, rushed from the train to the buses, fighting and scrambling in a most unseemly manner, to be first in the queue. The gravel road zig-zagged up one side of the valley to where a large tourist hotel marked the entrance to the site. A ring of forest-covered peaks enfolded the Inca city, as protectively against the tourists now as it had done 500 years earlier against the invading forces of the conquistadores. It was only in 1911, that an American, Hiram Bingham, had stumbled upon it during his South American travels. I scampered on ahead of the crowds, past startled llamas grazing peacefully on the terraces, so that I could get shots of the virgin archaeologoscape, before it was swamped by the swarming multi-coloured visitors. Feliks true to his contrary way, set himself to record the endless string of tourist variations.

There sat Macchu Picchu, smugly secure in its emerald setting, backed by the dominant peak of Huayna Picchu waiting for the latest batch of sight-seekers to arrive, ready to show off its exquisite shapeliness to an expectant and breathless audience. It was almost too perfect in its majestic isolation. Tumescent clouds hovered above, threatening to drop their rains over the abandoned city.

Pablo Neruda:
> *Entonces en la escala de la tierra he subido*
> *entre la atroz maraña de las selvas perdidas*
> *hasta ti, Macchu Picchu*
>
> *(Then on the ladder of the earth I climbed*
> *through the lost jungle's tortured thicket*
> *up to you, Macchu Picchu) Translation by John Felstiner*

My curse or blessing is the urge to battle against emotional glooeyness, defending my supposed watchful validity. I just managed to beat it down the few times it began to flood over me: mostly in the face of nature's magnitude.

*Thus I may be prejudicially armed against Neruda's sonorities. And he
must have seen his Macchu Picchu when still unpolluted by the tourists'
invasion. Polluted, or, to me (watchful, not kneeling to), revived into this
century in its grotesque contredanse of not quite confrontations. The myth city
gripped in the Cordillera's fierceness, raised from the dead, becomes a stage for
the futile antics of non-pilgrimages. And, properly, these circumambulating
corteges – not imagining any need for a ritual and the climax of an altar – are
redeemed (but not aware of) with the only available/left-to-us act of worship
(sacrifice?): the copulating young pair (meaningfully German/Polish) on the
highest pinnacle above Macchu Picchu.*

Bit by bit, the tourists began to spread over the whole site, like ants,
nosing into every crack and corner. I could see Feliks some twenty
terrace levels below settling on a rock to draw the invading hordes.
I watched as two and then three young women sat down near to
him, shyly at first but soon drawn into a growing circle of curious
voyeurs which ebbed and flowed as some people remained and
others left. By the time I joined him, he was holding court with four
girls while continuing to sketch the changing scene in front of him.
Lena, who had come from Puno with us on the train, joined our
group, but soon she and I decided we needed exercise and we set
out to attempt the hour-long climb to the top of Huayna Picchu.
   The trail was narrow and steep, and the stepping stones,
occasional remnants of the Inca construction, were slippery from
the humid mist. At 3,400 metres the pressure on the lungs was
painful and breathing came in gasps and gulps. But I found that
going slowly was just as uncomfortable as going quickly, but took
longer, so I tried to keep moving at a faster pace. Lena fell behind,
but I continued to push on, bathed in sweat, the thin air rasping in
my throat. The ruins lay like a relief model below and the drop,
from where we clung to the path way, was sheer. The last bit was
the worst. The Inca must have had tiny feet, because the remaining
sixty or so steps, painstakingly etched out of the rocks, only allowed
room for a toehold and went vertically up the mountain. I felt my
nerve going but just ahead of me the only other person on the
mountain, was pausing for breath. The urge to beat him to the top
overcame the vertigo, and I scrambled the last thirty metres up to
the wide slab of rock which was balanced at the very pinnacle. All
around was sickening emptiness, but the view was magnificent.
Range upon range of forest-clad mountains stretched away into the
distance, fading finally into the incoming mist, and below, tiny
human specks moved about over the ruins. Further down, on either
side of Macchu Picchu, the hazy sun was reflected off the waters of
two rivers which meandered vaguely through the mountains.

My rival climber wanted a photograph of himself in heroic pose and we made reciprocal records of our achievement. As he started his descent, Lena arrived. We sat for a few minutes enjoying the lonely tranquillity and I drifted off into erotic fantasy. The phallic slab of rock, the height, the exhilarating thrill of the climb, and the best known, most photographed spot in South America, all combined to make this a moment to savour. I urged Lena to celebrate it with me. At first she felt it was too public and that someone might arrive at any moment: and anyway it was cold, and it was about to rain. 'Why not later when we get back to Cuzco?' she suggested. 'There's no time now; we'll miss the train.' The more we talked the more it had to be. I pleaded with her to think how we would be reminded of the moment all our lives every time we looked at a photo of Macchu Picchu. 'We'll never ever have such an opportunity again; it'll be a unique encounter.' As the rain began to fall my fantasy became hers, and we spread ourselves across the rocky slab. The reality outstripped the fantasy and we abandoned ourselves to our chosen moment. Later, we took off all our clothes, so we could feel the rain cool against our hot skin. We felt an intense euphoria as we stood absurdly aloft like mythical conquering heroes.

It was with light heads and bouncing steps that we raced back down the mountain, through the now deserted and sodden ruins, and on to the hotel to catch the bus to the train. As the bus zig-zagged down the mountain, following the contours along fifteen or sixteen switchbacks, a young screaming boy took the direct route down through the forest, emerging on to the road at each level as the bus approached, to give a tortured cry, before plunging once more into the forest crossing with the bus again on the switchback below. His race with our bus, punctuated by his outlandish cries, caught the imagination of everyone aboard; and when we reached the bottom, we were all delighted to see the little poncho-clad figure running into the station car park ahead of us. No one begrudged the 'in flight' entertainment fee he claimed as we transferred to the train.

The train ride back to Cuzco was tiring and we agreed that Feliks would fly on to Lima in the morning, and I would remain another day, fly to Ayacucho, and then spend a few days alone travelling down by bus and train, to join him and the BBC crew.

I left Feliks at the airport the next morning in the company of Pily, a delightfully flirtatious Peruvian woman, who promised to make sure he got to his hotel in one piece. She offered to show us Lima. I spent a lazy last day with Lena in Cuzco, before she left for Lima and Ecuador, visiting the disappointingly modest Temple of the Sun, the market, some of the many churches and museums filled with ornate religious carvings and murals, and ancient and narrow Loreto street, flanked by well-preserved Inca walls. We had lunch with our militant Israeli hippy friends and a bemused American businessman on holiday, who tried to speak up for Carter; and we watched a bullfight to the death, shown live on television in gruesomely loving detail in a small cafe, while thunder, hail and rain pounded the square outside.

North west from Cuzco, through the mountains was Ayacucho, a hot, dusty, sleepy, friendly town. It was poor and dirty, but pretty, with its thirty-three churches and its homely central Sucre square. The streets were strewn with rocks and mud, washed down from the surrounding mountains by the daily violent storms that pummelled the town for three-quarters of an hour every evening, to the accompaniment of high winds, thunder and lightning. In retrospect, the unusual turbulence might well have been a godly warning for the series of earthquakes that were to hit Ayacucho a few days later, killing thirty people and causing heavy damage. Ayacucho suffered two further earthquakes in the three following months making it South America's 'unluckiest town of the year'.

I spent a fruitful afternoon photographing in the market and at the cemetery where the townspeople were preparing to celebrate the festival of Tupuamara, one of the Inca kings. They were cooking meals for the dead, tending the burial niches of their departed loved ones, arranging flowers, nursing infants, feeding adults at roadside stalls, playing fairground games, gambling, promenading and consuming ice creams and cold drinks and a host of delicacies. Everyone was relaxed and comfortable.

As the afternoon wore on, more and more people arrived in crowded local buses, all dressed in their best clothes. The greatest activity was at the front gate to the cemetery, where everyone gathered to exchange gossip once they had paid their dutiful respects inside. The approach road was lined with makeshift stalls dispensing food and beer, and drunks rolled happily along, led often by patient youngsters sent by mum to make sure dad didn't get into trouble. The celebrations continued all night, mostly by candlelight, because the electricity only came on sporadically, and never over the whole town at the same time.

A filthy sewer of a stream flowed through the middle of town, in which children swam and mothers washed clothes, sheets and babies with equal vigour. Mangy, flea-bitten mongrels picked through the rubbish that lined the banks, and rats scavenged for the leftovers. Miserable shacks, made up of planks and cardboard tacked and gummed together, tumbled into the gully through which the dirty stream ran. Other shanty huts dotted the outlying hillsides. These were to be the worst hit homes when the earth moved later in the week, and it was the people who lived in them, the most vulnerable people of all, who suffered most.

My bus ride on through the mountains, which I had undertaken expressly to see the dramatic mountain scenery, proved to be a disappointment. The three o'clock departure time was delayed until seven and it was dark when we finally set off on the twelve-hour journey. Although I could just make out the swell of hovering mountains, sense their shadowy hugeness, I could see nothing clearly however much I peered. We stopped for dinner at eleven o'clock at a roadside hut, and ate potatoes and stew; then we thundered on through the night along the twisting mud track, climbing and dropping, lurching and rolling, dozing fitfully while our collective lives were entrusted to the doubtful abilities of the driver. He blinked rather more often than seemed normal and I hoped that he would stay awake until daybreak.

Huancayo was plopped bang in the middle of one of the richest and most fertile valleys in the Andes. It was also a busy, fast-growing, unattractive industrial centre. The bus arrived fifteen minutes after the daily train to Lima had left, so I booked on to another Hidalgo company bus for their midday run over the Andes and down to the coast. It was a pity to have missed the train, because the ride was reputed to be one of the most startling of South American experiences. But I discovered that the bus trip was every bit as spectacular.

Four hours out of Huancayo we reached the stark dramatic black slag heaps of the mining town Oroya, crouched in the lee of a wild mountain at 4,000 metres. Wall slogans exhorting the campesinos to vote *Socialista* or *Communista* or *Revolutionista*, which had lined the route through the altiplano, now gave way to *Belaunde para Presidente 80–85* as we approached the capital. We took a short break for lunch, and a coffee to keep the driver awake, and then set off on a run through some of the most extraordinary mountain scenery I have ever seen anywhere in the world.

At just under 4,800 metres, higher than the tallest peak in Europe, the mist shrouded the snow caps that towered above the Anticona pass, and peeked out occasionally between gaps in the cloud. Open cast mines scarred the landscape here and there, creating a burst of colour, as subterranean rock was exposed to the outside air. These small settlements seemed to have been dropped haphazardly into the midst of the savage terrain. A large deep crater lake lay still and forbidding in this remote and heroic world, and the busload of people fell strangely quiet.

The road at this point was not good, and was made worse by the fact that the driver had a disconcerting habit of overtaking into the face of oncoming traffic on blind corners, slithering and sliding on the clay track, made wet by the descending mist. The erratic driving, the lack of oxygen, the sliding zig-zagging road, the mist and the splendour of the scene produced an atmosphere of silent tension and drama in a bus that earlier had echoed to the lighthearted chatter of Peruvian travellers.

Then we were diving down through the deepest of gorges, with the river Rimac, red and polluted from the mines, crashing and bounding below. Above us, the startling railway, completed by the American engineer Henry Mieggs in 1893, clasped the canyon wall, suspended in space, disappearing and reappearing through countless tunnels and over soaring bridges. The blood red Rimac collided with the white Rio Branco, swallowed it up, and continued down the mountain towards the Pacific, only slightly diluted. Sometimes the canyon walls were so close they seemed almost to topple into each other high above the road, while at other times they stood before us blocking the way ahead until at the last moment we swept round their edge, or plunged into a dark tunnel.

At last the valley began to open out, and as darkness fell, the descent became shallower, and narrow parcels of flat green land appeared, wide enough to support farmsteads, which now took over from the precariously perched mining communities. Ahead were the blinking lights of Chiroco barrio, and beyond it the untidy dingy sprawl of suburban Lima. We sped into the city along a wide auto route, skirting the low hills on which rested a profusion of shanty towns or Pueblos Jovenes. And when I reached the centre, I found that there too, even at the very heart of Lima, was a broken, decaying inner city, with crumbling walls covered in slogans, and only the handsome presidential Plaza de Armas and the Plaza San Martin providing any sense of grandeur or style. Occasional glimpses of the courtyards of private residences, smart restaurants like the 'Tres Monedas' where we filmed, or offices showed signs of restoration and care; but for the most part, central Lima was in need of a thorough overhaul. The rich middle classes lived in the west of Lima, beyond Plaza Grau, towards the ocean, in modern districts like San Isidro and Miraflores on the coast, and only came into the centre for business or other particular reasons.

CHAPTER 7 FILMING IN PERU: the perspective changes

If the taking of photographs obstructed enjoyment of simple human contacts which make this sort of travelling such a pleasure, then the filming was far worse. Our efforts in Chile had provided a foretaste of what was to come, but there we had been a pretty amateur team without great expectations. Now suddenly we were in a different league: full three-man camera crew, director, big budget, three star hotels, flights paid for by the company, a schedule to keep to, and a proper film to show at the end. In short, responsibility and a serious job of work. No more wandering and recording on a whim; our time was now to be accounted for. We were no longer independent. It was churlish to complain of course since we had agreed to do it, and had even suggested the idea in the first place. However the original intention had been for us to carry on the journey in our own way with the film crew descending on us inconspicuously now and again to record *our* trip. But unavoidably in the event, it curtailed and inhibited our movements and changed the nature and the flavour of the adventure. The presence of a camera crew blocked everything and stultified spontaneous encounters.

Something that particularly exasperated Feliks was the crew's constant references to their past assignments and filming occasions. The anecdotal prattle distracted us all from the present, from what was going on in front of us. The tendency of travellers to compare everything to other or better known places he found equally infuriating: 'It's just like Cornwall,' they said; and 'When I was in India, we did the same thing.' It reduced the uniqueness of where they were by trying to assert their own experience over everything in an effort to display their travelling credentials. In their defence perhaps those travellers were instinctively trying to reassure themselves in an alien environment by reducing it to cosy, unthreatening familiarity.

Our time in Lima and indeed the rest of our visit to Peru was inextricably bound up with the filming. We spent long sessions discussing the schedule, where we would go, what angle we would adopt and what we wanted to highlight. Only in the late evenings when filming was over for the day could we pursue our own pleasures. But filming was a tiring business and Feliks had to conserve his energies for the next day. So I spent time with Marco, a Peruvian friend we had met in Copacabana, exploring Lima and enjoying his friends.

I dallied with Pily the flirtatious lady who had accompanied Feliks from Cuzco. She wanted so much to come out of her shell but found it very difficult, being unmarried and a virgin at the age of thirty-nine. 'Que lindo, Dani,' (how lovely) she whispered. But nothing could alleviate her fears; she was sad and guilty and religious, and wished things were different, but lacked the courage to make them different.

The British ambassador asked expressly that we be positive about Peru, and that we refrain from doing what he called the 'usual BBC hatchet job'. He spent a long time extolling the virtues of the Belaunde government, 'elected under impeccably democratic conditions', and suggested that we film the mining and the fisheries and the agriculture and avoid the slums. 'Show the progress,' he begged. He and other British diplomats in South America had obviously born the brunt of angry official reactions to past British television investigations. Show the good news, they said, not the bad.

Between filming sessions, I was able to spend time on jironde La Union, the central street market, and wander San Martin square which was always alive, day and night. Groups of men, young and old, gathered in the square for long political arguments, or to view the porno magazines which were spread out for sale on the pavement, a side product of the new liberalisation policy and freeing of the media. One woman who sold them, kept her eight-year-old daughter with her, the future of whom must have seemed depressingly predictable.

During the day, other mothers walked with their children, and tourists joined the outer edges of the debating crowds while barefoot beggars pleaded with outstretched hands. Sometimes acrobats and magicians performed. But at night the hookers, male, female and transvestite prowled the square, sometimes standing in little knots talking while they waited for customers. A few stalwart old women kept food stalls, cooking eggs and savouries and making sandwiches and snacks; 'I'm here every day,' said one when I stopped to chat one night, 'from eleven in the morning until five or six the next morning, seven days a week!'

Pickpockets thrived in the early evening as the foreigners from the nearby big hotels strolled out before their evening entertainments. A crazed old lady harangued the crowd, and a sad hunched girl picked knits from her head and crushed them on the paving stones. Well after midnight tough pre-teen kids roamed the streets and squares, pretty, cheeky, sometimes violent, and usually sleeping rough.

In the early hours of one morning, I was returning to my hotel across the square, and caught the eye of a girl with long black hair. She smiled, I stopped and within moments she had manoeuvred me behind one of the statues. Her hand was inside my trousers, and things were getting a little heady. 'Come to my place,' she panted huskily. How could I refuse. But as we searched for a taxi, she seemed to change her mind. 'Another time,' she suggested. I protested but she disappeared quickly. Our brief groping resulted in the loss of $10 that she picked from my pocket, and the discovery that she had been a very convincing transvestite.

My curiosity about the rough bawdy parts of town derived perhaps from a subconscious seeking out of that violence and danger for which South America is so known. Tramping the late night streets was not so much the fidgetting of an insomniac or the search for pleasure, as an amassing of visual and completely unique moments which could never be experienced at home. I had an addict's restless need for action and challenge and it was possibly my subconscious and partly unfulfilled expectations of that excitement that pushed me on. All the same, when you were on the road and alone, and you didn't know the ropes, it was better to tread carefully. Danger always lurked for a stranger; he was easy game. But if you kept your wits about you, and you didn't show off, you could usually pass without bother. And after all, to miss out on the brothels and the dope dealing and the sex shows and the cock-fighting, and the clandestine gambling that flourished beneath the surface, would have been a shame. There was, in those seamy backstreets, away from the inhibiting formality of the elegant clubs, a lively irreverence, and a raunchy rude spirit that transcended the glumness and depression of the poverty around it and got the adrenalin flowing. Life was more fun on the wrong side of the tracks. Besides, here was the still living world of a past Europe long since sanitised and rendered mercenary and cynical. The brothel/ courtesan life of the nineteenth century was out in the open then and the respectable middle classes vigorously pursued their pleasures unashamedly and unhampered by guilt. The heroines of Toulouse Lautrec and his contemporaries came from this world, a world in which they themselves grew up. I coveted that brash uninhibited stylish harmony, that pandemonium of street erotics, and was able, here in South America, to reach back into the living past. But even in the briefest of encounters, I still needed the 'romantic' element, that personal exchange and friendship which gave credence and softness to my lusts.

Feliks confirmed that he too, in his earlier days in the cities of pre-war Europe, had sought out this world, away from the gentility of polite society. We both felt also that alone on a long journey a traveller is vulnerable to romantic fantasies, and is perhaps over prone to embellish even his most fleeting affairs with rhapsodical tenderness. But at the same time such relationships established along the way afforded a more intimate contact with the heartbeat of an unfamiliar country and inevitably helped in getting to know a place better.

One evening, Marco and his friends took Feliks and me to a cock-fight. We had accumulated an extra group of people around us, including six French travellers I had met in Ayacucho and an adventurous miniature blonde Canadian teacher, barely out of school herself, encountered that afternoon in the market between programme meetings. We all piled into the back of Marco's custom-built pick-up truck and sped off through the streets of Lima to the down-town venue, where fights took place three times a week. All was quiet outside, but inside the door, crowds jostled eagerly to pay a £1.25 entrance fee. The small amphitheatre and balcony were full to capacity with men betting vociferously with each other and with the ten official numbered bookies. Anything from $20 to $200 changed hands for each fight. At floor level, the enthusiasts were restrained by wire netting which enclosed the sand-strewn fight area. Above the arena, at first floor level, the balcony encompassed the wire cage from which the elite of Lima society, slumming for the evening, could observe the show with pisco sours in their hands and young fashionably-clad girlfriends hanging on their arms. Here too were the owners and their families, agonisingly distanced from their beloved strutting cocks, which they had entrusted, under the rules, to experienced handlers below.

The crowd bayed for blood. Cock-fighting aficionados were proud of their sport. With disdain, they dismissed bullfighting as mere childsplay. Here in the sweaty, bloody close atmosphere, the true lovers of blood sport gathered to indulge their passion.

Beautiful, lovingly-groomed roosters were carried in, their feathers shining healthily. The handlers caressed and fussed and coaxed them, stroking the heaving chests of the frightened birds as they circled the cage showing them off to the crowd.

Then on the count of three they were thrown into the centre of the ring where they circled each other, sometimes cautiously, barely moving, sometimes haughtily, stiffly dipping their proud heads, and at other times darting into a premature attack, only to be dragged apart again by the handlers. Often the two birds would ignore each other completely. Then the handlers would gather them up, and proceed to half throw them at each other, infuriating them, teasing and baiting them, letting them peck painfully at each other's heads, just enough to arouse their ire.

They were provided with deadly curved knives, strapped to their ankles, with which unconsciously, they would slash and stab at each other until a mortal wound was inflicted. These short terrible spurs glinted under the hot bright lights as each bird underwent the final preparations.

Bets were laid amid a cacophony of sound, as the punters shouted their offers and others drew attention to the various attributes or failings of the two preening creatures.

A few more parries by the handlers to raise their fighting spirits again and suddenly there they were, in the centre of the arena, face to face. One had to die, sometimes both; there was no escape. It was raw and brutal. If they tried to hold back, lacking heart for the battle, they were gathered up once more and swung at each other, forced to flap, induced to claw with their killer feet. Then once again they were thrust to centre stage. Suddenly one would attack; they would dip and dive amidst a flurry of feathers, duck and sidestep over and under each other, but always lashing out with that deadly dagger, until one would strike home, piercing the heart or severing an artery. The stricken bird would falter, continuing bravely to flap and attack, but too weakened to worry its opponent. The victor would stand arrogantly to one side, watching the loser in its death throes. The whole action tended to last little more than a couple of minutes, or three at the outside. The lethal daggers reduced the fight to a game of chance and a very short one at that.

A lucky strike ended the contest.

It was a sickening sight, but we watched five fights, none of us much enjoying the spectacle, yet persevering out of morbid fascination and some misplaced investigative sense of duty. In one struggle both cocks were mortally wounded and sank pitifully to the ground, waiting for death to overtake them. The crowd went wild. Everything depended on which head hit the dust first. Every one watched spellbound as the two heads sank lower and lower to the ground. Finally the black and gold bird keeled over and a triumphant roar went up from one section of the crowd.

The defeated birds were casually whisked up by the wings, sometimes still dying, and carted unceremoniously out of the arena; very different treatment to the cossetting they had received before the fight. The victors were smoothed and gentled while the dagger was detached from their ankles and then, after a victory tour of the ring, they were carried out if still alive, to be prepared for future fights. The more famous owners were always pointed out respectfully by the knowing audience who were delighted to find a bunch of gringos straying so far from the beaten track. They were keen to inform us of all the nuances and complexities of their bloodthirsty sport. One of the owners, a bulging, mustachioed man, came down from the balcony with his family and accosted Feliks, eager to see his drawings.

In contrast, we explored the more esoteric levels of Peruvian society. Diplomatic and society receptions led us to subsequent meetings and conversations with political figures and commentators, who gave us informed opinions about Peru.

Fernando Belaunde was three months into his second term as president. His first term had ended twelve years earlier when a military coup, with left wing reforming promises, drove him from office. Now he was a right of centre democrat, and had come to power with a great fund of popular support. He had quickly set about restoring the trappings of democracy and when we met to film our interview with him in the palace courtyard, he was preparing to formally hand the newspapers back to their rightful owners, restoring the freedom of the press. He was sombre and impressive and gave a statesmanlike performance. The ceremony, attended by the whole Peruvian press corps, was simple and effective. He seemed genuinely moved by the event as he pledged himself to the defence of democracy and free speech.

Later the editor of *El Comercio*, the leading right wing daily, celebrated the release of his newspaper with his rival editors in a bar across the road from the palace. I asked him if he was satisfied with the outcome and he said: 'We must wait and see. We back

LIMA

President Fernando Belaunde Terry

democracy, and Belaunde represents democracy at the moment. So
we will support him for now. But we feel he is a little soft on the left,
tolerating strikes, that sort of thing.' Yet this same editor had a lot
of admiration for the left wing paper *El Diario*, which had also been
liberated by Belaunde.*

When we spoke privately to Belaunde, he talked enthusiastically
about his pet project, the road over the Andes to the jungle, which
he promised would open up Peru. But he was not too keen to
discuss the growing problems that were being aired by the
international experts, nor the human suffering that was caused by
the influx of inexperienced campesino colonists from the mountains. His supporters pointed to the stability that had come to Peru
since his election, and the freedom people felt to speak and to meet
and to publish. But his critics accused him of not tackling social
problems, of dragging his feet. They expected serious trouble in the
future if he failed to address himself to the needs of the peasants.

While we were filming in the slums one day a local man
approached me on his way home, and started to rail against the
government. 'You're quite right to take pictures here,' he said
angrily pointing up the hill. 'There is no lighting here, no running
water. And here we are in the centre of Lima, in the heart of the
country. It's disgraceful. It's a bad government; they do nothing.'
Behind the Presidential Palace, beside the river Rimac, old down-
and-outs dozed drunkenly on the pavement or picked through the
refuse and rubbish piled high along the banks. Our film director
had invited a local guide to talk, on camera, about slum poverty. 'The
tourists rarely see this Peru. They are not interested. They come,
knowing what they want to see. It depends though on which
guidebooks they have read and from which countries they come. The
English, they like history and archaeology, but the French are more
intellectual and they want to see the museums and contemporary
culture. The Americans are the most relaxed; they like the people, and
have read books about anthropology. The Germans are the hikers, the
outdoor types.' Feliks questioned the choice of location as a typical
slum, since alcoholic bums were a common worldwide feature from
New York's Bowery to Hong Kong's Kowloon, Moscow, Bombay,
Soweto and London's Charing Cross arches.

A retired United Nations official, who invited us to tea at his
smart villa in Lima's San Isidro suburb, reported that socialist
feeling in Peru, although very strong, was deeply divided into ten or
more groups, each propounding different left wing philosophies.
'They refuse to unite,' he observed. 'Hugo Branco for instance, is a
hero of the resistance and a Trotskyite. He remains completely
uncompromising and separate and sabotages any attempts to unite

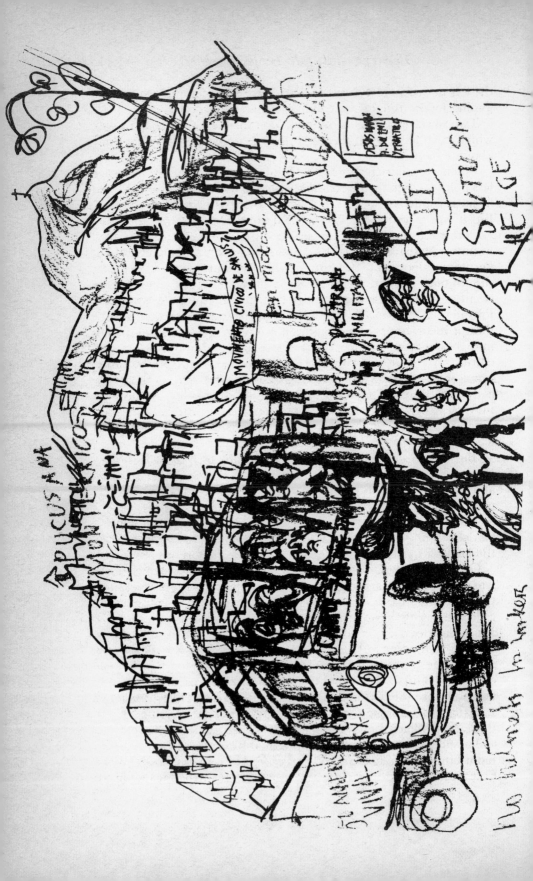

the left in this country. But at least there has been some success in joining forces to fight the coming municipal elections.'

Two weeks later the left alliance won the local elections in Lima, which must have given the Hugo Branco group something to think about.

When we suggested that the campesinos in Peru seemed even less political then they were in Bolivia, our UN friend observed that in both countries they were more motivated than they appeared. But it was true that many were still politically naive.

Carlos Zusunaga was the leader of a new centre-right party, Freinte Centro Democratico, and he spoke articulately about Peru's problems and the future, when we dined with him at the sumptuous, pseudo Victorian style Club Nacional, built in the twenties by the same Polish architect who had designed the Presidential Palace. He saw one of Peru's greatest problems to be that of incorporating the majority campesino/mestizo population into the modern world without destroying traditional values and culture. In his view the impact of present western technology was providing little benefit to the mestizo/indian population: 'Politically, the "Indians" are not exactly bystanders,' he said, 'because they do things in their own way. But up on the altiplano, they are illiterate and not very active in party political terms. Most political leaders don't even bother to visit them.'

'But I've never seen a country so politically busy, so ridden with slogans,' said Feliks. 'There are hammers and sickles, red stars, and slogans everywhere, in the tiniest villages, even on the mountain slopes.'

'Political slogans are not decisive in political results,' replied Carlos. 'And in fact those that did vote do not necessarily support the left. They did after all vote Belaunde into power.'

Outside the Presidential Palace, the daily changing of the guard was a raucous affair. Soldiers goose-marched barely in step and the trumpets blew off key. The stern Indian faces of the young guards reflected Peru's Inca ancestry, and in the Rafael Larco Herrera Museum, a vast display of pottery heads, dating back a 1,000 years, showed a stunning variety of expressions and detailed facial types and bore testimony to the fact that people had changed very little over the centuries. The characteristics and the expressions on the faces of those soldiers and of Lima's daily stream of shopping and walking pedestrians, could easily have substituted as models for those pre-Colombian potters.

To satisfy the requirements of the film we needed to visit the mountains again, to explore once more the campesino life of the Quechua Indians. So we flew north east to Cajamarca, across fierce mountain chains, with patches of green amidst the red and brown parched crags, and landed in lush pastureland and a cool fresh climate, exhilarating at 3,200 metres. Within an hour we were installed in a fine old restored inn, with rooms on two, colonnaded, balconied floors, surrounding a central courtyard. Behind the town rose a steep hill, half way up which was a stone seat from where the Inca Emperor Atahualpa was said to have reviewed his subjects. It was here that the conquistador Pizarro ambushed and captured Atahualpa, held him to ransom, and demanded that two chambers be filled with gold and silver to the height of the Inca leader. Although the Inca carried out the requirements of the ransom, Pizarro executed Atahualpa anyway and ended the Inca empire once and for all. One ransom room, a dank, bare, poorly-tended chamber measuring about four metres by five, and three metres high, still stood just off the main square behind the cathedral. A large faded mural had been painted above the steps leading to the chamber depicting Pizarro and Atahualpa in the ransom scene. While I was there, a school party holidaying from Tumbes, down on the coast, noisily married me off to one of their classmates. A mere $2,000 was their asking price and I nearly agreed. The guard was quite appalled by our charade in the holiest of holy places and threw us out.

There was time to explore the town. The market was in full swing, with handsome, eagle-nosed, dignified women, wearing richly embroidered shawls and fine, high-crowned, wide-brimmed, panama straw hats, tending their well-stocked stalls, and coping as usual with sprawling squalling offspring. Apart from the uniqueness of the local costumes, the now familiar scene differed in one respect. Nearly all the women and young girls constantly spun wool on little spindles, whether they were negotiating prices, suckling babies, sitting discussing the world or simply walking in the town.

The men were in greater evidence than I had seen elsewhere in Andean markets, and wore the same hats and occasionally tended some of the stalls. To Feliks they seemed physically more exciting, more forceful than in Bolivia. The main Plaza des Armas provided a gentle and exceptionally photogenic tableau of a town and its people at peace with themselves. I had to constrain myself on my use of film in Cajamarca. I had estimated that a roll and a half a day on average would see me through to the end of the trip, but here I was in danger of using up a two-week quota in a single afternoon.

I climbed the hill to Atahualpa's throne and looked out over the town and the country beyond. A tiny girl sat in the king's chair, her grubby bare feet dangling over the edge. Maria Luz was seven years old and wore a torn grey school uniform. She was a lovely, serious and articulate companion. She told me about Cajamarca, her school and how difficult it was being a campesino girl trying to handle town life and a school where most of the other children were richer and more sophisticated. She drew a picture of me and I did one of her. Hers was far better.

Later, in the town, I followed a funeral with crowds of mourners walking behind a slow-moving hearse. School was breaking for the day and children streamed out on to the streets mingling with the cortege. Groups of youngsters ambled home, chattering to each other. But one girl walked alone, a few yards behind her classmates. She talked animatedly to an imaginary friend next to her, imitating the expressions and gestures of the girls walking in front. She was a sad, lonely, little creature. Here in this small town there was a definite sense of town versus campesino, the latter regarded as interlopers, outsiders, there to sell their wares and leave. They trudged in from the surrounding countryside laden down with wares and babies strapped to their backs and set up shop in the market. In the same way that the people of Lima looked down on the mountain people, the Cajamarca residents regarded the campesinos as a race apart, lower class and inferior.

We spent the next day out in the hills, driving along dirt trails through some of the most luxuriant landscape we had seen in South America. It was a scene of idyllic rural life, with small farmsteads and villages along the roadside bathed in stillness and sunshine, and cattle and pigs being driven along to market. Farmers hoed and tilled the fields, and streams coursed down from the mountainsides. Yet the lushness concealed an underlying hardship that had brought much tragedy to the region during the previous three years. A campesino mother stopped to talk to us, spinning all the while, her baby strapped snugly to her back. She spoke in a lilting sing-song voice, her speech full of diminutives, in the linguistic style of the Peruvian peasants.

'The last three years have been very hard. No water. The little cows died and the little pigs. I lost six of my nine children in the drought.' She talked on in a matter-of-fact tone, resigned to the struggle of life, not expecting anything better, just waiting for what each new day would bring. She was twenty-nine years old and looked to be in her forties. If drought had ravaged this harmonious land, what hope was there for the people of the barren, desolate Bolivian and Peruvian altiplano, or for those in the shanty towns clinging to life above the vast metropoli of Lima, La Paz, Santiago, Valparaiso, Rio and the cities of Argentina.

We stopped to eat on the outskirts of Cajamarca at a run-down

Revolutionary turned commercial traveller

restaurant across the road from the Ché Guevara petrol station. A huge portrait of Ché which hung outside was the station sign. The restaurant specialised in 'puy' – guinea pig – the special delicacy of the region. The camera crew took one look at the kitchens and left for the more acceptable eateries in town. Next to the unhygienic lavatories, three old ladies in black were beating in the skulls of the guinea pigs, and then skinning them, beheading them, and washing the tiny white corpses, while pigs, chickens and dogs sniffed about. But the puy was delicious, a cross between roast duck and pork.

Sitting round our table eating lunch was a curious mixture of people. Two out-spoken radical students, a university lecturer and the janitor from their college, argued, along with our driver, that Belaunde had shown very little interest in reform since he won power. He had better buck up his ideas, they said, if he wished to retain the support of the people. We were joined by a large fat man in a glittering, white lace shirt, who seemed to be the epitomy of the local bourgeois businessman. But he quickly disabused us of our first impression. Over the next two hours, we learnt that Pedro had joined APRA, when it was the leftist political party, (now it stood to the right of Belaunde) in the early sixties. He had gone to Cuba to study and had made friends with Guevara and Fidel Castro soon after their revolution, and had returned to Peru to join the resistance to Belaunde's right wing, repressive regime in the mid sixties. 'Havana and the experiences there enchant one, and would induce anyone to follow that correct path,' he told us. There was a lot of support in Peru for Ché Guevara in those days, he went on, and even now he was still widely regarded as the peoples' hero. Pedro spent two years in the hills until he was captured; then he spent seventeen months in Belaunde's prisons, being tortured and starved.

'They squeezed my cohones and put me through the water torture. I was degraded. I had to watch my close friend taken up in a plane and thrown out.'

Pedro was released when the reformist military putch in 1968 ousted Belaunde, and for a time, he says, there was hope. 'They tried to push through radical agrarian reforms, but finished by selling out like Peron in Argentina.' He explained how their cooperatives didn't work and how the country fell into chaos. Another military coup, this time a right wing one, brought back all the torture and repression which lasted until this year, when democratic elections were allowed and Belaunde was returned to power. He won, said Pedro, because the favourite APRA leader died before the elections. 'Now there is something like democracy and freedom of speech.'

Although our companion was an intensely political man, he was reluctant to enter into politics himself, because he felt it was a corrupt world and he would have to compromise too much. He believed in world revolution, although not in the rigid dogmatic style of the communist block. He preferred a liberal socialism, he said, along the lines of the new Chinese model. But he was not shy about speaking out. He was depressed by the lack of political motivation of the Indians, by their passivity, which led to Ché's downfall in Bolivia. 'Our experiences were very similar,' he said. 'We made the same mistake expecting the support of the campesinos – he in Bolivia and me in Peru. The peasants saw the gun fire of the army and got frightened. I won't say that there were not peasants who offered their lives, but in the moment they didn't do what they promised. The campesinos stay outside the system, whether it's left or right, and their lives change very little, while the leaders line their pockets.' Many of his colleagues had opted for the easy life, for 'military boots', as he put it. He blamed the United

States for supporting unconditionally all the rightist military regimes, and arming them, while at the same time torpedoing reformist and liberal governments. 'It's not that I'm a convinced communist,' he declared, 'I just wish the Americans could try to understand South America more, and behave more correctly towards us. We simply want justice, democracy and freedom from oppression – the very things that the United States believe in.' He despaired of the divided leftist groups in Peru, of the Trotskyite Branco who he regarded as a clown. 'All they need is one representative leader to rally behind, and they could win. They fail to see how the right keeps them weak and divided. But at least there's one good thing. We are free to talk; before, we didn't dare.'

Belaunde might have been the most widely travelled Peruvian politician, the one most closely in touch with the hearts and minds of his people, but there were still a lot of sceptics scattered around the country who still needed a lot of convincing.

Next morning we drove back to the coast, to Trujillo, Peru's second city, set on the desert strip between the Andes and the Pacific. On the way down, we stopped every so often to film the scenery, the aeroplane arriving from Lima from over the mountain-tops, and the campesinos working in the fields. I managed to fit in a little training too, taking off on a run ahead of the car, while the crew were setting up a shot, and managing three or four kilometres before they caught up with me. I was surprised how little the altitude, at 3,000 metres, affected my breathing, and I felt distinctly light-headed as I loped along through the mountains past surprised shepherd boys and startled flocks of sheep. On another occasion, I climbed up to a series of shallow caves, high above the road, because we had been told they were Inca tunnels, but they penetrated only a few metres into the mountainside.

The landscape became progressively more barren, until by late afternoon, we hit the flat, hot, dusty desert and joined the coastal Pan American Highway – north to Ecuador and south to Lima and Chile. I was filmed hitching beside the road, since, within a few days I would be travelling back up along this road to Quito. But first we planned to spend a day filming in Trujillo and at the archaeological sites nearby. We arrived at night in the midst of a dramatic, torch-bearing, political rally in Trujillo's main square.

Our mornings were still spent discussing with the producer what we should film, the strategy and the synopsis, to the extent that very often we ran out of time to film the subjects we wished to cover. Then we would spend more time discussing what we should drop. While we waited in the hotel lobby to start filming, Feliks fell into conversation with Jaconda, a glamorous Lima girl, who was in

Tourist and Quechua Indians, Cajamarca

Trujillo for a business meeting. She was dashing and alert and thought it a wonderful idea that we should meet in Lima.

The film crew were very patient and very professional. They were, in the union-bound world of British television, that rare breed of 'guerrilla' camera team that relished shooting ad-lib, and took pride in getting it all done before breaking for the day. Their grumbles took the form of frustration over delays, inefficiency, lack of planning, rather than the usual gripes about the quality of the hotels or the difficulty of the terrain. The cameraman – a shaven-headed Australian called Chuck – was an adventurer in film making terms. He was a perfectionist too, always keeping his eye out for the unusual shot, preferring to work through for fifteen days or more, to the end of a shoot, before taking a break. His assistant Tom was bred more in the style of the union rep, sometimes obstructive and with one eye on the rule book; but he was a joker too, always recounting tales of other assignments. But his long association with Chuck had instilled in him the same pride in getting the job done no matter how hard the conditions; as a result, they formed a flexible and talented team. The sound man was quiet, thoughtful, and personable, and liked to join in discussions about what we were doing and seeing. Like all sound men he was unobtrusive, often underestimated or forgotten even by his camera colleagues, but he offered up good suggestions during shooting.

South of Trujillo, through the desert, was the village of Moche, which ten years earlier had been devastated by an earthquake. Its continuing existence shows how remarkably resilient the human spirit is. Cities fall, and are rebuilt, and people live on. The town was undergoing a process of rejuvenation and reconstruction, and despite the nightmare they had been through, there was a festive air and a flamboyant humour amongst the people here on the coast that contrasted sharply with the dour melancholia of life in the mountains. Here the music was gay, the drink flowed freely, and the women sang and danced the marinera. One woman swept Feliks into the circle of clapping dancers for an impromptu award-winning duo performance.

A mile or so along the coast, a few hundred metres back from the shore, rising like two great earth mounds, were the Pyramids of Moche, the largest pre-Colombian remains in South America. They were made up of thousands of adobe bricks, little different to the ones that were currently being used to rebuild the village. After a cursory visit we decided that after all, we had had enough of ruins. We preferred the here and now, the living to the dead. 'I'm interested in current life,' declared Feliks. 'This 'antiquarianist' looking back is escapism; it dominates our society today. If it's impressive in itself, that's fine; but I don't want my observations about a pile of stones to be shaped by a mass of literature. I'll leave that to the academics. Moreover we spend vast amounts of money preserving old ruins for the tourists, while neglecting the poverty-stricken people living in modern ruins across the road.' He slept in the sand, while I climbed to the top to photograph the surrounding plain, and the crew gathered some necessary sequences, including the disinterested and prone Feliks.

However, we were still not finished with ruins. Complaining bitterly, we went on to Chan Chan, north of Trujillo, which, we were promised, was of spectacular interest. More adobe walls, much of them reconstructed with newly-made friezes hewn into their lower portions, copied from one or two original patterns. The walls had been tidied up and many had been built anew. But after Macchu Picchu and Pisac, everything was proving to be less than thrilling, and since we lacked the burning zeal of the archaeologist, our curiosities had been more than satiated. Their value for research and study was no doubt of great significance, but their general appeal was limited. Our interest lay more in the way the campesinos today still built their homes like little fortresses in the style and with the same materials that their forefathers used. The dilapidated, abandoned and earthquake-mauled remains of their modern compounds looked little different from some of the antiquities we had seen.

We made for the airport to catch the plane back to Lima, and stopped off at Huanchaco, a small fishing village a few kilometres from Chan Chan. The local villagers were sitting in the late afternoon coolness on the sea wall, watching the sun setting behind the little, short-sterned, flat-bottomed tortora reed boats, or caballitos, which were stacked upright on the beach. The church bell rang out from the top of the hill above the village, and a tiny girl ran to fetch her brother because she was too shy to be photographed on her own. This was a far more fitting and satisfying end to the day than Chan Chan.

Political activity in the days before the municipal elections was at fever pitch and everyone seemed to be involved. Any equivalent period of local electioneering in Britain would have appeared pedestrian and apathetic in comparison. For our last day of filming, we drove thirty kilometres south of Lima along the coast, past row upon row of extensive low hangars packed with battery chickens, to the village of La Lurin, where the flags were out and political speeches rang through the streets. Leaflets poured from cavalcades of horn-blowing cars and trucks, and children ran into the road to collect the literature for their parents. One scantily supported party

with only two cars, watched dispiritedly as the widely attended
rally of one of their rivals ended to wild applause and swept out of
the square. Then before they could move up to take the stage on the
steps and patio in front of the church, a travelling folklore troup of
musicians arrived, after winding their way through the town like
pied pipers, collecting an audience for their free midday concert.
They were students from the University of Lima, hailing from all
parts of the Peruvian sierra. Their music was flute based, using the
traditional Zampona, or multi-barrelled 'pan' flute, and the single-
barrelled Quena. Violin, bongo drums and the shrill whistle so
beloved in South American music, rounded off the ensemble. The
leader's girlfriend performed the dances. The wretched politicos sat
mournfully across the square. When the band had finished, we took
them first to lunch where they accompanied a touching fin de siècle
conventional old harpist on the stage, while Feliks drew, and then
off to the stillness of the hills to record their music for subsequent
use in our film. There they dispensed with their raucous rousing
tunes, and charmed us with the subtlety and feeling of their
playing.

I began to look forward to the next two weeks travelling on my
own. The film crew were going off to Brazil to make a film about
football and Feliks was due to fly on to Quito in Ecuador where we
would meet for a week's visit. Then we were going to continue
again separately, up to Bogota in Colombia, to rejoin the crew for
the next instalment of the film. Feliks and I were now agreed that,
when our interests conflicted, we would split up for a few days. So
while I went off overland, he pursued his own curiosities and made
early contacts in the cities where we planned to spend some time.
Next day we dispersed, and I prepared to fly east to the jungle and
then make my way to Ecuador by land.

Alone in Lima, I had a chance to relax and to fill my remaining
two days as I wished. Much of this was spent wandering the streets
and enjoying the life of the cafes. Jaconda, our friend from Trujillo,
had returned to Lima, and we went out dancing one evening. Our
first, brief but keen impressions of each other were confirmed by
closer acquaintance and when the clubs closed, we were reluctant
to separate. But to spend a night together was not a simple affair.
No respectable girl, she assured me, would ever be seen going into a
hotel in the city with a man. The normal procedure for middle-class
indiscretions in Peru, like it was all over South America, was to go,
during the day, to one of the many motels on the outskirts of town,
where rooms for courting couples, complete with plush red
upholstery and sycophantic service, could be rented by the hour or
for the day with no questions asked.

'But I don't like those places,' she said. 'They make you feel like a whore, and besides I might bump into someone I know.' The clandestine nature of all encounters made everyone jumpy and guilty.

I left her at her front door and made my way back to my hotel, dallying for a brief conversation with a tough young hooker who was trying to get into a locked house. The male voices inside refused to open the door unless she agreed to sleep with them all, and she discussed the pros and cons with me on the doorstep. She finally decided that they were a better bet than I was, and yelled her acceptance to their terms through the letter box.

I met Jaconda next morning and we hit on the bright idea of hiring a car. If it was impossible for us to be together in town, then we would drive out of Lima and spend the day along the coast. I got a Volkswagen Beetle, and we set off across the desert, collecting her swim suit from home on the way as a pretext for our expedition. We visited her favourite beaches, but they were crowded with holidaymakers. We changed direction and wound our way back into the hilly sand dunes, the car wheels spinning in the loose sand, and with farm dogs barking and chasing us as we passed. Finally we found a concealed spot surrounded by dunes, with the desert stretching away to the east and the ocean washing against the coast below us. With rare and grateful abandon we spent the afternoon free of prying eyes and guilty thoughts.

Having the car for a while gave me more flexibility so that I did not have to rely on the Lima taxi-drivers, whose knowledge of the city was a good deal worse than mine. Many operated privately using their own cars. I had spent hours with them, circling various districts, hopelessly lost, until finally, out of desperation, I had taken over control of the search. Since the price of the ride was always agreed in advance, clocking up extra mileage was not the reason, and tipping was not normally expected anyway. There was simply an overriding smell of defeatism emanating from each driver; a hopeless sense of doubt, it was as if they had long ago, given up believing in their ability to find an address. They were used to failure.

I meandered about Lima, visiting churches, beaches, cafes and avenues that I had noticed before in passing, but had not been able to explore.

The flamboyant priest in charge of visitors to the catacombs beneath San Francisco church, told me I was *caprioso* because I preferred to go round alone rather than wait for the slow-moving, Spanish-speaking, group tour. And after I had been round the impressive but run-down monastery, which was undergoing painstakingly detailed restoration, and had wondered at the vast tombfuls of skulls and bones and scorpions and dust in the cellars, the same priest bade me farewell, saying: 'Thank you, congratulations.' Why? Was it because I had broken the rules? or because I had survived the scorpions?

I photographed the main squares and the statues and called at the embassy to collect eagerly awaited letters and pore over the British newspapers – always two weeks old, but a welcome link with home (Foot breaks foot, Reagan election reactions, rowing news). I noticed when I re-emerged that one of the car headlamps was missing, but decided that it must have happened before I hired the car. For safety I locked the spare tyre and windscreen wipers away. But when the silver metal trimming around the car disappeared as well, during another two-hour stop, I realised that even as I drove around Lima, things were being ripped from the car's superstructure. Next day the reputable hire firm insisted that I should bear the cost of all these thefts and informed me that the insurance, which I had paid in advance, did not cover these items.

The daytime and early evening scenes around the cafes of Miraflores were a different proposition to the night time ones in downtown San Martin. Barefoot children sold flowers and washed cars. Pretty women in the regulation smart baggy jeans, high heels and accessories cruised the shops and the fashionable meeting places. Dark coffee-skinned mestizo girls, tall, pale, leggy girls from mainly Spanish parentage, broad-featured, black-haired beauties, shorter and plumper, from more Indian backgrounds, all mingled in a continuing stream of disconcerting loveliness. Teenage girls on roller-skates, wearing satin shorts and bright smiles, displayed their skills provocatively. The men, on the other hand, showed far less propensity to beauty; features which in the women were exciting, seemed coarse and pinched in the men. Admittedly I had the tendency, when out on the street, to look through and beyond the less attractive plain women and men, and focus mainly on the people I found good looking. That was after all my pleasure. There was a special type of South American beauty, generously proportioned, tall, loose, stylish and graceful. Brazil streamed with such spectacular girls, but they were also there, although perhaps in fewer numbers, in all the countries we visited.

Chile had the reputation for the brightest and most liberated women, and their growing feminism and awareness was beginning to spread. Two hundred years ago, the combination of Chile's abject poverty and literate European population had produced a climate where it was possible for women to go out to work. Gradually they won an independence and an economic freedom which set them apart from the rest of the continent. But women elsewhere were slowly following suit, and the male-dominated societies of Latin America were under severe pressure. In some cases this liberation was interpreted by 'macho man' as a growing pool of available females for their consumption.

Two girls, one with a breathtakingly shaped bottom, accepted an invitation for tea, and we talked about some of the prevailing attitudes in Peruvian society. They knew that more liberal ideas held sway in Europe, and they said they would love to let their hair down a bit, but that it would make life impossible for them in Lima. Yes, of course, they would like to try for good jobs, have children on their own if they wanted, or go topless on the beaches like the girls did in Brazil and in Europe; but men here just would not be able to cope. They would just stare and touch and jeer. As if to illustrate their point, the driver of a car that was passing in front of our cafe, slowed down as he approached a girl crossing the street, reached out and grabbed at her breasts. My companions shrugged resignedly and laughed at my astonishment.

The flow of political cavalcades with honking cars, flag-waving crowds, roller-skating girls and loudspeakers was uninterrupted on the last day's electioneering. Three short honks on the car horns meant PCP the Partida Communista de Peru, while two long blasts, followed by three short ones represented Action Popular Party. On the eve of the election, Lima ground to a halt, submerged beneath the mass rallies that filled the avenues and squares. San Martin was full of chanting, militant left-wingers, supporting the '38' party. Number '34', less left and combining most of the liberal parties, drove through other parts of town, while the very right APRA party, and Belaunde's slightly less right Corrego party, derived their greatest support in the middle-class areas of Miraflores and San Isidro. There, smartly dressed, middle-class boys pasted Corrego leaflets to the lamp posts.

I settled at the Haiti bar where youngsters rushed in to beg at the tables, between clouts from the waiters. A young Cuban exile sat down at my table, and we talked politics while we watched the noisy cavalcades. He had come six months before to Peru with his pregnant wife, and he was not happy. 'The life I left in Cuba was far better than it is here for me,' he complained. 'Things like housing, medicine, technical training and employment in Cuba are guaranteed, but here it's many problems.' He hoped to go to Canada where he was sure life would be better, and he echoed the feelings of many South Americans I met, who believed that the United States were to blame for most of the troubles that beset the continent today. The eternal paradox remained. The Latins resented their dependence on the Yankees and the support they gave to the dictators while pining for, and relentlessly imitating, every feature of their way of life.

I drove to Callao, through the back streets of the smart coastal suburbs of Lima, and then along the coast. I knew I had arrived when I saw the rubbish dumped two metres high on the beach, along the whole length of Peru's leading seaport. Driving inland a few blocks, I came across some of the most shocking, numbing poverty I had ever seen. Only India and Ethiopia had anything to compare with it; but here there was a seething sense of anger, a threatening atmosphere that at first I only felt, but which soon manifested itself more obviously.

One or two children playing football in the street kicked their balls at the car as I passed, or hit the roof with their fists and feet. A scowling man on the street corner shook his fist, and a patrolling prostitute angrily spat in my direction. Yet I was only driving a battered VW. I kept my camera on the seat next to me, and occasionally raised it to my eye for a moving shot, down an alleyway, or at a group of people. But I made sure that no one saw it. The spontaneous anger was directed solely at the car. The kicked football may have been in fun, a variation of a local sport, the scowler may have been a drunk and the prostitute may have been in a bad mood, but the sense of foreboding was ominous and I did not dare to stop the car. Cardboard and wooden shacks pressed tightly together, flies and rats and dogs picked over the filth, and people with flat, empty expressions, hung around with nothing to do but wait and squabble and play football and drink, if they had a peso, and fuck and produce more kids to swell the miserable ranks of hungry mouths and hopeless lives.

It is possible that I over-reacted to the horror of the scene and read more threat into it than in fact existed, because normally I would not have shied away from such a place. Here was, after all, the raw material of the photographs I took, and the sort of world I often chose to explore. But all at once, strength and curiosity failed me.

I carried on to the end of the peninsula. Here, where the navy had it's headquarters, just a mile further down the road, elegant homes lined the sea shore and pretty colonial squares rang to the laughter of pale-skinned children dressed in gingham dresses and white socks and slacks. Fresh-faced girls, daughters of the ruling classes, roller-skated along well-maintained pavements, blond and brunette hair flying in the wind. Three rowing clubs faced the sea. No film could have highlighted the contrasts more vividly, as I cut from one scene to the next, and I had to go back to the slums to make sure I wasn't imagining the whole thing.

Later, back in Lima, I was taken to a sumptuous sports club overlooking the Pacific Ocean, with tennis courts, squash courts, football pitch, full length swimming pool, gymnasium, basket ball and conference hall and a membership of thousands paying $1,000 a year for the privilege of belonging. I met the Peruvian rowing team, rich aristo-Hispanics to a man, butch, young, arrogant, good-looking body builders, posing with weights, while fashionably track-suited, slight, adoring girls, claiming to be the women's rowing team, sat on the sidelines. I bored them with training talk, and the massive workloads that the British women's Olympic team which I coached in London endured in their daily preparation for their big races. They all looked a little blank. 'That sounds very painful,' said one. 'We like to enjoy our sport.' I invited them to Henley, but doubted if the name of Peru would ever appear on the lists of victorious Olympic rowing champions.

* By mid-1982 guerilla activity in the central mountains suggested that there was growing dissatisfaction in the countryside and the Belaunde government found itself under considerable pressure.

CHAPTER 8　A Journey to the Jungle and Back over the Andes

I wanted to get a preliminary taste of the upper reaches of the Amazon, which I thought would be deeper, thicker and narrower than downstream. I suspected that the effects of Manaus, the roads being cut through from coast to coast, and the bulldozing clearance of the Brazilian forests, would have destroyed much of what the Amazon had once been. Feliks still refused such titillating pre-tastes. He was determined to wait for the right moment – and that moment was to be at the Colombia – Brazil border just before Christmas, when we made our final and decisive crossing from the Spanish Andes. He wanted to experience the full impact without dissipating it in any way.

I flew east to Pucallpa, back over the Andean chain which I would be re-crossing yet again by land a few days later. The flight was a mere two hours and the change to thick rain forest rapid. Soon we were over the wide open, forest-cleared landscape of Pucallpa. I stepped from the plane into a wall of suffocating heat and almost immediately the sweat began to stream down my body. I caught the bus to town and checked quickly into a small neat but cheap hotel with a fan. Then I set off for the river Uyutali, one of the many wide tributaries which make up the Amazon Basin.

Decrepit rattling buses ground along rusty dusty mud tracks, crashing their worn out gears and scattering the ugly black vultures that swarmed about the town looking for scraps. People hovered on street corners and watched the flow. Movement was slow in the draining heat even though it was not yet midday. I wanted to get straight out of town and on to the river, joining in with the normal local traffic of boats and fishermen and small traders visiting the villages and settlements, upstream away from the immediate influences of modern town life.

The banks of the river were teeming with children and chickens, dugouts and launches unloading bananas from upriver, and people bargaining for prices and arranging their passage. One of the many drivers of taxi-boats with an outboard engine agreed to take me to the only village in the region which was fully Indian; the rest he said were mixed blood mestizo.

He dropped a group of girls off at the local mission and then navigated on past isolated villages, with dugouts pulled up on the shore, and children splashing in the water. Sometimes a canoe would pass by, with a family on the move, or a couple fishing with nets. The forest lay well back from the shore which had been cleared for settlement and subsistence farming. Cattle grazed, and there was a delicious sense of peace and tranquillity after the bustle of Lima and the desperation of Callao.

Three girls were bathing at the point where we came to land, and they turned shyly away covering themselves. But they followed me up the path to their village. Neatly laid out straw and wattle huts stood on either side of a central walkway. Their wooden floors were platforms raised over a metre on stilts. Women sat on them cross-legged weaving and preparing ornaments and rugs. A crowd of children kicked a football towards me drawing me into their game. Some men invited me to buy them drinks. The girls wore stylish short coloured blouse tops and wrap-around skirts. They had wide smiling faces, jet black fringed hair, pale skins and clear shining almond-shaped eyes and were, without doubt, the prettiest people I had yet seen, and the most open and relaxed in temperament.

The girls played football too and what's more, they also wanted me to invite them for a drink. Although there were things for sale, I felt no pressure to buy. But I felt I was intruding too. People were friendly but not over-awed. They were not over welcoming, they were simply getting on with their lives. My presence was just a small diversion, and I liked it that way. I would have liked to stay for a few days, in the way I had been able to, so easily, in Africa. I sensed that there would not have been any objection. But such unscheduled stops were not possible within my tight programme, and I returned to Pucallpa.

On the trip back, I tried to sort out some confused thoughts in my mind that had begun to trouble me. I questioned my puritanical attitude to money. Why did I flinch so at the mercenary way children and women demanded payment for photographs as soon as they saw my camera? Did I resent the signs of commercialism creeping into every aspect of life, affecting everyone everywhere? Why did I refuse on principle to hand out pennies to beggars, and why did I argue the price so determinedly with shoeshine boys who were overcharging, or with market women selling their wares? Was it because I didn't want to lose face in front of them by paying their first asking price? Was it because it was the norm to haggle? Or because I was always low on funds and couldn't spare the cash? Or that I was basically being mean? Or do I have the puritans' streak that is obsessed with the idea of the noble savage; the liberal wet who wants to preserve purity, and the picturesque traditional ways, and resents the impolite intrusion of such sordid considerations as money which bastardise all relationships and situations? Somehow the loss of such qualities as innocence and honesty and nobility and pride seemed bound up in the undignified scrabble for money. But perhaps that is just a load of hypocrisy. People are poor, and every extra penny helps. So why could I not just contribute towards keeping the economy turning over? The same really applied to my attitude to prostitutes which was based not on a moralising, critical viewpoint, but on the simple fact that money changing hands had such a stultifying effect on the encounter. I always felt that to make love to someone with any pleasure, required desire and affection and some commitment, or lust at least, on both sides. But when money changes hands it is a clear statement that the desire is only on one side, and that the act is dependent on the cash payment, and is devoid of any affection. What silly romantic qualms; pay the lady the price if it's a fuck you want. If not shut up and zip up or join a missionary group. Feminism and equality had no place here; women's lib had me firmly by the balls.

The children and the old ladies I wanted to photograph, the prostitutes and the shoeshines, were all trying to earn a living in a tough world, and they had a far more realistic view of it than I, with my patronising ideals. They were far more practical. Why not pay the pennies; everyone would be happy then – I would get the pictures, they would get the money. After all, if the *Daily Express* in London wanted to take some pictures of me, would I not charge them for my time? But still, my middle-class western sensibilities balked at the sight of kids scrambling round begging and fighting for tips. It was so 'unseemly'.

After years of travelling on a shoestring, I was finally beginning to come to terms with the harsher mercenary aspects of life. There was no escaping the fact that I was a European traveller, from a cosseted and pampered world, and my romantic quasi-liberal misgivings about the corrupting influence of money and tourism had little place in the real world. It was all very well for me to have my ideals while others starved.

Pucallpa had that earthy optimistic feel of a turn-of-the-century boom-town. Cocky and hustling despite its isolation from the rest of the world. But the twentieth century was catching up. Japanese motor bikes zipped by and some modern building and tarmac roads were in the process of being laid out, and quick service 'chicken'n chips' restaurants were dotted along the sidewalk of the main street. Fashion conscious girls paraded in the early evening.

It was election eve in Peru, and the cinemas and churches were supposed to be closed. No beer was supposed to pass the electorates' lips for fear that intoxication might impair their judgement on the day, or worse, prevent them from voting. But of course, in typical irreverent fashion, no one took a blind bit of notice of the ruling.

I ate chicken and drank beer at a main street cafe, and watched the arrogant urchin kids picking the scraps and bones from discarded plates on the tables around me as if doing the restauranteur a favour – a 'I wouldn't stoop so low, but since you insist', look on their faces – cleaning up, so to speak. They shared round the bones, lazily lounging on the wooden partition that surrounded the eating area, chatting loftily to each other like diners at the Savoy. They polished off unfinished cokes and beers, discussed particularly tasty morsels and looked down their noses at the assembled customers. When the waiter chased them off, they didn't scatter, but strolled away coolly, hands in the pockets of ragged jeans, only to return a few minutes later, unperturbed. It was a funny/sad theatre of manners, with the young boys salvaging a little dignity by their bearing, in the face of a humiliating situation.

As the cruising crowds began to disperse for the evening, I walked towards the outer edges of the town, past the barking dogs, towards the jungle night noises, the chirping and the whistling in the undergrowth. A wide variety of music and singing mingled with the jungle sounds and I made for one of the sources. People were gathered outside a bungalow watching a family performing a ritual before a homemade altar, with flutes and drum, singing and dancing. They circled and chanted, rested for a while, and then started up again. I passed by them at different times during the night and they were always hard at it. A little further on another party was in full swing. This one looked more conventional, with young well-dressed teenagers dancing to records, and the older people sitting outside in the courtyard of the little bungalow. Again a small crowd had gathered to watch. An old woman sat and surveyed it all from her rocking chair, and explained to me what was going on.

The party was a fifteenth birthday celebration, equivalent to our twenty-first, when a young girl was launched on to society. The poor girl had to stay away, across the street, hidden from view, while all her school friends danced and drank with her family. Then at eleven o'clock, she was led in triumphantly by her father, to great applause, a plump, plain girl dressed in pink tulle, deeply embarrassed. She then had to dance first with her dad and then with a favoured uncle while her assembled friends looked on, smirking, giggling, joking. She then moved to the centre of the room, turned her back on the boys, who had all gathered together, and threw her bouquet over her shoulder. The gallant who caught it, in this case a particularly popular good-looker, gave a short speech, and then invited her to dance. Still everyone else stood back, until their dance was finished. Then the party took over once more and the drink flowed freely again. The twenty-year-old daughter of my rocking chair friend, a slightly balding, sweet girl, laughed at me when I suggested a dance. She protested that that was not for the likes of her. Her mother agreed because her daughter was, she explained, a little retarded and everyone would feel awkward. She was chirpy enough though, even if the idea of a dance was given a firm veto. But we were able to talk. The mother expanded on a tale of woe. Her son dealt in drugs and had disgraced the family, and her husband had run off. But her friends were kind.

The star of the night had shed her embarrassment by now and was flinging around the room; and although the party was lively and informal, there seemed no place for me. As I walked on through the dark town, I noticed that many people were sleeping out in doorways and on the sidewalk, and a few odd-ball characters slinked about in the shadows, or gathered in huddled groups, murmuring. A transvestite, out of place in such a macho outpost, wandered disconsolately alone.

The trip back to the Pacific coast was the most exhilarating and least conventional part of my whole South American journey to date. And for that I was thankful. The first part of the journey by bus, from Pucallpa to Tingo Maria, crossed the low-lying rain

1. Villarica, Chile.

3. La Paz market.

5. Inca Terraces, Peru.

6. Cajamarca market.

7. Carnival, Rio.

8. Carnival, Rio.

forest region leading to the Andean foothills, except that most of the forest had been devastated and tamed. Thoughtless, unplanned clearance, had stripped the land of its protective cover, and far from growing rapidly back, as popular myth would have it, the trees of the Amazon had failed to take new root. Hillsides looked scarred and bare with felled trees lying scattered and shorn of their leafy greenness.

After a few hours, the first rolling hills of the Cordillera Azur appeared, and the landscape began to look wilder. Near the road, there were plantations of coca, raw material for the cocaine business which centres on Tingo Maria, where it starts its clandestine journey to the fashionable coke sniffers of the West. Control of the trade is hard, because the economies of the producer countries here in the Andes rely so heavily on the crop, which provides their peasant populations, as well as the middle-class dealers, with a living. The United States, while trying to persuade the governments concerned to put an end to the trade (which is directed mostly her way), knows only too well that to do so would endanger the position of those governments, because of the hardship which would be caused by the loss of such a vital currency earner. And should those governments come under fire at home, with a resultant threat to the relative stability of the region, then Washington would suffer, by losing tame allies and allowing less amenable regimes to take over. So the Americans have at the moment to grin and bear it; turning a blind eye to all but the most outrageous floutings of their drug laws. One of the prices she must pay for retaining the loyalty of obedient, stable, right wing regimes in South America is the continued unofficial tolerance of the drug trade, or at least a careful restraint on the imposition of punitive measures to stop it. And unless she can come up with any equally lucrative alternatives for the peasant populations of Peru, Colombia and Bolivia, things are going to stay exactly the way they are. Even the United States' much vaunted civil rights position has had to take a back seat in the effort to keep Latin American dictators on 'our' side.

Waterfalls began to sprout from the rock face, cascading down the matted green cliffs, as we edged up the gorge. Endless police checks slowed the journey. They would walk through the bus, examining passports and sticking slim spikes into the baggage. They then smelled the tip of the spike, testing for drugs and for contraband meat.

Around Tingo, the landscape was lush and lovely. The bus climbed on towards Huanuco from where I was going to cut north west into the mountains along less worn trails, well away from the bus routes. A little girl selling cold drinks settled into the seat beside me. 'I'm going to Lima,' she said grandly. 'OK,' I replied, 'let's go.' She giggled with glee and got off at the next stop. But she left me with a cold homemade drink which gave me diarrohea. On the whole though, most of the maize, cakes, fresh papaya and pineapples, sold at stops along the way, were fine.

It was after eight when I got off the bus, and together with Alberto, a nineteen-year-old Peruvian student on his way to the coast, went in search of a hotel. Rooms were scarce so we agreed to share a room. Alberto, who had seemed to be a quiet, unassuming sort of fellow, was keen to be out and about. In fact, he was hell-bent on a visit to the bordellos on the outskirts of town.

There was nothing surreptitious in the way he set about finding the place. He approached everyone we met, asking directions, until finally, at the end of a dark road leading out of town, we found it. A few cars were parked outside, and inside the entrance, a group of young boys peeked and sniggered at the buxom middle-aged women who stood at the doors to their respective bedrooms, chatting to each other, and to any of the passing men who cared to listen. Most slunk about peering into the rooms, or waited outside the door of their favourite girl, until she had finished servicing an earlier customer. Even my hot-blooded companion Alberto balked at the array of motherly figures who smiled golden-toothed grins of welcome. 'Yesterday in Pucallpa, I was with a sixteen-year-old girl for 400 soles (50p),' he complained. 'But here they want 800 and they are all like my grandmother.'

On the way back to town, he wanted to know about London's prostitutes. He found the idea of sex without paying hard to believe and the £20 charge for a prostitute had to be a downright lie. Here you fucked prostitutes and you went out with and married nice girls, with whom you later made babies. There was very little in between. We abandoned the quest, ate a kebab and went to bed.

In order to get transport out of Huanuco and over the mountains towards La Union, you had to go to the market place – on this occasion in the pouring rain – to where a line of trucks was parked. Co-drivers called out destinations and guided prospective passengers to the right truck. The cost for my ride was a mere $3, and no wonder. People were making dark prophesies about avalanches and collapsing roads as the rain thundered down. The front halves of all the trucks had been converted into makeshift, covered seating areas for passengers. To be more precise, there were three benches which should seat three people on each, but could be made to take up to twenty adults, or even thirty passengers, if half were children, or chickens, pigs or goats. Behind, in the open section of the truck, many more passengers could stand, along with the cargo and the baggage. The driver was usually hemmed in on all sides by feeding mothers and girlfriends or mates, and was hard pressed to turn the steering wheel, let alone cope with any emergency. This was alarming, considering that all the tracks in the region were 3 metres wide, slippery and muddy and soared hundreds of metres above the valleys and precipices of Central Peru. Small windows, which you had to bend double to see through were cut out of the wooden superstructure. I chose to sit close to one, in the vain hope that if, in what seemed the likely event of our overturning, or going off the edge of a 300 metre drop, I might have a 0.0001% chance of extricating myself through the said escape hatch to safety. Some hope. I even tried, ever so nonchalantly, to rehearse my escape during one of the many stops, under the curious scrutiny of a couple of children travelling in the back, and found that I could actually manage the feat in well under a minute. Somehow, I did not feel that that would be fast enough.

I'd been told the bus would leave at seven-thirty in the morning, but the driver revised our time of departure to eight-thirty. We were fifteen in the cab, room to stretch out I thought. At eight-thirty, the large taciturn weather-beaten, grumpy old driver got out and disappeared.

At nine-thirty he returned with a couple more passengers. So the seating arrangements was revised: passenger, driver and two passengers in the front; then me and four other passengers in the middle row; and then behind me, directly behind me, a snivelling coughing little girl – (I can still feel her sneezes dribbling down the back of my neck) – with four other children and three more adults on the back bench. In the rear under a tarpaulin, there were more. Right, I thought, we're off. We faced a sixteen-hour journey, probably more with all the rain, and I imagined the driver would be keen to get going so he could do most of the trip in daylight.

Slowly we moved off. But it was a false alarm. Instead we toured the town, looking for more passengers. At nine-forty-five we picked up another large, elderly woman. She had a nervous chicken with her, and she clambered into the tightly-packed row behind me. My little sniveller was now joined by a squawking, flapping chicken. Next we had to fill up with water, and repack the back. There I was, with one of my bags on my lap, a feeding mother next to me and another in front, the little sneezer over my left shoulder, and the prospects of a hazardous drive in thunderous conditions before me, loud squeaky mountain music issuing from the tape machine on the dashboard, repeating the same four Peruvian highland tunes, and I felt completely happy.

We repacked the truck yet again and moved some of the kids into the very back, including, wonder of wonders, the little sniffler. But now another man got into the back row and a woman whined to the driver for a front row seat and, eventually, even though everyone else had failed, she secured a place next to him. It was now ten-fifteen and still we crawled around the town. In front, a dust cart laboriously collected refuse, but our hero made no attempt to pass. One guy sat up on top amidst all the rubbish, while his mate ran alongside grabbing the boxes and heaving them up to him. He emptied them and hurled the box back down. The truck never stopped.

Our next port of call was the petrol station. The tank was underneath my seat so we all had to get out. On again and suddenly the town fell behind, the rain stopped, the chicken quietened down, and we rolled off towards the mountains, towards a little bridge over the tumbling river. But it was not to be. We didn't cross the bridge, but turned back down a bumpy side road to town, and joined the traffic jams once more, stopping briefly to buy something, and then carried on into the centre for more loading. Patience and good humour were beginning to evaporate. A new woman and her baby were squeezed in next to me and more repacking went on behind. We were now well over thirty people crammed into the little truck.

Finally, at eleven-thirty, we trundled off, over the bridge, and leaving the woodlands behind, we climbed into rocky scrubland, bumping along the narrow precipitous track running with water. Below the trail, on the valley floor, a red, muddy torrent raced by. Little farms clung tenuously to the steep mountain slopes, their fields tilted at crazy angles. We stopped twice for meals in lonely, muddy, wet villages. Often the lunch stops proved frustrating. A strong dislike of foreign travellers seemed to persist and the simple process of ordering food could take ages while all one's fellow passengers were happily advancing through their meal. Once or twice I lost my cool and became every South American's caricature of the ranting eccentric Englishman who can no longer cope with the inefficiencies and frustrations of Latin life. 'Agua mineral, por favor,' I asked. 'No Ai,' came the curt reply. 'Yes you do,' I said pointing to a bottle of mineral water and to someone else drinking one nearby. After much irritation and wasted time, I got the bloody drink. Foreigner baiting. Great sport.

I sat glumly pondering over the frustration and negativeness and hostility I had encountered so far on the trip. I was beginning to come to the sad conclusion that most of the charm and fun and adventure of travelling rough had been knocked irrevocably out of me by this South American experience. I couldn't tell though if it was me, tiring of this sort of travel, of suitcase living and language problems, opting for a softer life. But all the same, I doubted if I would ever again take on a similar six or eight month trip.

'Coming to his senses at last,' I hear you say. 'Finally growing up and accepting his responsibilities.' I suspected that in future I would restrict my journeys to two or three month assignments at the most, and for a specific purpose. I would forsake this wanton ambling. But then again, perhaps it was just a passing misery and the next day would bring a more positive outlook. Yet I was left with the overriding impression that the continent was ultimately rather charmless and ungracious compared to Africa, India or Asia.

'Eeyie, aiee, yie, yie' went the wailing high-pitched music over and over, as we splashed on across the darkening mountains. The worst danger now was that the driver would fall asleep at the wheel, and I urged the good ladies next to him to keep him talking, madly making sleeping signs to explain what I meant. They tried, but they soon fell asleep.

Half the passenger load had left the truck by the time we arrived in La Union; it was dark, silent and empty. Only the most ramshackled, rat-infested pension, sleeping three to a room, had a free bed, and the lights did not work. But since there was little temptation to stay up and explore the deserted little town in the rain, I bedded down with two strangers who were already fast asleep. In the next room were two Peruvian boys who were travelling on next day like me to Huaráz, looking for work, and they agreed to show me where the bus was. But they had gone when I awoke next morning at seven. I despaired of ever meeting a Latin I could rely on.

I remembered that when Feliks and I were discussing our itinerary in London, we had planned to make a five-day horse-back trip along an Inca trail from La Union, with the film crew in tow. Such an idea seemed laughable now as I trudged through the muddy streets, looking for a truck west. The rainy season was in full swing and even in fine conditions it would have been far too tough an expedition.

I found the truck going to Huaráz; well, not quite to Hauráz but to Huallanca; but from there, I was assured I could catch the bus on to Huaráz; and when I arrived in Huallanca, I found that in fact, no bus existed. But I did have a splendid little trip through steep rocky gorges, so narrow their walls almost met overhead, with grey torrents rushing alongside, and sometimes even along the track on which we rode. The first hour of the ride was made more

pleasurable by the company of a local teacher, a very politically
active man, who told me that his '38' leftist party had made great
headway in the national local elections. He spoke enthusiastically
about 'a new deal' and declared quite openly that he taught
outright communism in his classes. Behind were the two fellows
who had left me sleeping that morning, and I felt secure sticking
with them since we were all heading the same way. Also in the
truck were six girls and their brother who were going to a fifteenth
birthday party in the next town, and in front, next to Chino the
driver, sat the local policeman reading a pornographic novel.
Above the driver's head hung a Ché Guevara pennant, and
alongside it, a picture of Christ at the Last Supper. The words
'Power from the barrel of a gun' were written above them.

The territory we crossed was rough and tough, the scenery wild
and remote. Pretty soon, I would have had my fill of the splendours
of the Andes. I had also decided to put a stop to my pursuit of Inca
ruins and the trails which proliferated throughout the region,
because I wanted to spend more time making better contact with
people. I would simply be rushing up and down mountains to be
able to tick off this or that ruin and say 'wasn't Chavin beautiful'.
As it was, I was seeing breathtaking countryside coloured red, rust,
green, blue and purple topped with white flashes of the distant
peaks; and all around was the sound of tumbling water.

But I was having a relatively fruitless time communicating with
people. Even sitting as we were, huddled together in the truck,
there was little talk between passengers, and my thoughts drifted
back to Africa where the endless hubbub of chatter, and the
warmth of friendship and humour and the unabashed interest were
part and parcel of every journey, however short. Travelling in
South America was more like a ride on the Bakerloo Line to Oxford
Circus at eight-thirty in the morning rush hour.

I was dropped off at a little mining village, about 3,800 metres
up, with the assurance that, later in the day, something would pass
by on its way over the towering Eastern Cordillera ahead and on to
Huaráz. Once again my two companions disappeared without a
word. I tried asking the drivers of the huge Volvo transport trucks
waiting to be filled, if they were, by any chance, possibly going in
the general direction of . . . 'No,' they answered one by one, each
pointing a different way to the best place to wait for onward
transportation. First they had me waiting in the wrong place, then
they told me there would be a bus; then nothing for three days; then
that may be one truck would leave later in the day; then, many
trucks would be leaving next day. Confused and hungry, I chose a
spot to wait rather than find a meal, in case I missed something.

But there was no one else waiting there, so I didn't feel too hopeful. Maybe everyone else knew something I did not. And where were my two young friends – if I could call them that?

I sat disconsolately on a rock writing my notes, and watching two enormous pigs sniffing about for scraps in the rubbish beside the road. The air was thin and cold and an icy wind blew down the valley. I thought of making my blanket into a poncho, and mused to myself, as I watched a campesino man standing against the side of a building, how men in South America seemed to piss an awful lot, and always chose to do it in public. There had to be something more to it than just a weak bladder. (Maybe it was the same reason that when their soldiers harrassed peasants while searching for guerrillas, or fought wars and tortured enemies, they liked to cut off a man's penis preferably in front of his family. Maybe they were just very cock orientated.)

How patient they were too these people. They would sit at a junction, like the one I was at, for hours, day and night, day after day if need be, waiting until some truck or cart came along. And they were never perturbed if a driver decided not to stop, or not to take them. They seemed, the campesinos especially, to accept everything without a murmur. Often I would be travelling on a bus which stopped at two or three in the morning to pick someone up who had been standing in the cold and rain for hours, and often we rolled past old peasant women sitting alone, on high cold mountain roadsides, staring out across the valleys into the distance.

Finally a nice man from Juliaca joined me who was also going to Huaráz. He was going home on leave, but worked here at this remote mine because he could earn a lot in a place where few wanted to come. 'There can be good pay at the mines, but it needs long service before you get the best wages,' he said. It was pretty depressing working up here away from the world, especially for someone like him, who enjoyed the friendly warmth of the coast where his family lived.

At last, just as I was despairing of ever finding a lift, along came a huge lorry, one of the vast Volvo transporters. Perched at the very back were my two 'friends' and the driver waved to me to get up with them. My companion declined, and I soon found out why. As I went to throw my bag up into the back, they all shouted to me to stop. I clambered up the side and swung my leg over, and then realised what the problem was. The whole cargo was a muddy, molten mass of liquid 'plata' – oily, slurpy silver. I crept gingerly along the rail to join the other two sitting on the tailboard. Below them was an empty narrow section where I put my bag. But it wasn't safe there either and soon it was covered in black muddy slime as the foul liquid sloshed back over us while the lorry climbed its long swaying, jerking way over the Cordillera. 'It will be very cold,' warned the boys; but at that moment I was more concerned for my bags and the slurping that threatened to pour over us. In the normal manner of things in South America, no sooner had we started than we stopped, this time for lunch. I dined on two eggs and bread because the soup stew tasted foul. While the others finished their meal, I got ready for the ride and wrapping myself up in my blanket, settled uncomfortably on the edge of the thin tailboard.

At first it was exciting, and adventurous, trying to avoid the oozing slime as it ran slowly back towards us whenever the lorry lurched upwards. The exhilaration of the breeze, and the increasing spectacle of the red and black mountains and snowfields, and the roof of the world stretching far far away, peak after peak, through the clear air, was awesome. What a sense of freedom and elation there was at the sight of the vast expanse of jagged white pinnacles unfolding over the crest of each successive slope as we pulled up above the snowline. A great, greeny-blue glacier hung above the track.

I had not realised quite how vulnerable we were back there and it was only after a couple of hours that the cold really began to seep through, and the pain began to numb my backside and legs. My fingers clasping the sides of the lorry were frozen stiff. Then the hail started to fall and the wind whistled and we moved up into the icy mist that was descending about the peaks. Again and again we seemed to reach the top and begin the descent, but there were many descents followed by further ascents ahead, and the weather was becoming too hard to bear. The driver and his mate were cocooned in their cab and showed little sign of coming to our rescue. Two more hours of swirling damp cold mist reduced the three of us to chattering frozen snowballs, completely unprotected and with no imminent sign of salvation.

But then fate stepped in. We had been hotly pursuing a slow-moving truck some three kilometres up ahead, which was the only other sign of life on this desolate piste, and finally, after much hooting and cursing, we swept by in a flurry of skidding muddy snow. Two hundred metres further on, we blew a tyre and slithered to a halt, blocking the road. The other lorry was forced to stop too, and in an instant, I saw my chance. I made desperate signals to the driver of the other truck and detecting a friendly response, clambered, nay fell, from my precarious perch, and on numbed legs, made for the warm welcoming shelter of the rival cab. I felt little remorse deserting my companions since they had, after all, walked out on me twice before.

We edged by the stricken Volvo, and as they dismally waved goodbye, and we lumbered off down the mountain, the heavens well and truly opened, and the real storm began. Lightning crackled across the sky, the rain obscured the windscreen, and the thunder roared directly overhead. And even within the security of the snug little cab, tucked between the driver and his mate, I felt awfully vulnerable and exposed, 4,500 metres up the Andes.

After an hour the storm eased a little, and the landscape took on a softer more grassy character. Horses grazed, unconcerned by the thunder, alongside pigs, cattle and sheep. Curious sprouting cacti, some four metres high with thick black stems, looking uncannily like human figures, dotted the landscape. The dying ones produced bright yellow flowerings as a final defiant flourish.

We rolled out of the Cordillera Blanca and into the central Santa valley with its tumbling green lushness; rust red cliffs above topped with majestic snow caps on the eastern side from where we had just come; while ahead rose the barren dark Cordillera Negro, the last barrier to the Pacific. But before I crossed them I wanted to travel north, down the Santa Valley through the Callejon de Huaylas.

We turned on to the first tarmac road I had seen for days which followed the valley through to Huaráz, set in some of Peru's most glorious mountain scenery which drew mountaineers and hikers from all over the world. But this was also the scene of one of the country's most devastating earthquakes which had destroyed people and towns throughout the region only ten years previously. The damage was still being repaired, and as I made my way down the valley the next day, villages, like Yungay and Caraz, and many of the valleys running out from the two Cordilleras, were still cruelly disfigured by the scars left behind by the avalanches and the upheavals.

The road alongside the Santa river was only tarred for 240 kilometres north before it petered out into a thin dirt track as it reached the Callejon-corridor – and the crossing of the Black Mountains, and so onward transport was scarce. Most traffic followed the main southern highway. But I teamed up with a trio of German hikers and we hired a collectivo. The driver, however, wanted to take the southern tarmac route of course, the one which carried all the buses and normal traffic. But we were adamant, and reluctantly, he finally agreed to take us on the ten-hour journey down to Trujillo at high cost.

The ride was a joy. Because we had paid for his time, we were able to stop along the way, to photograph, to explore a little, and to see the astonishing point where the two vast ranges of the white and black Cordilleras of the Andes came together and all but kissed, their towering walls within inches of each other, high above the gurgling Santa river 500 metres below, which holds them apart. The extraordinary beauty of the scenery was the perfect finale to this central Andes trip and although I was to spend a further month in the greener softer mountains of Ecuador and Colombia, I now felt content to turn my attention to other things and forget about the Andes.

CHAPTER 9   ECUADOR: a calm interlude

I caught the night bus through Peru's northern desert to Tumbes on the Ecuador border, at the point where the cold Humbolt current flows away from the South American coast. From here the coastal vegetation changed dramatically from inhospitable sandy desert scrub to thick tropical forest.

Ecuador was an incomparably different country. A mellow, green, soft land, with rounded, forested mountains, gentler people, and without the grim, humiliating poverty further south. Although it too was a poor country, and the slums of Guayaquil, and the country's main port and leading city, as bad as any on the continent, the character of the Ecuadoreans seemed to transcend the worst aspects associated with shanty life.

Leaving Peru, left a sour taste and a sting in the tail. The border guards tried to extract bribes, to 'help' the procedure along they said, and when I refused, they delayed my crossing by a couple of hours out of spite. The local Peruvians streamed through, but I was shunted to one side with a couple of Norwegians under various pretexts. We began to make a nuisance of ourselves, opening our bags, spreading our belongings around on the floor, and generally getting in the way, until it became clear to the customs officials that we had no intention of greasing any palms, and they reluctantly let us through.

The Ecuadoreans by contrast were most welcoming and hardly wanted to see our passports. On both sides of the frontier, a bustling market was in full swing. Black marketeers did a brisk business, blatantly changing the money that they carried in bulging smart briefcases for the crowds crossing back and forth.

The bus to Guayaquil had to stop eight times during the short four-hour journey for military police checks. Foreigners had to get out to show passports at each stop, while the police examined our luggage and took bribes from the many contrabandists who were riding the bus. The police left their luggage conspiciously alone. The smugglers were mostly garrulous old ladies, pushy and chatty, weighed down with easily identifiable contraband boxes of washing powder, lavatory rolls, toys, soap – anything that they had been able to buy more cheaply on the Peruvian side of the border. It paid them to tip off the police to turn a blind eye, because they could still make a decent profit when they sold to the shops in Guayaquil. On this bus, a self-appointed drivers' mate also took his share of bribes, threatening to turn the women over to the police captain, and hassling the lady next to me for three payments within as many hours. He became so unbearable that the driver, responding to the angry protests of the contrabandists, drove off smartly after one stop, leaving the unpopular conductor running along the road behind us. Great cheers greeted the move, but he caught up an hour later, having hitched a lift from another bus, and proceeded to exact an expensive revenge.

At each stop children sold melons, coconuts, pineapples, chunks of meat on sticks, delicious roasted bananas with cheese slices, sweets, cakes and sugar cane juice. Enterprisingly they served cold drinks which they poured into plastic bags to save the valuable bottles for cash on return.

Banana groves spread out for miles in every direction. Tucked along the roadside at irregular intervals in constricted clearings stood wooden huts balancing on stilts, with washing flapping in the breeze, and children playing while the evening meal was prepared over open fires. Bright blinking fireflies darted about in the undergrowth beside the road, visible even from the racing bus.

The tropical greenness and humidity of Ecuador was a spectacular change from the dry desert plain and the fierce snowstorms I had experienced just a couple of days before in the Peruvian Andes. The music too was different. Gone were the flutes and the high-pitched singing. Romantic ballads and guitar music were favoured in Ecuador; less rousing, less interesting perhaps, but more soothing.

I proposed to stay no more than a night in Guayaquil. It's reputation as a haven for thieves and muggers gave it little attraction. At its centre, it was a modern, noisy, dirty, lively, high-rise city, and only the commemorative statues of Bolivar and fellow liberator San Martin, clasping hands at their famous meeting beside the Guayas estuary, gave any true sense of Latin American history.

During a late evening stroll, I passed a group of middle-aged men, all with guitars, sitting on the sidewalk, in a not-too-salubrious part of town. I hovered for a while, curious to know what they were about. Cars pulled up, with one or sometimes two young men inside, and the guitarists would leap to their feet and surround the car, pleading to be selected. 'Take me, take me, please . . .' they cried as they offered their services. One of them came to ask me if I required someone for a serenade. For 600 sucres ($24), three of them would go with a young suitor to serenade his sweetheart with three songs, professionally performed. 'It is traditional here in Ecuador,' my new friend told me. 'This is the only place left where we still practise the ancient art. In Peru it is not allowed. Only here in Ecuador.' When I looked doubtful he added, 'Well in Mexico they may still do it . . . and in Colombia too I think . . .' They were a charming unpretentious group, and very proud of their skills.

Near the big hotels, pneumatic aggressive prostitutes offered, 'fuckee, suckee, and ass fuckee' for $20. Smart boys cruised the streets late at night in their Chevvy jeeps and Japanese racers. Neons flashed all night, and insomniacs gathered at the roadside stalls and snack bars to drink beer and cooling fruit juices.

On the second floor of my dingiest of dingy hotels, which smelt of piss and vomit, the doors were inadequately padlocked and the walls paper thin. I spent a fretful night listening to the nocturnal rantings of a lone, mad American in the next room. 'I believe in traditional values,' he raved; was he asleep or awake? I could not tell. 'I don't believe in priests and rabbis and stuff like that.' He seemed to bang his chest, and punctuated his words with loud obcene farting noises, blowing raspberries and coughing in an unnatural and exaggerated way. 'If only I were a movie star' – fart, cough, bang – 'it's enough to give anyone a nervous breakdown.' Then he would have discussions as if he were with a friend, imitating another's voice, discussing elections, hamburgers, ex-creta, in a reasonable conversational tone. Then more mad raving. 'I wouldn't be able to exercise on a homosexual level . . .' He finally tailed off around four in the morning and was gone when I awoke.

My journey by furiously-driven buses through Ecuador towards

Quito, took me east across rolling, misty green hillsides to Cuenca, the country's third city, a beautiful, unspoilt colonial town with cobbled streets, and a warm atmosphere. The market women wore trilbies or red peaked hats and sold baked pig and roast guinea pig skewered over an open fire; the young girls were flirtatious and kept lovesick boys staring up to their windows throughout the night, with promises of a blown kiss or a possible assignation.

The streets were alive in the early evening with students like Ketti, who was on her way to night school. I went to meet her after college, waiting with other impatient boyfriends for the half-past-ten bell. We joined her colleagues who thronged the bars and cafes behind the school and talked with her sister until midnight. The boys here were friendlier and brighter than those I'd met further south. Back at my hotel I had to wait half an hour to use the bathroom while a couple made noisy love under the shower. Cuenca seemed to have that effect.

Riobamba was a less attractive town. Over-endowed with nine markets, it squatted comfortably in one of the series of fertile basins, which make up Ecuador's central territory, surrounded by three snowcapped volcanoes, Chimborazo, Altar, and Tungurahua. Local elections were taking place in Ecuador too, and as usual in South America, the streets were alive with politicking. It was heartening to see such universal enthusiam as cavalcades of cars toured the streets, to the accompaniment of rousing music.

Small, scuttling, red poncho-clad figures wearing trilby hats, half ran and half walked between markets, usually bent low by heavy loads – splashes of colour in the grey wet streets. In true campesino tradition, they went about their business, oblivious to the noisy electioneering going on around them. Some of the men were drunk after a hard day in town watching their wives negotiating in the markets. As the rain began to fall, and the stalls closed down, they all piled into the backs of trucks for the journey home. Some stayed all night, joining the down-and-outs sleeping in the open under the empty stalls, close to where old ladies tended their all night food and coffee stands. A few people picked over scraps that even the dogs refused to touch.

Although people did not die in the streets as they did in India, the hopelessness and filth was the same. While the squares and parks were spotlessly maintained, many of the streets where the poorer people lived and worked were squalid and strewn with refuse, the walls daubed and disintegrating.

I went to the cinema near the railway station. Three hundred local lads sat on seatless ledges, shouting greetings to friends and whistling for the film to start. They were a brash crowd. Only three

women had dared to come with brothers or husbands. *5 Man Army*,
a subtitled western about the Mexican wars, enthralled them, but
everyone talked through *All that Jazz*, and kids noisily sold colas.
This was participation cinema at its best.

Next day I went to Banōs, travelling in an old 'Co-operativa' bus
– much cleaner and more reliable than the zappy commercial
companies and with more careful drivers. There I bathed in the hot
healing springs beneath towering green cliffs. The air was icy.
Squealing children and short, thick-bodied Ecuadorean men and
women in ill-fitting costumes, floundered about in the murky pools;
I hoped an ache in my shoulder would undergo a miracle cure, but
it didn't. Nor did the waters appear to help the beggars and
cripples who sat in strategic positions throughout the dirty pretty
town to waylay the stream of visiting Ecuadorean and foreign
tourists who came to bathe. One young boy, with no arms, wrote in
a notebook with his toes and attracted amused crowds. But another
beggar, a pure white-haired and skinned old albino woman without
legs, attracted little attention.

She sat outside the entrance to the church which was next door
to a small, well laid-out museum. Here the curator had an array of
arts and crafts from the jungle communities just two hours away
down the mountain side: some stuffed cheetahs and wild birds, a
variety of snakes and scorpions and five shrunken human heads.

The rains poured down as I set off on the last stage of the trip to
Quito. The clouds hung low over the snow-capped volcanoes which
I knew were there, but which I could not see. However the clouds
could not conceal the delight of gentle Quito spread across the
valleys and lower slopes of the volcanoes Pichincha and Cotopaxi
and the Cerro Panecillo, eighteen miles south of the Equator. At
over 3,000 metres, Quito was a cool, hilly, white-washed village of a
town, with red roof tiles and cobbled streets running back into the
hills which toppled down to the very edges of the old quarter. All
around there was rich verdant farming land, and despite the air of
continual bustle and life, a tranquillity and peace hung over it all
quite unlike any of the other towns we had visited.

I went directly to the hotel Auca where I had arranged to meet
Feliks. He was in the coffee bar, and we marvelled that we could
cross vast distances separately and keep meeting up with such ease.
We spent the rest of the day comparing notes.

ECUADOREAN ENCOUNTERS

*A telephone call: Carmen something (an Ecuadorean name) in Polish. Soon
this timid young girl comes to my hotel rooms – her mother Polish, her father
an Ecuadorian, who came to Poland on some educational exchange scheme, and*

*stayed on. She, Carmen, brought up in Poland to reach a diploma in painting
at the Warsaw Academy of Art, urged by her father to visit his country and his
family, came to Quito. And the painful clash between her Bohemian-
European ways and her conservative grandparents, who, disappointed in not
confronting an imagined blonde of traditional manners, wanted her to wear
(passé for her) longish dresses and stay under their guard while they searched
for an appropriate husband. And so she side-stepped them, fell in love with,
and married hastily, a young Ecuadorian architect-cum-musician, who played
the nightclubs and soon surfaced his macho instincts; they were parted now.*

*There arose an instant compatability between us, both of idiomatic
Polishness and our common profession. We took a bus: swaying in its
congestion, paying those tiny sums of sucres, being part of the ordinariness of
Quito – a feeble but still real pleasure for me, contrasting with those detached
car/taxi rides. Then some walking after centre-of-town businesses, by-passing
my routine stops (the British Embassy and the sumptuous Quito Hotel) and,
at her command (since she wanted to show me her precious sites), emerging low
down, below the scarp of smartness, at the homely old church in the village
square. The church contained her favourite naive paintings, but it was
puzzlingly closed and I wanted to see her work before dark.*

*But, before this, I was to see her special offering. We took a precipitous
path behind the church, edging among the pine trees, the immense gorge and the
colossal mountainscape crowning great distances below and afar. The path
wound round stony edges, until, unexpectedly, we stepped into the ruins of a
grandiose hacienda. She was preparing me for it: it was haunted; a friend she
brought there after dark backed away in haste, intimidated; her patron and
master(?) had lived there until some twenty years earlier, but now abandoned,
open to the elements and vandals, crumbling yet persisting, it became sublime,
with odd inner half-open darkened twists, life-invoking graffiti. Its solitariness on that bulwark in face of the aloof prospect of huge distances – their
centre advancing at us in the shape of densely wooded, threatening prominence.
And the vultures.*

*Then we zig-zagged upwards on foot (beyond my invalidated prowess and
training, but done) to her house on top of the village, and her room, suspended,
still higher, over the same stupendous depth, the window taking it all in.*

*All this, from the outset, and culminating in her room (her drawings,
spreading to meticulously obsessively patterned immensities bigger than her
floor space, outstripped the modesty of the term, being complete works
impossible to be achieved differently, or stretched out into further media); all
this carried the accompaniment – a flow of her confessional talk; she was there,
in Quito, on her own. And the tale was of doubts, regrets, unfulfilment; of
longing for Poland and her milieu there – the strongest regret and, somewhat
hopeless, emotion; of 'jobs' only, and wrong steps and reaching the edge of
'composure'; conscious of losing grip on herself, apprehensive.*

She took me (it was dark already) on short walks, to me immense, to La

Galeria, an art gallery of fashion where we found a Peruvian sculptor, preparing his vernissage for the following day – with sumptious women probing ahead for choicy purchases (such is art patronage intensity there), to another (miles away) closed already, to a vegetarian eatery run by a stylish Polish-Jewish woman, mostly for selectively jeansy young North Americans, with concerts thrown in.

Next day Daniel arrived and, at a meeting arranged at the Quito Hotel lobby, he unhesitatingly pointed to the shape among others at the entrance: 'Here is your Polish girl.' Such was the Polish physical prevalence in her mixed origin.

My departure nearing, I tried clumsily to leave her with more support. I took her for supper to a charming old Polish diplomat-collector; to another with the German dandy-bookseller-publisher and his worldly German business-woman friend. I sent her some literature and wrote to her, and several months later sent a telegram, but never had any reply. And my Polish diplomat told me on a visit to London that also, after one meeting, he lost sight of her. She did not reappear.

Footnote:
Two days later, officially invited as guests of the British chargé d'affaires, in the be-pennanted limousine within a formal cavalcade we arrive in front of Carmen's village church, which was closed to her modest call, now open, but ceremonially, and for pride. We enter it between the two lines of presidential guards, soon after comes the vice-president (now president), and finally, trumpeted in and escorted by adjutants, the president. As San Francisco monastry was the other day the mere backcloth of the past to the orchestration of revolutionary banners, slogans, songs and speeches, so the gold-glittering altar has a serving role in the spectacle of earthly power: the long table in front of it, garnished with the top men of the country (behind them stand erect their adjutants and attendants), faces the congregation of courtly worshippers – Cardinal Arzobispo de Quito, a minute figure, being late, hurries and trips upon the steps to the altar, habitual for him in hieratic ascensions, but now blocked by the live demi-gods, amongst whom there is a chair for him. Consequently, this ritual of longsome speeches of self-congratulation and practical promises superimposes hollowly over the claims of eternity exuding all round it.

Alan White, the British chargé d'affaires, and the hospitable Spanish wife of the head of the British council take me to Senor Galo Plaza Lasso, the former (before intermediary upheavals) president of Ecuador, internationally respected figure of South America. Cannot wish for more: cloud-capped mountain-chains accompany or cross us, eucalyptuses give way to high cacti; campesinos in their market day finery frieze the roads; and the warning-reminder – a crossroads holy statue hedgehogs with improvised nailed-on plastic symbols of revolutionary labour – pink arms holding hammers.

But beyond, the calm grace of the remoteness of rurality (costumes and gestures in accord with the land), till one reaches almost by chance the walls of the estancia and enters another era – the unhasty vague Indian domestics within a cobble-stoned quadrangle held by the silence of three-winged old-print sedateness. The anticipated/imagined colonial Spain opens up. There is, in the coolness of the lobby and the antechamber, the assurance of style: the past accumulated in harmonious layers exists by its seigneurial right. Yet then the huge galleried interior, rebuilt by the host, serves for his entry: and there (I am the last to hold to the uniformity of a standstill-past) this majestic relic presents his contemporariness by his faultlessly correct (a shade comme-il-faut eccentric) anglicised country casuals of wools/cashmeres/silks; but also his has-been presence in political vulgarities: behind him high on the wall a pair of immense full-length portraits – identical in size, identical in details: black tails, white ties, red-blue-yellow ribbons across the chests – his father an earlier (beard and curved moustache), and he the later (young and smooth) president; logically and properly bad paintings, in accord with the surrounding array of dedicated photographs of the world's mighty. These speak of his commitment to the international UN contredanse. But now he is back: 'I've always been a farmer.' Though not quite. His role as an incorruptible elder statesman, with a variety of top international engagements behind him, makes him needed still. And he tells us, with some satisfaction, that he acts constantly as an intermediary at the highest level and that, recently, during a gathering of several South American leaders, he was selected to give a key speech.

We move to a pretty lean-to greenhouse (plants and birds), his wife properly secondary; and, after leisurely drinks, we eat deliciously, with an Indian girl, starchly folklorish, serving, and hear of his endless squirish activities. Indeed, he is convincing, his grace and handsomeness and worldliness contributing when he holds forth on salvation through paternalism (though the term is avoided). He is even more convincing on our long drive over his 2,600 hectares of mountainous estate. The grand vistas, horizons lost in clouds, tender with the decorative peasantry hieratic at cultivation and crafts, securely bowing to the father-figure. There are many questions though, and the answers don't carry beyond his presence.

Quito was preparing busily for Quito week, and the inhabitants of the old town were white-washing their homes. On the other side of the city grandstands were being built for the great Quito parade. Every morning at six-thirty down Avenidas Sucre and Venezuela, past the hotel where we were staying in the heart of the old town, came hundreds upon hundreds of ranked, mini-skirted drum majorettes, in the North American style, rehearsing for the big day. The monotonous theme music for this year's event was the same for

Plaza de San Francisco, Quito. Left wing
pre-election rally

everyone, and every school, college and institute produced a band and performers for the parade, all of them stepping along in well-rehearsed harmony. With their brows furrowing with concentration, most of the girls counted out the choreographed steps under their breath, but just loud enough for their colleagues to hear, desperate not to lose the rhythm. The curious droning that was apparent on the day, and which sometimes rose above the sound of the bands, was the breathy counting of the anxious performers.

In the evenings there were street peñas, traditional musical shows, and as 5 December approached, street parties and dances began in earnest.

All over town, neatly pigtailed Otavalo Indians, dressed in their distinctive white, cotton, calf-length wider-than-sailor trousers, black trilby hats, scarves, sandals and dark blue ponchos, sold their traditional woollen sweaters, ponchos, blankets, gloves and scarves. They merged well with the white and blue colour scheme of the houses of the city. In commercial terms, the Otavalo were amongst the best organised Indians in South America, and this was apparent from their smart appearance and efficient sales operation. But they were not a political force even though they had managed to win for themselves a high degree of economic independence and financial security. From their base in Otavalo, a two-hour drive north of Quito, they had spread out over the Andes into Colombia and Peru, selling their wares, but keeping themselves very much to themselves. I saw them derided in Quito by raucous town youths, who mocked their pigtails and their costume and their small stature, and tried to bait them into a fight. But their discipline and their loyalty to traditional values and culture remained strong and while the world wanted to buy from them, they saw no reason to change. Compared to the independent, radical tin miners in Bolivia, who chose confrontation, the Otavalo had settled for peaceful co-existence with the changing governments of Ecuador, content to follow their independent and separate private enterprise route.

There was a large community of expatriate Europeans in Quito and they went out of their way to make us welcome. Acknowledged grande dame of this group was Olga Fisch, a deft Hungarian collector of local art and folklore, who ran the leading crafts shop in town. She was also a source of inspiration to the indigenous artists, encouraging them in their work, and even directing them into more commercial and lucrative efforts for their mutual benefit. She had created a naive art form amongst her artists and stimulated a market for their work. She took a shine to us and invited us to her inner sanctum for tea to show us her own magnificent private collection of Inca and other South American artifacts. Her close Polish friend Antoni and Feliks had known each other in London before the war and in Singapore in 1950, where he had been a high ranking UN official. He was a widely travelled man, with a caustic sense of humour; he had chosen to retire to Ecuador, he said, because he had grown accustomed to 'service'. He had his cook of twenty-five years with him, and he liked the sort of life that was no longer possible in Britain, Poland or the United States. Although he could no longer afford the seven servants he had been used to in the old days, he still managed to live pretty well here in Ecuador. 'But oil has spoilt Ecuador,' he said; 'too much money going into too few pockets.' Like our taxi-driver had said earlier: 'So few of our leaders have the interests of their countrymen at heart.'

On one occasion, we were taken by the enthusiastic and kind-hearted wife of a diplomat, for a tour of Quito's further-flung attractions. Also in our car load was her house guest, an Ecuadorean girl, whom she was helping through school, and an American dancer, whom we had met in the lobby of the grand Hotel Quito where she was performing nightly with her touring dance troupe. We visited the hot springs, set in luxuriant swelling hills and picnicked in a gentle village square where local men played coin-tossing gambling games. In the small church, a series of pictorial representations by a Quiteno naive artist, showed a miraculous Christ emerging from a tree trunk, and restoring health and life to victims of a variety of mundane accidents and car crashes.

We returned to Quito via the Equator which was marked by a monument and a huge globe, as yet still incomplete. Two nights later, I was driven by a shyly tender, ex-patriate German woman to the same spot, now deserted and rainswept, and she parked her car across the Equator line. We made love with our heads in the northern hemisphere and our legs in the southern hemisphere.

As foreign visitors to Quito, we were given celebrity status. In Peru and later in Brazil it was the newspapers, in Quito it was television as well. A popular daytime programme spent twenty minutes interviewing us live, and rashly insisted that my Spanish was good enough for us to dispense with the services of a translator. While Feliks was persuaded, much against his will, to draw the interviewer on the air while the camera watched over his shoulder, I prattled on in pidgin Spanish to the bemused presenter, and no doubt to an even more confused Quiteno audience.

The Quito week celebrations culminated in a five-hour parade before forty-year-old president, Jaime Roldos, and the gathered diplomatic corps. An endless stream of floats and bands and high-stepping schoolgirls wafted by to the same turgid tune. Folklore dance and theatre troupes from the many different ethnic regions of tiny Ecuador, jumped and somersaulted and held mock fights down the wide avenue. Some represented the Indian peasants under the whip and yoke of the oppressors, and an Inca monarch in full regalia was born by costumed followers at the head of the procession. A tough-looking Cuban brigade, putting in a guest appearance, was led by a handsome, one arm withered, grim-faced, pole-throwing drum major. His single-handed performance in front of the stands was the highlight of the day, as he twirled and threw the long stick dexterously about his body and up into the air. Behind him, his intense-featured, khaki-clad colleagues forcefully pounded their drums, heads held high, battle suits open-necked and crumpled. The girls in the group presented a particularly fierce heroic front. Next to the coy local performers, with their beauty queens, formation dancing and cheer-leaders, this was an impressive display of Cuban youth – long haired, bold and exotic. Behind them came a white mestizo group, their faces painted black, representing Esmeraldas, Ecuador's negro coastal region. Feliks, who was standing in for the occasion for the wife of the British chargé d'affairs, was well placed to draw, sitting three seats along from President Roldos. I spent the hot morning equally well placed, out on the piste, photographing at close quarters.

At either end of the mile-long parade route were the inevitable stalls selling fruit, empanadas, llapingachos (potato and cheese), baked pig, cold drinks and maize to the assembled thousands. A busy young Jugoslav film student called Andrjei, who was filming his way through South America for Belgrade TV, complained that he found the girls unexpectedly unappetising. 'They are so short and heavily built,' he said. 'I don't find these Indian mestizo faces very pretty.' From the endlessly parading ranks of provocatively-costumed young people, only a few striking exceptions stood out, and more often than not they were either from the black-mixed tropical coastlands where the Indians were scarce, or they displayed a strong Spanish influence in their racial background.

The rest of the day and night was given over to street parties. Bands played coastal music, guitar-based with repetitive rhythmic riffs, on every other flag-bedecked street corner of the old town, while milling crowds danced, and drank hooch from bottles purchased from young boys for £1 a litre. Although drink was supposedly prohibited after midnight because of the local elections, no one seemed to be checking. Mothers, kids, drunks, families, working men, Otavalos and students mingled and swayed from band to band, passing through the crowd, clinging tightly on to each other. One drunken student stayed closed to me for an hour, discoursing at length about the state of mankind and how awful it was to be a single man in Quito. He wanted me to go back to his room with him since he had long ago abandoned the futile pursuit of women. I was not convinced.

At the 24 de Mayo street, half-a-dozen tough hookers were bantering with a semi-hostile crowd which was intruding on their attempted transactions, criticising the prices, and denigrating the general appeal of the girls. Twenty or thirty men would herd round, whenever someone entered negotiations, but after a while the presence of the crowd would make him lose his nerve and he would move on. Some customers were brash and pushy, some experienced and friendly, while others were bashful.

One girl, aggressive but not unattractive, chatted to me between business discussions. She wanted $8 since it was Quito week, and trade was brisk. One black man with a bleeding ear harangued a black girl – (his wife ? his girlfriend? it seemed such a family sort of a quarrel) – while the inevitable crowd gathered to watch. She took off her shoe and hit him with the sharp heel, and as he went to retaliate, the other girls waded in to defend her, scratching and kicking out at him. For twenty minutes they argued and tussled, until, with a final stinging comment which brought hoots of laughter from the 'audience', she flounced off with her girlfriends, leaving him chastened and humiliated.

Before leaving Ecuador, I wanted to go down to Esmeraldas, an eight-hour bus ride through the jungle. Feliks was still busy in Quito, but Yolande, a rebellious Argentine girl, whose military father was working in Quito, decided to come with me instead. We had met by chance in Quito's main San Francisco Square and she had spent two afternoons showing me the city. The mood of the coast was entirely different to anything we had yet experienced in Latin America. The people were predominantly black, freed slaves from further north, who had settled there a century before. While the diminutive serious Indians of the Sierra scurried along the streets struggling with heavy loads, the mixed black and Spanish/mestizo people of the coast were just the opposite. They were long and leggy, with haughty looks and laughing eyes, and both men and women exuded an easy confidence and style which I had missed on the journey so far. People here seemed sexier, more liberated and earthy. I remembered this loose elegance on my first visit to Brazil eighteen years earlier, and I had expected it to be a common feature of the whole continent. After three months, I had begun to think that I must have imagined Brazil, or that I had

confused it with Africa. But now here it was again, and I felt
relieved, almost as if I had come home. I could once more look
forward to Brazil with high expectations.

We took a tiny, yellow-walled room in an affectionately ramshackled, wooden hotel, just off the main square. A stuttering fan
barely stirred the hot air. Noisy rats scampered behind the walls,
and even noisier neighbours screwed all night.

In the morning we sat downstairs having breakfast in front of the
hotel watching the Sunday 'paseo' of handsome people strolling by
in their smartest gear on their way to church or to vote in the
municipal elections. Queues formed under the watchful eyes of
gun-toting, coca cola drinking soldiers, as the population of
Esmeraldas went to the polls. Down by the riverside slums, which
lay below the level of the main town, vultures flapped clumsily
amid the refuse, and people lazed in hammocks. A mother, younger
than one normally saw feeding in the street, suckled her baby,
while she talked to her girlfriends.

Yolande and I stayed in Sua, just down the coast from
Esmeraldas, with an Italian family who had quit the high life of
Milan in favour of peaceful Ecuador, and had four days earlier
bought a tiny wooden hotel and restaurant in this village on the
Equator, on the western shores of South America. Just like that.
They looked after us well, and fed us good Italian home cooking.
But there was little time for beach bumming, since I had to move
on to Colombia where Feliks was flying ahead to meet the film team
in Bogota, and Yolande had to be back at college. Besides, lazing
on a sandy beach beside the Ocean, with tropical rum and fruit
cocktails and a delightful Argentine companion may appeal to
some people, but 'holidaying' was not on the programme!

For two days we played chess and I read *The Farm on the river of
Emeralds* which told the touching and frustrating story of an
American ex peace corps settler and his local fisherman partner,
who bought a farm outside Esmeraldas; it gave an extra and
illuminating insight into the tough life of the peasant blacks along
the coast. We returned to Quito where I had a final Ecuadorean
evening with Feliks before setting off north by bus to the
Colombian border. We were anxious for each other's safety and we
parted like comrades in arms setting out for battle; so fierce was
Colombia's reputation. We were due to meet up together again
with the film crew in Bogota within ten days.

CHAPTER 10 COLOMBIA: the wild west revisited

Colombia really ought to hire a public relations firm to improve its image. For weeks the grim warnings about violence, murder and robbery had prepared us for a battle arena. We were advised always to carry $15 or $20 in cash to give to the young hooligans, those famous street urchins of Bogota, when they held us up, as they undoubtedly would. If you failed to provide them with something worth stealing, they would stick a knife into you anyway to compensate for their disappoinment. A few dollars was not enough. 'What if you are stopped and robbed by one gang who take your offering, and then further on you're stopped again?' enquired Feliks sensibly. 'The second lot will probably kill you,' replied an English journalist with relish. He worked between Quito and Bogota and took a delight in dramatising the world in which he lived and worked. He demonstrated vividly how many journalists need dramatic events to function and give colour to their lives. He recounted his most recent report about a child killer he had interviewed in gaol, who raped and murdered 300 eight-to-twelve-year-old children in Peru, Ecuador and Colombia. 'He showed no remorse whatsoever,' said our friend. 'He's in solitary now but he won't last a minute when they put him in with the other prisoners.'

Other people told of watches being ripped from wrists, and how it was normal practice, when getting into a taxi, to wind up the windows, lock the doors, and hold one hand over your watch. Others had lost glasses and cameras and jewellery, torn from ears, wrists and throat; yet despite these constant warnings, I often saw tourists in Bogota, walking the streets with cameras slung carelessly over their shoulders. Although many of the stories were no doubt true, we suspected that the victims were as much to blame through their own carelessness as the eminently talented robbers, and that incidents were magnified enormously to thrill listeners. Even so, both Feliks and I approached the country with trepidation. We took extra precautions, tied our luggage to our waists, and doubted the integrity of everyone. Every fellow passenger on a bus was suspect, and all bus and railway stations were danger areas.

Colombia displayed all the trappings of 'wild west' America in the good old days: stetsons and rip-roaring bars, brothels and gang warfare, speakeasies and organised crime. A steady diet of US films and television 'cops and robber' fare had turned Colombians into sophisticated wide boys, worldly-wise, ambitious, often corrupt and very Western orientated. Yet they were also amongst the most open, friendly and stimulating people on the continent, with a zest for life and pride in their cultural heritage. Furthermore, in over 150 years of independence, Colombia had experienced only three periods of military dictatorship, and was considered one of the most stable democracies south of the Rio Grande. But even in such a supposedly liberal and egalitarian climate, a section of the population felt unable to express their dissent freely without resorting to guerrilla warfare. The 'MI9' group hijacked planes and bombed strategic targets and carried out assassinations against a regime they deemed repressive and entrenched.

I arrived from Ecuador across Colombia's southern border to the tune of the usual customs chorus of bribery demands. I kept an especially tight grip on my baggage, because I had been assured that the worst perpetrators of robbery were the local soldiers and policemen. I planned my overland trip to Bogota like a military exercise. I caught a speedy microbus north to Pasto and Popayan, through still more immense, mellow, thickly-forested mountain country, less cultivated than neat Ecuador, and punctuated occasionally by stunning great gorges and vertical cliffs. We followed the thin asphalt line of the North-South-Inter-American Highway, as it snaked far ahead across the rising ranges. The soft contours of the beautiful landscape belied the country's violent reputation and the well-publicised presence of marauding guerrilla fighters who were proving to be such a thorn in the side of the conservative liberal government of Dr Julio Cesar Turbay Ayala.

Repeatedly the road climbed over the cool, breezy passes at 3,000 metres and plunged down to the oppressive, steamy, tropical jungle heat of the basins at 1,500 metres, often in the space of half an hour or less on its long journey north to Bogota and beyond to the Carribean coast. In the hot, low-lying basins and valleys, the people were mainly black, while in the towns higher up the mountains they were mestizo. The mad bus drivers – especially on the Boliviano line – tore through the tranquil countryside on the narrowest roads, cutting up the traffic, in a test of virility with equally suicidal lorry drivers. They grinned sheepishly to their 'mates' whenever they negotiated a particularly insane manoeuvre to the accompaniment of angry horn blowing and cursing from their victims. We thundered through one village where a group of children were playing in a schoolyard; a white ball rose above their upturned faces, hovered for a moment, and then dropped back into the crowd. Men with long machetes hanging at their hips, strolled to work. Other macheteros were already slicing away at the roadside, clearing the undergrowth. These were South America's lowest paid manual labourers. A crowd of schoolgirls in the bus in front waved and shouted to attract attention and gyrated cheekily to music I couldn't hear. They swapped sweaters and blouses with each other, stripping down to bras, teasing wildly for the benefit of the bus passengers from the security of their swaying, swerving vehicle.

Normal dress on the mountain slopes was still the poncho, as it had been in Peru, Ecuador and Bolivia – so unlike the in-vogue ski-style padded jackets worn in Argentina and Chile. Farmers worked the sun-dappled green mountainsides in fields that tilted at precarious and virtually untenable angles.

Popayan, in the fertile Cauca valley, was a unique town, an ideal place, I thought, for a calm introduction to Colombia. A favourite holiday retreat for the aristocratic European-descended Colombians, this cool, lovely, whiter than white colonial town sat above the humid valleys brimming with sugar plantations, amidst gentle bamboo groves and palm trees. Its quiet, wide, clean streets carried little traffic, and people sat out in the shaded squares or at the open cafes that encircled them. Spacious churches, monasteries and cloisters were in the best Spanish colonial tradition. A new bridge built in the same style as the defunct one next to it, linked the newer and more commercial part of town with the historical quarter. Here, near the bus depots and the cheaper hotels, was the hangout for the muggers, the dope pedlars, and the bent police, who had a reputation for planting drugs on unsuspecting long-haired travellers. I had been well warned.

I left my valuables in my room, and taking a photocopy of my passport with me, I spent the evening in the cafes, watching the passers-by window shopping at the shining, luxurious store fronts. Old women sold lottery tickets, and pretty modern misses, coolly confident, stopped to chat and share a drink with friends. Schoolgirls with muscly legs in elegant uniforms, sat in coffee bars. In one street a student demonstration was in progress. They were noisily boycotting their classes, chanting in the street outside their college, because they questioned the fees being charged for their studies. They believed that evening classes should be free, and they also wanted to know where the money they had already paid had gone. They suspected the assistant head teacher of embezzling most of it. But they were well behaved and adopted recognised and legitimate tactics of peaceful protest. When one or two of them struck a passing car that hooted at them to clear the road, their colleagues told them to stop. They were an appealing bunch, and dispersed quietly when the classes were over and the blacklegs came out to go home.

I turned back across the bridge, heading for my hotel, hands pushed deep into my pockets to protect keys and cash. Two girls flirted with a policeman against the parapet. As I made my way through the bus station, I noticed a crowd of soldiers leaping off the back of an open truck and fanning out across the street. Three approached me and grabbed me, shouting that I should accompany them to the truck. I tried to explain that I was a foreigner, but they were young and nervous and would not discuss the matter. Instead they raised their sub-machine guns. 'Periodista Ingles,' I protested, as they frogmarched me over to the truck. The officer in charge also refused to listen. I tried showing the photocopy of my passport and the letters I carried from the Colombian embassy in London, and from the acting British ambassador in Quito, but it was all to no avail. 'Why are you doing this?' I asked angrily. 'Why won't you look at my documents?'

It was a repetition of the mindless arbitrary mass arrests that are part of the normal currency of everyday Latin life, whether in a democracy or a military dictatorship. It was the way of things. To be stopped and searched, or stopped for questioning was one thing, but to be violently apprehended, knowing that in the general scheme of events you stood an even chance of never being seen again, was quite another. If you resisted arrest you could be shot on the spot, no questions asked; if you went quietly, you faced the possibility of torture, of death or a term of imprisonment for no other reason than you happened to be there at the time.

A few people, mostly women, stood idly by watching, and some detainees tried to shout telephone numbers to them asking them to call a parent, a brother, a friend or a lawyer. I was half lifted and half thrown into the back of the truck, along with the motley gathering of students, drunks and ordinary indefinable men who had been tasting the various delights of the local bars and brothels. 'Can you accompany me to my hotel, just there on the corner, to get my passport before you take me in?' I asked; but there was nothing doing. Once again I was in the soup. Once again my anger subsided into resignation and then anxiety.

For twenty minutes we waited in the truck while more strays were rounded up, then with a catch of thirty-odd men and boys, guarded by twenty gun-toting boy soldiers, we were driven off through the streets, back to the central police station. We were ushered into a courtyard, which was both the drill ground and a basketball court, where we joined another thirty-eight prisoners. Through the night another 150 men, of all ages, classes and types came trooping in; and as usual none of us had any idea why we were there.

A drunk lay gasping at our feet where we were lined up, searched and roll-called. He was barely conscious and after a while, they propped him up against the wall and studiously ignored him. Later he staggered about, crying to the police, pleading to be set free, much to the amusement of the rest, who were glad that he was diverting police attention away from them. 'Some Colombian democracy,' complained one student. I asked him if it was normal. 'No,' he replied, 'this sort of thing doesn't happen very often here but they enjoy themselves when it does.'

After a while we all began to relax as more people were brought in. Friends began to meet up and groups formed, discussing what had happened. The cigarettes came out. Although everyone was annoyed, the jokes soon began to fly. Surely they couldn't suspect us all. I asked a police captain what was going on, trying to establish my foreignness and my credentials as a journalist – that I was here in Colombia to make a film about the country for British TV. 'Ten men broke out of jail at ten o'clock this evening,' he said. 'We're rounding up all the single men we can find. But it won't be more than a few hours and then you can go home.' 'May I phone the British consulate?' I asked. With a pained expression he replied, 'Really, that won't be necessary.'

One man sold lottery tickets while others tried to contact any friends they might have in the police force. When finally they decided to dismiss their eager young cadets and line us up for re-identification, it was five in the morning. The process of release looked like taking all day as each person was interviewed separately, but I managed to catch my captain's eye and he signalled towards the front door for me to slip out.

With my luck as it was, I expected a mugging to round off the evening as I made my way back through the dark streets to the hotel where a drunk man was trying to book in with a prostitute. The young boy on the door insisted that he should pay an extra charge for the room, but he was refusing. And so it goes.

If you carried your passport with you it got stolen; and if you left it at the hotel you got arrested. Catch 22.

That night John Lennon was assassinated in New York.

Next morning I went to photograph the old town. As I loaded a roll of film near the bridge, two policemen approached and decided to search me. I turned out my pockets and emptied my shoulder bag. They wanted to open up the film cassettes too. One took a shine to my sheath knife and pocketed it; he laughed when I asked for it back. They were rude and rough, and enjoyed my visibly mounting anger. I took out my letters of 'safe passage' from the embassies and, for a change, these had a dramatic effect. Their faces fell, and they hurriedly repacked my ransacked bag. Sheepishly, the light-fingered one returned my knife, and when I suggested that I take a photograph of them to commemorate the occasion, they declined with nervous ingratiating smiles, saying that time was short and they had to get on. Then they scuttled off.

I had a yoghurt for breakfast with a student of computers called Carmela. She had spent a year in the States and wanted to leave Colombia. 'The poverty and the stealing depress me very much,' she said. She warned me that the police were the worst robbers and could not believe that I had escaped intact, the night before, from my visit to the police station. She wanted to talk about English politics, world communism and Chile; she told me I would like Cali – 'the girls are so beautiful' – but that it was the most dangerous city in the country; and that I should try to see a Colombian-made documentary film about 'our mad country' called *Locombia* – 'the nickname we now give to ourselves.'

In the bus to Cali, Colombia's third city, I decided that I liked Colombia even though they kept arresting me, and even though I had to chain all my belongings to me. What an illiberal lot they were, though, these South Americans when they got their hands on power.

Two old men sat in front, one talking incessantly to the other, who remained sound asleep throughout the journey. A friendly teenager wanted to discuss football with me, insisting that Colombia's national team was the best thing since sliced bread, but in my paranoid distrust, I suspected him of trying to set me up, and kept the conversation brief.

I left all my gear under lock and key at the bus station, and armed with toothbrush and alarm clock, I set off for the centre of cosmopolitan Cali. A huge Christ statue watched over the city from the hills above, and three crosses faced it from the next hill. In the main square, lounging young black men eyed the strollers, and one tried to chat me up. 'Quiere cocaine? Una chica? Un hotel? Un guia?' Carmela was right though; Colombia's beautiful women had made Cali their home. Haughty and naughty, in smart baggies or shorts or tightly-fitting skirts, and in sloppy sweaters and cut-off jeans and T shirts that read 'kiss me' and 'virgins have more fun', the enfants dorées of Cali strutted their stuff along trendy Avenida 6. Every main South American town had its equivalent smart street: Miraflores in Lima, Amazonas in Quito, Providencia in Santiago, La Prada in La Paz, Quinze in Bogota. The bright young things hung out all day in the sidewalk cafes and bars, and I joined in after a stroll up and down.

Equally pretty street-trading girls with barefoot kids, passed between the tables selling home-crafted trinkets, 'chicklets' gum, Marlboro cigarettes and lottery tickets, while fire-eaters and shoeshine men, and cheeky street boys, entertained us from the pavement. Down the road, at an open-sided modern hamburger stall, a young woman responded to two begging street urchins by offering them a hamburger each. Gleefully they accepted and sat importantly beside her at the counter. But the waiter refused to serve them. I offered to share the bill with her and ordered the round again. Grumbling the waiter went off to make up the order. When the boys had finished, they said 'thanks', got up to go, and then asked me to make a further contribution to their funds.

It was after eleven o'clock and the streets were clearing, when I suddenly realised that in this supposedly dangerous city, I still had nowhere to stay. Anxiously, I made for the old part of town with its cheap hotels. Every passer-by appeared to me to be a potential mugger. The Hotel Flores took me in, and although the young student night porter suggested that a fourteen-year-old hooker round the corner might appreciate the price of a meal, I was now suffering a severe attack of xenophobic agoraphobia. I called it a day.

I arrived next evening in Bogota, its suburbs enveloped in darkness, victims of a power cut, after a twelve-hour bus ride over the spectacular Quindo pass. As usual, the driver was fearless and treated the narrow hairpin bends with scant respect. The towns we passed were dusty and unkempt but considerably better off than

their equivalents south of the Equator. Bogota itself displayed all
the trappings of a modern large city, with towering office blocks
and wide avenues and a mountain backcloth.

In the teeming downtown area, lottery ticket sellers and
Marlboro merchants chanted their wares in a fast, oft-repeated
stream of words which provided a continuous background sound to
the noise of street life. Those famous cheeky urchins who lived out
on the streets hunted in packs, checking for possible victims.
Beggars squatted against walls, their hands out, muttering unintel-
ligibly and girls sold snacks from makeshift stalls. Prostitutes, both
young and middle-aged, in short skirts and white socks, stood in
the doorways along La Decima. Lepers, with fingerless hands,
toeless feet and deformed faces sat on the pavements in hopeless
public agony. They were the first lepers I had seen in South
America although they were a common sight in India and Africa.

I went to keep my rendezvous with Feliks.

BOGOTA (before Daniel's arrival)

*Again and again, this vigil-wait for Daniel. Santiago was easy, though he,
after his imprisonment in Paraguay, had to cover immense distances with only
the approximate date of meeting as a point of contact. Santiago was easy
because I was already involved in engagements, and, returning to the hotel on
my second afternoon, I found him in my room, more or less on the date we had
proposed a month earlier. The joy at uniting in victory over stretches of time
and swelling bulging oceans and continents milling with unpredictable
humans: the emphatically supremely convincing confirmation of kinship. These
treasured moments, these endorsing encounters we repeated, thanks to the
fragmentation of our South American expedition, several times. The holy
moment passes, becomes confrontation, in all its nuances: discords, alliances,
manoeuvres, tripping on trivialities.*

*Again, another compressed, therefore more anxious a wait, in La Paz, close
to our departure, in the hotel room. Daniel, having heard of the great impact
on me of the Moon Valley, arranged to be taken there in the morning in a car
by some young Bolivians he had come across the night before. He should have
returned hours ago. Bags were packed and we were due at the bus stop. And,
unavoidably, my imagination raced with visions of tragedy, of the boys
(nothing easier), for the sake of his camera, throwing him into the sharp-edged
ravines of that deserted world; I imagined his impaled death, the search for his
body – the full-scale paternal tragedy woven out.*

*And then he strolled in – not only debonair, but also having had a haircut,
and offering an amazingly sangfroid tale: the boys had failed to come, yet,
shortness of time and distances brushed aside, he made it on the back of a lorry
and a bus. This was, after the torture of my imaginings, a veritable
breathtaking resurrection.*

The Peruvian wait was hard indeed. Those Andean Cordillera passes held terrors, such as the most recent cutting-off heads of two camping young Germans – by wandering bandits? by campesinos? But Lima's re-uniting was defused by a TV director's fussing presence, and true tenderness reappeared only in Ecuador. I lived in old Quito long enough – that is some ten days – to feel domesticated, yet anxious, Daniel being late and not in touch; his over-Andes trek treacherous and unpredictable – Lima to Quito. Days went by, my messages at the hotel mini-reception trying to direct him to me from hour to hour; and when, unusually for me, I sat one evening, flattened somewhat, in a dreary cafe attached to the hotel, suddenly he stood on top of the back door steps, sprightly and not damaged.

Then, finally, Bogota, as from then on we did not part until it was I who left – Rio for London.

Again the vigil-wait, this time differently tense, his lone passage taking him through most violent, knifing-to-death country. Again the great joy, underlined by the tale of Colombian imprisonment and clashes with the military.

And then his nightly walks in Bogota within the killer quarters – days were enough for me – held me in tension. But it had to be: this was the errantry for one of the heroic breed, however drug-and-gutter-bound Bogota's life-death arena was. Also, it may be so, those hours were his own, free from all obstructions.

Feliks had already made friends in Bogota, and we were given a Sunday tour of the town. In one particularly infamous district, just behind the Hilton Hotel, we sat in a car with local English residents while Feliks sketched the lounging locals in their doorways. I had been in and out of the car all morning, photographing the city, and now my camera lay on my lap as I sat in the back seat, the window half wound down in the heat. Suddenly two hands shot in through the window and grabbed the camera, but the strap was wound round my hand; for a few moments we pulled back and forth, and then my assailant let go and jumped away from the car. I passed the camera to the person next to me and leapt out after him. He ran off a few metres, turned and stood crouched, waiting. Then he was off. I started after him, but as I chased him up the street, I began to think that it might not be such a good idea. He could have a knife, or some friends round the corner, and besides I still had my camera. So I gave up the chase and returned to the car.

There was a brazenness about the incident which was startling. No one in the street had made any move to help. They just watched and grinned. It was all part of the sport. But then why should they help? There was probably little mercy shown to traitors in these tough neighbourhoods, so why risk going to the help of a gringo against one of your own. At least we felt that we had been tested and had not been found wanting. It was part of the running battle between the haves and the have nots, and according to the rules here, I was in the former category.

It seemed that one of the prices the democracies had to pay for their freedoms was an element of social lawlessness. The southern cone military dictatorships suppressed lawlessness and political opposition by extreme methods; for the obedient, the streets were safe from the common brigand. Violence was institutionalised. In the democracies, drug pushing, contraband traffic, robbery and violence thrived in the atmosphere of relative political freedom and lack of suppression. For even the richest and most reactionary Colombians I spoke to, they preferred their way. 'I would rather our democracry with all its faults, the lawlessness included, than Argentina's militaristic suffocation,' said Antonio, a wealthy Bogota industrialist and landowner.

The ruling classes in Colombia lived, in some ways, as if in a state of siege. The more palatial homes were patrolled by armed guards and many kept ferocious dogs. Middle-class suburbia too, took extreme precautions to protect their property. They were firmly European bourgeois in outlook, and they took pains to establish Colombia's classy international credentials at every opportunity. 'We have a world famous eye surgeon, you know,' they would tell us proudly. 'Our artists Botero and Obregon are internationally known.' 'You've heard of Garcia Marquez, of course, and the renowned harpsichordist Rafael Pujana? They are Colombians!' 'We are a very culturally and educationally minded nation; just look at our museums and our five universities here in Bogota.' The whitest, most European of Colombians, would claim, in a burst of inverted racism, that they would never be ashamed to admit having Indian ancestry if they had any, but of course they didn't. Those with duskier skins and broader features were less inclined to make such claims.

Well-to-do Colombians were justly proud of their long democratic tradition. 'We have a large middle class, and we are a very political people,' explained Alana, a well-born society hostess. Colombians claimed strong links with Europe and the United States and they travelled widely. Their college days were spent at universities in America, France, Britain and Spain. But they were united in their refusal to take part in our television documentary which, we intended, would show them relaxing at home. 'We're fed up seeing cliché films making us out to be insensitive brutes and contrasting our supposed wealthy lifestyle with the slums of Bogota.' They suspected the BBC's motives no matter what we claimed to be our own intentions. Throughout the southern hemisphere, the ruling classes were rejecting western Europe's arrogant and hypocritical view of the globe. 'Look to your own back yard,' they said, 'and leave us to take care of our own.'

Yet they acknowledged the presence of a vicious mafia and the rampant corruption in their society. The Turbay government was considered by some to be immoral since positions in government were often given to relatives and friends*. We were told of mafia people who tried to go straight once they had made and laundered their money, sending their children to smart schools. That was against mafioso rules. They were shot dead. Drugs and emeralds introduced a pretty rough breed – gun-toting, unprincipled and ruthless and although guns were illegal, they were universally carried. 'Even the New York gangsters fear the Colombians,' said Maria, a Bogota photographer, in a burst of curious national pride. 'When their mafia settle scores, they kill the enemy leaders. But our mafioso kill the wives, the children, the servants, even the pets – everything.'

At lunch in a beautifully preserved and well-lived-in hacienda overlooking its own lake out in the Savannah, a couple of hours from Bogota, a young American businessman, and fellow guest, defended the tough stance of the militarists. 'Shoot any transgressors; Reagan's right to let people here do things in their own way. We're far too lenient back home.' Even the well-tweeded à l'Anglais Colombian 'chic' choked a little over their roast duck and best imported French wine as they listened to him speak. They could recall the senseless and brutal killings – La Violencia – in the fifties when the liberals and conservatives, reviving their traditional rivalries, fought pitched battles which resulted in the deaths of 200,000 people. Yet by the end of the decade, they were partners in government.

Overall however, Colombians possessed an aggressive but positive uplifting spirit. Ecuador, though similar in landscape, had a less racially intermixed mestizo population and seemed less exuberant, apart from its coastal region. The harsher landscapes of Peru and Bolivia seemed to be reflected in the sad melancholic character of its people, although they also showed a tough resilience and pride. There was certainly a dramatic and heroic undercurrent to life in the Andes fashioned by the grandeur of the mountain landscapes, the mystery of the jungle and the unpredictable violence and terror of volcanic eruptions, earthquakes, military coups and bloody massacres. Life seemed transitory, too dependent on human whim and acts of God. There was an uncertainty in simply getting through each day and an almost fatalistic submission to events by the large mass of the South American people which I found disconcerting and depressing. How safe and comfortable England seemed seen from such a perspective. Yet people from Europe still came to settle in Ecuador, in Colombia, in this fierce land full of promise.

But within the context of the smouldering savagery of the continent, the homes of the wealthy were settled and elegant, full of art collections and imported books, unruffled, above it all. The ruling class, European North American in style, sat comfortably and serenely atop a populace that was wholly South American: two different peoples, apparently inhabiting different worlds.

It was always a pleasure to catch up on news from home, and a pile of letters awaited us in Bogota. Despite our long absence our nearest and dearest had not forgotten us. Their support and concern were always a help when facing an alien world. Chatty gossip, newscuttings and love were good therapy. I finally had news of my Oxford rowers too. The newspapers front-paged our new lady cox and the sinking of one of the trial crews. Reading between the lines though, it was clear they were a powerful prospect for the annual race against Cambridge and I relished the thought of returning to coach them. There were telegrams and phonecalls as well. Bogota was certainly proving to be a reassuring half way house.

In the interests of the documentary, we flew to the north coast town of Santa Marta to film the 150th anniversary celebrations commemorating the death of Bolivar, which were to be attended by nine Latin presidents.

The rhythm of the Carribean was immediately apparent as we touched down in Barranquilla, Colombia's main northern port: the tropical heat, the slow and lazy movements of the people, the green palms, the white sands and the blue azure sea. Jamaica lay just across the water. We hired a decrepit old van to take us along the famous drug dealers' coastal route to Santa Marta, one of the world's great dope processing centres, from where light aircraft distributed the stuff to the lucrative markets further north and east. Colombia's highest mountains, the Sierra Nevada of Santa Marta, stood massing in a haze of purple ranks beyond the town, their white helmets unexpected in the burning tropical climate.

Soldiers with automatic rifles lined the roads for miles between Santa Marta and the commandeered complex of hotels where the presidents and their entourages were stabled. 'MI9' had hijacked a plane the day before to mark their disapproval of the occasion and everyone was jittery. Armoured vehicles crowded with soldiers and military police patrolled the region and manned the road checks.

Nine presidents at the 150th anniversary of
Bolívar's death, Santa Marta

The great event itself was ultimately unsatisfying. While most of the locals preferred not to interrupt their day of leisure, and swam from the beach opposite, the presidents of Colombia, Ecuador, Peru, Venezuela, Panama, Costa Rica, El Salvador, the Dominican Republic and Spain, gathered under a long tarpaulin-covered platform to view representatives of their respective armed forces and those of all the other countries that had helped in liberating South America from the Spanish. The United States were conspicuous by their absence, but a small, rather motley detachment of British soldiers, led by a loudly commanding sergeant major and a bagpipe – playing Scots guard, were an eccentric but edifying distraction from the stream of variously and colourfully uniformed (each country searching in design to distinguish itself from the others) meticulously-drilled ranks, all trying to out-step each other in neighbourly rivalry. Their formal parade costumes were in vivid contrast to the battledress khaki of the working soldiers. But overall the speeches dominated the proceedings. The addresses were longwinded and over-embellished, embedded somewhat in the tradition of nineteenth century oratory. Bands played, announcements echoed stridently and Belaunde, with a cunning sleight of hand and good PR sense, scored a diplomatic point over his fellow presidents by walking over to the gathered crowds, shaking hands and talking to the masses. The other presidents looked on sulkily.

Suarez of Spain, who was to resign a few months later, cut a dashing and thoughtful young figure as he surveyed the scene, with the hint of a bemused and condescending smile on his face. Duarte, of El Salvador, was a slippery little gangster type in a flashy tie; so too was Gusman of the Dominican Republic. The Panamanian looked like a handsome Gaddafi in a white suit, while Carazo of Costa Rica, appeared large, smiling and simple. Turbay, the host, was a big man in his fifties, in a bow tie and glasses, with an honest academic look, but seemed desperately pleased by the sound of his own voice. Locals ran sweepstakes on the length of his speeches. Herrera Campins of Venezuela, was a big burly bear, about seventy years old, who gave the impression, perhaps deceptively, of being unashamedly corrupt, and not too bright, and who also talked at great length.

Belaunde seemed to be the most accomplished statesman of the group, and he hugged the young Ecuadorean Roldos like a long lost brother. A month later these two were practically at war, accusing each other in the most vitriolic terms of unprovoked attacks across their mutual ill-defined border in the mountains of southern Ecuador.

SOUTH AMERICAN MILITARY FASHIONS

The military versus the civilian government – a shaky axiom: Napoleon and, till the First World War, most European crowns were, so to speak, military; and since then, Corporal Hitler, Marshals Pilsudski and Petain, Generals Franco, De Gaulle, Eisenhower, Amin and Jaruzelski. And are Vietnam, Belfast and Afghanistan militaristic or not? Soldiers in the north west quarter of this globe are less seen because the ultimate weapons are concocted in secrecy.

Militarism, to simplify: the South American states are run by the ruling class with the military as their tool, excluding the campesino and the city proletariat who are the revolutionary material and the excuse. The European nationalisms are millenia old. Tribe language/territory divisions justify Europe's national passions, sustained against internationalisms of Christianity – a thousand years' assault – and today's marxism. But Spanish-speaking (Portuguese Brazil is a separate matter), Spanish-mestizo-ruled Latin America eulogises Bolivar, their unifying hero, yet splits into numerous discordant and warring countries – artificial creations based on former colonial provinces. The original tribal inhabitants are not included in this game; the ruling class belongs to the Spanish tradition, with the countries often complementary in their resources; yet our oft-repeated question 'What about the United States of South America?' is always shrugged off, even at Santa Marta during the rally of nine presidents of the continent.

All this, without Europe's or Asia's justification, is in need of exaggerations and verges on the grotesque: mental and physical. And so the academics and cultivated aristos within each country tend to overvalue the characteristics of each as unique and superior to those of their neighbours, to isolate the archaeological pre-conquest past presented as a border-to-border independent case. But the visual demonstrations of national identities (here this awful word is apt) had, for a century and a half, to be modelled on a fragmented Europe, as indeed their whole way of life tends to be: sporting and naval outfits, male manners and tweeds from Britain; Paris for women; army drill – Prussian.

But I am too rash. These are of our time; in the second half of the last century – witness the old prints, and, above all, the statues – the clashing armies and their commanders wore those touching French-inspired kepis and frilly Napoleonic epaulettes (I say touching, because this shape was for me always connected with Latin American heroics); these and the top hats plus whiskers and the banners; and to find all this there – also in some ceremonial guards' uniforms – helped to link 'my' legend with reality, often terribly bleak.

And so each city in each of these high Andean countries is heavily populated by monuments, most of them probably erected at the beginning of this century, since, somehow, the architectural styles of the past seem to have arrived greatly delayed. Their themes are heroic deeds and victorious leaders, while across the borders similar heroes raise their swords and win – possibly in the same encounters. Multitudes of them, since obviously aggressive and plentiful arguments for so many patriotisms are sorely needed. In La Paz there

*crouches/attacks, bayoneted gun in hand, an ordinary infantryman or partisan
in bronze; all true to my history pre-vision: he wears the Frenchified kepi, but
also sandals over the huge bare feet of a universal campesino.*

*The banners: Ecuador's and Colombia's oddly are identical, both the
colours and their distribution, the yellow stripe being wider than the blue and
the red; only the heraldic emblems differ. But no one seemed to know why the
stripes vary . . .*

*Uniforms but primarily the hats: in Chile, ultra-modern and west-
orientated, the airforce (and its uniforms to the last stripe) is modelled on the
British. But across the frontier into dictatorial Bolivia and amazingly the
military headgear matches their oppressive role: stiffened wired-upward
structures with peaks flat over the eyes, they are exact replicas of Germanic
shapes. And then one learns that in the early Nazi days, impressed Bolivians
invited Roehm, still Hitler's favourite then, to come and redesign the drill and
outfits of their forces!*

*The sheer contrariness – the need to differ (even the trends in political
systems may respond to this?) – strikes the eye on entering Peru: the police-
cum-military cap is a negative to the Bolivian verticals – here the horizontals
tend to be enforced: the peak stands far forward and so the top – wires are out,
democratic softness prevails!*

*Ecuador, enriched lately and patronised by the States, goes for the toy
policeman à la USA, and plays at toy-guardsmen at the presidential palace.
Colombia, though, accepts Europe's traditions and has the palace guards in
their 1900 German-copied pickelhauben. Colombia staged the meeting of
nine presidents of Latin America which was dominated naturally by the
military parade of their representative units. Brass helmets, hussar-shakos,
endless varieties of colour-schemes, of stepping drills, here on display was the
pathos-ridden pomp of Latin America's competitive insistence on enforcing
differences – the designers' field-day.*

*However, all this faded out. Wherever one went, in which ever country,
when there were conditions of emergency, battledress and equipment were
worn, and the soldiers took on a uniformal US – model look.*

The celebrations wore ponderously on, as the venue transferred to
Bolivar's home and memorial tomb, attended by a more select and
gilded audience. The only really moving moment, after all the
presidents had laid wreaths and made speeches, was the solitary
wail of the haunting bagpipes, played during the sounding of the
cannon salute. All else was silent and heads were bowed.

People fainted in the oppressive heat, and the only refreshment
available was water from the garden hose. Lines of dignified guests
queued for desperate paper cups of water. Only a very few honoured
invitees were allowed iced drinks from the special VIP room. Soldiers
toppled from their places as medical orderlies passed along their

ranks, popping ice cubes into the parched mouths of their surviving colleagues, before carting the unconscious off to the shelter of the surrounding trees. 'I don't know what came over me,' said one of the fainting Brits who had volunteered for the assignment as a bit of light relief from a Northern Ireland winter.

It was early afternoon when we finally regained our luxury beach hotel, half-an-hour out of town. Hot and exhausted, we fell into a stupor of poolside inactivity, and only emerged the next morning urgently aroused at six o'clock to catch the best light for a final burst of background filming in town. But breakfast at a cafe on Mainstreet before we began work, effectively cancelled out the purpose of the early start. Irritated by the delays, and while we waited for the next bout of filmic activity, I wandered on to the beach and fell into conversation with a group of boys and two challenging girls who played teasing games and demanded to be filmed. The girls invited me to their hotel room across the road – 'just to see where we live' – smuggling me past the hotel porter. They were on holiday from Bogota, and young Liliane's parents had entrusted her to her older girlfriend Maria. We had barely got into the room before they stripped off their bathing costumes. Maria disappeared into the shower and Liliane and I fell on to the bed in a lustful and wholly unexpected embrace. It all happened so quickly that it was over almost before it had begun, and there was Maria, standing over us dripping wet, claiming a fat fee for Liliane. I was disarmed and a little bemused. I had not realised they were working girls. I suggested weakly that I had already contributed to the happy encounter in kind, but Maria disagreed. They were not professionals, she said but needed the money to pay for the hotel room; it would have been churlish to argue.

The film crew were still discussing the next shot when I rejoined them, feeling much refreshed, and far less pent up about the continuing indecision. After a few more shots, we wound up for the day and retired once more to the beach hotel to wait for our evening flight back to Bogota.

Avenue Jimenez in the centre of Bogota, was the special preserve of the emerald street-trade. At first we hesitated about filming and drawing there, because we thought we might be running a serious risk when we revealed our cameras. But there was nothing underhand or secretive about the way the dealers went about their work. Over a million dollars of business was done every day out on the streets in front of the big emerald trading and refining companies. The dealers parked their smart Japanese imported jeeps and British landrovers, the fashionable cars of the moment, bonnets nosing into the curb, in spaces carefully kept clear for them

Campesinos visiting Santa Marta

by the accommodating policeman on the beat, who took his pay-off quite unashamedly. Anyone who was not a dealer, trying to park here unaware of the local parking pecking-order, was chased off by the ingratiating cop.

'This is the safest street in Bogota,' one dealer told me. 'Every man here carries a gun, and everyone knows what would happen if they tried anything, so no one does.' Even so, there were dramatic shootouts and corpses appeared with unnerving regularity on the outskirts of town.

Handfuls of emeralds were displayed by the dealers to potential buyers, and they did a brisk trade between themselves as well. Whenever an innocent like myself wandered on to the scene, he was immediately surrounded by salesmen extending opened paper packages full of stones, urging him to buy. The prices varied alarmingly, for what seemed to be gems of equal size and quality, and there were fakes galore. You needed to know your stuff if you wanted to trade with these men. They usually met for lunch, after a busy morning, at a second floor cafe called El Mosaico, and this was often the best place to do business, because the gems could be examined in detail with magnifying lenses and weighed on the little scales they all carried, which were, unless you checked carefully, extremely inaccurate – in the dealers' favour, needless to say.

We celebrated the end of filming with lunch in a finely designed restaurant that had been converted from an old house. We drank potent, hot rum cocktails and watched a pair who sang traditional Colombian 'llanos' and coastal songs. A black group of songsters from the coast, and later an energetic dance troupe of three boys and three girls who performed a variety of local dances, completed the afternoon cabaret. Dick, the sound recordist, commented on a curious pair who had just walked into the restaurant, and I glanced in their direction. He was a bulging man in his late sixties, wearing dark glasses, and would not have looked out of place as Al Capone's favourite hit man. She was a bright blonde teenager, in the tightest of tight skirts. Not wishing to appear rude, we got on with our meal, but a minute or two later, the waiter appeared with a cryptic message in Spanish. 'Me estas admirando o a mi novia' it read. (Are you admiring me or my girlfriend.) Big Al was clearly a little paranoid. Our whole table turned in amazement to stare at the glowering gangster doing far more pointedly what he had objected to in the first place. Our director explained to the waiter that Feliks was an artist. Then to us he whispered, 'Watch it he's the type who carries a gun.' We were loth to get into a he-man shootout over a Latin's wounded honour, so we buried our noses once more into our ajiaco de pollo stew. When we looked up again they had gone. We imagined his bodyguards, lined up with sub-machine guns in the road outside, waiting for us to leave. But there was no need to fear. Macho man had simply changed tables, and was seated out of sight behind a convenient pillar.

I was getting more than a little concerned about Feliks' health. Although he looked healthy and brown, he had lost weight, and he had developed a weakness in his ankle. Several times he had missed his step and had fallen full length. At first I thought he had simply tripped, but during the next couple of weeks, it happened more and more often. I got panicky about this, since the most testing part of the journey, the trip down the Amazon, lay just ahead, but I kept my anxieties to myself. I felt that he, for his part, was trying to pass it off with a joke in order not to worry me, but that he was in fact quite concerned. For someone who was always very vigorous and physically fit it obviously undermined his confidence considerably. But he was determined to complete the journey and not fail others and himself. He told me later, back in London, that it had not been fear that had dominated his thoughts each time he fell, but irritation and embarrassment at his loss of mobility, and a sense of relief that he had not broken any bones.

On top of this he was beset by a variety of uncomfortable ailments and a burning thirst which made him drink a lot of mineral water and which consequently led to a continuous need to pee, a need that cropped up at the most inopportune moments. (Driving in the country around Bogota with society ladies, he would have to come out into the open with pressing requests for roadside stops.) We tried to pinpoint the causes. I reckoned that the combination of strong sun, altitude and too much fruit and mineral water were responsible for his less serious complaints. We devised some specified exercises for his foot, and I suggested that he drink less fruit juice and eat more – particularly yoghurt.

QUOTE FROM THE TRANSCRIPT OF THE BBC TELEVI-SION FILM: WORLD ABOUT US.

FELIKS: In this relationship between son and father – which we were conscious of from the beginning, since it is how we chose to go, the two of us, rubbing against each other, finding a way to harmony through disharmony – I felt at first a lot of disharmony in the sense that I had been still in my old shape of competitiveness with what Daniel is obviously better at: getting to grips with life and being springy on his feet, as it were. So possibly, because of that, in some way I had a sense of playing second fiddle and feeling that this was not as good a

journey as my former journeys were. But then came my
collapse. I got this awful accident, this failing of my
right foot, which made me fall about. It started in
Bogota. The foot wouldn't hold me so I was falling on
my face a great many times. During one single walk
around Bolivar's house, I fell three times, and I had to
lean on Daniel, and he held my hand, and it became
part of the whole game that really I was a cripple more
or less. It has gone now, luckily, but I was a cripple and
the potential of a crippled father being led and taken
care of, and with great tenderness, by the son, produced a new situation, a sort of crossroads in my life,
and in our attitudes to one another. In other words, I
accepted the situation of an older man with his
limitations, his muscles not being on top form and
relying on the younger man, and I think this created a
harmony which I never experienced before; and I hope
now, when I am better, this close harmony will go on,
because I feel happy in it. I feel that I am settling to the
beginning of harmonious old age, close to my son.

The British film crew flew home to London, with my exposed film
and notes and Feliks' full sketchbooks, and we prepared ourselves
for the jungle.

* The Liberal Government of Turbay was defeated in the 1982 general election
and Belisario Betancur's conservative party came to power announcing an
amnesty for all guerillas.

CHAPTER 11　THE AMAZON: smouldering giant

There was in fact little preparation to be done. We had been taking anti-malaria pills for two months, and we expected to pick up hammocks and mosquito nets as and when we needed them. The flight to Leticia, which stands at the confluence of the borders of Colombia, Peru and Brazil, first took us south westwards by way of Cali, before turning east, much to the annoyance of two English girls, who had just flown from Cali at three o'clock that morning, to catch the plane we were now on. A crowd of noisy young men joked and drank and played their tape recorders at full volume. Feliks was convinced they were members of the cocaine mafia. I was equally sure they were students returning home to Leticia for Christmas. (We saw them later swaggering along Leticia's main street and relaxing boisterously in one of the popular open cafes. They seemed at home, which we both took to confirm our earlier, divergent, suspicions.) We flew out of the mountains and down over the thick dark green tufted carpet of the rain forest, cut by lazy brown meandering waterways, to land at Leticia airport.

In the cool of the evening, following the late afternoon downpour, the 'paseo' of Leticia was in full swing. It was a rough and ready, fast-living border town, throbbing with vitality and youthful opportunism. The main streets were paved for a few hundred metres to the edge of town, where the jungle took over, but on the whole there was a raw feel to the place. Youngsters on zippy Japanese motorbikes toured round and round the six blocks that made up the centre, most of which consisted of wooden buildings. The houses were two storeys, coloured blues and greens and pinks and yellows, with shady, covered verandahs running the length of each one.

Busy, narrow, market streets ran down to the river bank, where large paddle-wheeled steamers were docked, loading and unloading alongside a host of smaller river craft, ranging from delicate dugouts, to canoes with outboards, motor launches and an amphibious plane. Leticia was one of the major river ports of the upper Amazon, three days downstream from Iquitos in Peru, and five days upstream from Manaus, the hub of Brazil's Amazon region. Here at Leticia, the river was relatively narrow, you could see the far bank clearly and you could feel the forest closing in on you. But lower down the vast expanse of water resembled a sea, and a distant thin line was all you could detect of the jungle on the opposite shore.

A huge, snorting, squealing pig was being unloaded from a canoe by three struggling men. A daughter stood watching, holding two chickens by their feet – so silent and submissive when upside down. People smiled and chatted easily. A girl bathed her three babies outside the stilted wooden shack where she lived, at the river's edge, with her seven sisters and six parrots.

Back on the main street, the modishly-dressed young women strutted confidently. The men wore sharp, well-tailored slacks and monogrammed shirts, and drove the latest model sports-mobiles, all so out of place in this remotest of remote jungle towns. It was of course all part and parcel of the massive drug network. Here Colombia's narcotics mafia reigned supreme, uncontrolled, a law unto themselves. They handled their lucrative traffic without much fear of being brought to account. The pay-offs were high, but the rewards were enormous. Their ruthless and brutal reputation was well documented and they were feared by the North American mafia rings.

For those who preferred a safer business, the tourist trade was growing fast. Mike Tsalickis was the most enterprising of the local operators. He owned nearby Monkey Island, in mid river, with its jungle tourist hotel, in addition to his other hotels in Leticia. His fleet of small outboard motor-boats took visitors for expensive jungle trips, where they could spend days camping and visiting the up-river villages, all services provided. They were accompanied by a guide and a cook, who supplied food and drink, tents, mosquito

nets, hammocks and any other items deemed necessary for full
European comforts. He had imported a whole village of Indians
from Peru, promising them a guaranteed income from the tourists,
as long as they remained permanently at the ready to greet visitors,
bare-breasted and in loin cloths. Business was booming. His three-
day trips, which two years earlier had cost $40, now cost $400.
Other agents had set up in competition with him, and the scene of
the greatest in-town activity was at the tables of the sidewalk cafe
outside the Anaconda hotel, where they touted for business.

Across the street, a stage had been set up for the Christmas Eve
show that night. It was here that 'Alberto', mister smooth and
nonchalant, in dark glasses and languid expression, detailed his
terms for the hiring of one of his outboard canoes, and a guide.
With our TV producer, we were seeking suitable locations for our
next bout of filming with the new Brazilian crew we were meeting a
week later, in Manaus. I was anxious that we should locate our
Amazonian sequences upriver, in the area where we now were,
because I was convinced that Manaus would provide little in the
way of jungle atmosphere. It was a big town, and I was sure it
would have a wide sphere of influence from years of rubber booms
and constant trade. We would have to search long and hard there,
to find the sort of remote forest we wanted. We invited the two
English girls from the flight along for the trip which we planned for
the following day.

We watched the Christmas show performed on the makeshift
stage, set up across the street from the Anaconda. There was some
desultory singing, a little guitar playing, some contemporary
dancing, a stand-up joker doing a lot of talking while everyone
wished everyone a happy Christmas. With the Amazon river
providing the backdrop, it was a touching scene.

When the others had gone to bed, I took to the streets, as is my
wont. Music poured from most homes, and I could see people
dancing and drinking inside. The whole town was pulsating to a
Christmas beat. All the houses had gaps between the wooden slats,
which allowed what little breeze there was to pass through the
buildings. Otherwise the oppressive heat would have been too
much to bear. A local treat was to visit the post office, because it
was the only building in town with air conditioning. Shadowy
figures tottered along the dark potholed and puddled muddy
streets, and offered swigs of beer or hooch from their bottles as they
passed. The church was full for midnight mass, and outside,
children played in their best clothes, and the girls preened and
flirted with the casual young men. Some of the more dashing girls
cruised this busy church scene on shiny motorscooters, while joyful

halleluyahs emanated from the congregation inside. Down the street, the Anaconda hotel disco was closing and the late night dancers spilled into the street and made their way home, their singing and shouting ringing clearly through the still sultry hot air.

As Feliks began to rely physically on me more and more we slowed down our pace and I in turn became calmer, less hurried and more pliant. Our new relationship became a theme for the film. His thinness, and his unsteadiness made him pensive but I was sure that it was only a transient phase, the result of so much hard travelling. When he returned to London, he would have full tests done, and with a few good meals and some rest, he would put this brief confidence crisis behind him. He still worked terribly hard though and produced many magnificent drawings. He began to relax into his new, more passive role and became happier once he had accepted it, conserving his energy, retiring to bed earlier, moving more slowly.

Our little group set off next morning: thin, bronzed Feliks; pale skinned producer; bosomy, slim bikini-clad Lucy and her shy, serious, schoolteacher friend Sara; energetic Chiri-Chiri, the curly-haired guide, in khaki dungarees – a cheeky wise-cracker from Bogota; Emanuel, the Brazilian driver, a plumpish, tall, good-looking twenty-year-old, who had lost a thumb in the engine of his outboard motor; me and little Camillo, the boss Alberto's cousin, who was learning the ropes and who became Feliks' special friend. Our craft was a narrow twenty-footer with a thatch roof covering the centre section under which we were supposed to sit.

We travelled for only an hour on the muddy brown, wide Amazonas, before turning off abruptly up a narrow tributary the Callaru, which flowed black and cool beneath overhanging creepers and high-rising forest. The jungle closed in around us. Exotic birds flew away screeching as we passed, and butterflies rose in coloured profusion. We encountered thick weeds that blocked our passage, but we hurtled into them, lifting the outboard engine up behind, and planing across them. Sometimes we didn't make it through, and we remained stuck, while Emanuel and Chiri cleared a space for the engine to operate, then backed us up to take a run at the tightly-bound weeds. We broke a couple of sheer pins and, while Emanuel repaired the engine, we sat in the burning heat, watching the teeming river life closing in on the boat. Forward they came, the ants, the huge furry spiders and biting flies, jumping from the overhanging weeds on to the canoe, and on to us. While we were moving, the gentle breeze concealed how hot it really was. But whenever we stopped we were assaulted by a heavy excruciating heat.

Amazonia

So we tried to do everything on the move, including eating lunch. I took over the controls of the boat, while Emanuel ate. Our Christmas lunch consisted of bananas, fish, root crop and beer. The water was cool and sweet, and it seemed worth risking the piranhas, the river dolphins and the snakes, for a quick dip. Further on we saw two huge, finned dolphins rolling and leaping from the water, rocking our boat from side to side.

In the middle of the afternoon, we pulled into the little village of Buona Vista, set atop a high steep bank, overlooking a broad sweep of the river. Children splashed in the shallows and women washed clothes and combed their long black hair, as they squatted up to their waists in the water. We were offered a large wooden guest hut, raised like the others, on stilts in the neat village, which had about thirty homes arranged round a central grassy open space. The young boys played football there in the evening. The forest rose in a dark crescent behind the thatch-topped huts, and I wandered alone for an hour enjoying the tranquillity. I was greeted everywhere with welcoming, often toothless, smiles. Most people had rotting front teeth, or had had them knocked out altogether because they thought it improved their looks.

Our host was a villager who had come originally from Iquitos, and it was in his guesthouse that we hung our hammocks. While Chiri prepared dinner, Sara and I went down to the river for a swim. Canoes slid silently across the water, returning from fishing and hunting trips further upriver, and on the far bank.

Christmas dinner was rice and chicken – sticky lumpy rice and very tiny morsels of very skinny chicken – washed down with beer. Night fell quickly at six-thirty, and we gathered after dinner to talk and smoke with the village headman. We smoked mainly to deter the massing mosquitos, and we got through three-quarters of a bottle of excellent Scotch. Candles lit up the faces of our little circle. Our host explained to us that, although he was better off than his fellow villagers because he spoke a little Spanish and because he could make some money taking visitors for walks into the forest and renting out his hut, nevertheless he took great care not to antagonise his neighbours or allow jealousies to build up. He was prudent in not building his home any bigger or better than the others, and he refrained from adopting airs and graces, or dressing up in smart clothes. He had seen people in other places trying to set themselves above their brothers, and had watched them fall flat on their faces. He valued the friendship and community spirit of his adopted village far more than the uncertain fellowship of passing, well-heeled strangers. The village enjoyed having visitors, he told us, because they brought money. Sometimes there were eighteen guests in a party, but at this time of year it was quiet, because the river was low and few could get their boats through the thick weeds. Emanuel our boatman puffed up his chest proudly.

The villagers were very shy, and spoke little Spanish. Unlike other, more frequently visited villages, they offered no local crafts for sale.

The night was fraught with whining mosquitos and loosening badly-tied hammock ropes which left some of us with our bottoms dragging on the floor. Since all the hammocks were tied to the same overhead beam every move, every cough and jerk, was felt by the others and that, combined with our inexperience with hammocks, meant that we spent a pretty sleepless night. Our host had promised to take us on a hike through the jungle next morning and so after we had breakfasted off huge palmleaves, watched by a semi-circle of curious little faces, we set off in single file leaving Feliks to dally in the river with young Camillo.

The Amazon in the straw-roofed boat ersatz exploration – but fine, though bothered with anglo-holidayish pranks.

My resistance and protestations at phony 'experiences', dictated imitations (ergo 'tourism') moving into the lead; but these are each tourist's own unique happenings – and so, having in my remote past 'truly' gone through much of those trials, I tend to misbehave when roped in now, but have to recognise some value emerging in such testimonies.

Over Callaru's dark tributary, butterflies painted in wettest watercolours, rather gigantic and challenged by equally gigantic bumblebees to jousts over the shore-scum; the bizarre-shaped bloodsucking (from legs only) flying bugs; in full moon, mosquitoes few and less bellicose, but making their entry under the nets. And the band of village children, in the morning, tracking me at shitting posture. As everywhere, there stands out among them a child-coquette, playing knowingly the game of hide-and-seek to the camera and the sketching-pad.

I fall on my face a lot, but form attachment with Camille, the mulatto boy in our crew, with whom I exchange drawings each of the other and swim and taste the calm of the day's village doings. Of course he is beautiful, at first reservedly proud – then unreservedly companionable, tolerant of my (for him) oddities – a perfect friend, brusquely lost for ever at the landing back in Leticia. The network of relationships in this world: he is a schoolboy from Cali, holidaying with his uncle, the white owner of the boat.

Over the village creek a dugout carries a fishing man: a few paddles, then the same hand shoots the spear steeply through the surface. But we, the swimmers, do not encounter predatory creatures, and, back in the boat, in progress over the black, narrow, almost static waters, all is lyrical and, oddly, without expansive ostentation in this, most tropical, passage: water – black-brown, between and under high thicknesses of vegetation – green, and within it a rarely glimpsed flower – always purple, no other. The silence of the still depths, yet composed of the past giant struggles: the overturned bulky white-grey trunks – some blocking our way. And in this closeness the sky's moods are of no importance.

The fitful vegetal, carpeting/invading from bank to bank the tributary's width, ensnares the boat; cutting, crashing, being caught (the damaged motor anxieties) by this virginal-seeming membrane offers the reverie of primary exploration – until: IMMENSITY, of sky-meeting, speeding – bright vast waters – disdainful of the idea of being discovered; of bad-tempered, purpose-changing clouds, cascading, rainbowing, sun-dressing.

Already at seven in the morning the air was close and sticky, and as we hurried across the first kilometre of secondary-growth forest, the sweat began to pour from our bodies. The villagers had cut away a lot of the forest in the immediate vicinity of the settlement, and we could see clumps of banana trees and other crops set in little clearings. Occasional long, straight, recently-felled trees suggested that a canoe or a centre timber for a new house was being prepared. We were introduced to some of the secrets of the jungle. Natural dyes from a red fruit produced a blue finish, while the colour green came from a certain leaf. Weeping rubber trees oozed a tasty sweet milky liquid when they were cut into with a machete. Whenever we stopped, the hot sun burnt like a furnace, and the nasty insects moved in for the kill. I smoked continuously to keep them at bay but it did no good. For some reason they found my sweat irresistible. My blue-shirted sweat-soaked back was quickly covered in ferociously biting insects, yet strangly none of my companions suffered more than the occasional nip; those merciless Amazonian guzzelers were utterly seduced by my smell. It took me a week of agonised scratching to recover from their kisses.

Abruptly we came to the real jungle. It was dense and dank; the sun was blotted out by an impenetrable tangle of dripping, crawling foliage. We slashed through with machetes, trying to follow an invisible trail that only our host could distinguish. At times we waded thigh deep in the swampy undergrowth, and at others we balanced above it along fallen tree trunks. Our boots were of little use in the deep acrid stagnant mire. Once as I strained to protect my camera while at the same time trying to photograph, I slipped and fell into the slime, nearly writing the damned instrument off altogether. It was so dark in there I could scarcely get a meter reading anyway. Great llanas hung thickly like ropes from the tall trees that struggled upwards towards the light far overhead. The vast knarled thickness of the trunks bore witness to their age. As we waded and ducked and stumbled and clambered on behind our barefoot, light-stepping guide, he told us how he had, as a child, been lost for eighteen days in the forest. He had managed to survive by eating wild berries and roots.

To my discomfort, he kept stopping to point to one interesting feature or another, or to answer questions, which allowed the insects to swarm in. He also thought we should stop to let the girls rest, but in a burst of justifiable feminist indignation they protested that their stamina was holding out better than that of anyone else. I felt bound to support them, since all I could think of now was diving headlong into the river to escape my buzzing tormentors. We battled on and it was with sweet relief that we arrived back at the village hours later. After a swim we took off on the next leg of our boat trip.

Our visit to the 'remote' Indian village of Mike Tsalickis was a depressing interlude. Unlike the villagers of Buona Vista, everyone here spoke Spanish; yet also unlike the people at Buona Vista, everyone here went naked save for a red loin cloth, to provide the tourists with the spectacle of a typical Indian village. A few desultory huts were grouped on a rise above a backwater off the main river, and the inhabitants sat around listlessly, displaying a meagre collection of trinkets for sale. Because they had been uprooted from their original home, they seemed to have forsaken horticulture and even fishing and hunting to a certain extent. They relied on what the tourists brought and the 'boss' Tsalickis provided, and what they provided was not nearly enough. One child stood with his mother, watching us. A festering sore on the back of his scalp was covered in swarming flies, ticks and weeping scabs, and we took him back to the boat to try and treat it with antiseptic cream and bandaging. A little girl intoned her demand for a hundred pesos per picture; some pretty wealthy visitors must have passed by recently. Twelve-year-old Carmen flirted with Emanuel, who chased the squealing girl gleefully between the huts. They were apparently old sparring partners already.

We ate lunch back on Monkey Island amongst the monkeys and the parrots in the deserted guesthouse. As we left for Leticia, an elderly American butterfly collector and a young Israeli couple arrived on their way down from Iquitos by river to Manaus. We had a farewell dinner with our boat trip companions in Leticia that night and prepared to leave Spanish-speaking Latin America for Portuguese-speaking Brazil.

Our crossing of the border from Leticia into Brazil was comical. We had two huge and heavy suitcases full of film stock and six bulging shoulderbags between the three of us, so we took a taxi to the border; but we were dropped at a point where the road ceased to be a road and became a pot-holed track. The driver pointed vaguely down it while demanding full payment of the fare. 'But you were supposed to take us to the border,' fumed our Portuguese-speaking film-director. It was encouraging to see that even with his command of the language, the same frustrations and misunderstandings that I always experienced occurred nevertheless. The driver continued to demand his money. We commissioned five little boys with a wheelbarrow to help us and while the driver tried to put his case to a very unsympathetic soldier, we tottered off down the track behind our little saviours, who struggled along under the enormous weight of our luggage. We fell into another taxi on the other side of the frontier and drove to the airport at Tabatinga. Once again the road was under construction, and more little boys were needed. We finally settled gratefully into the airport lounge to await our flight to Manaus.

The place was alive with noisy, easy Brazilians. At one table four middle-aged men, who were seeing off a friend, hammered out a percussion rhythm on table, bottles, spoons and suitcase. The waiting passengers began to jiggle and then dance and finally sing along. Brazilians enjoyed, indeed preferred, their own music to the widespread invasion of Western pop, and soon the whole check-in and bar area had turned into an impromptu dance hall.

I remembered how, only six months earlier, at the Moscow Olympics, I had been struck by the wonderful spirit and fun within the 300-strong Brazilian sports team. They were unlike all the other national teams present, moving about the sporting venues in large noisy groups, playing guitars and supporting their team mates at the different events, regardless of which sports they were in. The warmth, humour and good looks of their team were highly distinctive, but of course all the medals went to the more serious, less uninhibited athletes from the other countries.

As we soared above the Amazon, the green vastness of the jungle became breathtakingly apparent. It stretched to every horizon, intercut every so often by great meandering brown swathes of sluggishly drifting rivers, zig-zagging their way north-south across the thick forest into the gigantic main artery of the Amazon as it made its stately 4,000 kilometre journey from the Andes to the Atlantic. There were swamps and flooded expanses of woodland, but there were open spaces too where the forest had been cut away to make room for cattle ranching and to supply wood to the increasingly voracious markets around the world. To Feliks the forest clearance seemed minimal beside the great spread of virgin forest, and he questioned the fears of the worlds ecologists who

predicted devastation, major climatic shifts and barren deserts if
the little controlled destruction of Brazil's equatorial forests was
allowed to continue. I saw bare patches and he saw thick forest.
There we were observing the same scene yet arriving at completely
different viewpoints. 'It all depends on the basic starting assumptions of each person,' I suggested. 'I don't start with assumptions,'
replied Feliks 'I tend to challenge current platitudes on the strength
of "tabula rasa" evidence while you yield to sympathetic "liberal-
humanitarian" propaganda.'

Manaus lay 1,600 kilometres up the Amazon river, at the
confluence of the clear dark Rio Negro and the murky brown
Solimóes (Amazonas). They ran, distinctly separate, and side by
side, for ten kilometres before their two waters began gradually to
intermingle and they finally became the one Amazon.

Manaus had had many success stories in its history, many booms
and many slumps: from the glorious days of the rubber boom, when
the grand opera house (Teatro Amazonas) was built in 1896 and
the great Caruso and other European stars were tempted to the
Amazon by the rich pickings, through to its present day designa-
tion, albeit an artificial one, as a 'freeport' city. People flocked to
Manaus to make a quick buck, and there was a tough, mercenary
feel to the city which suggested that everything and everyone was
for sale. The modern centre was not very inspiring. More evocative
were the multi-coloured wooden shacks which encircled it and a
river front of crumbling, tall-stilted homes and dockyards that
tumbled in a crowd over each other to the water's edge, and
provided, along with the vast variety of river craft moored in front
of them, the best view of the city.

We had six days to wait for the Brazilian film crew to join us
from Rio. In our modern, nondescript hotel, visiting foreign
businessmen sat round the pool in the evening, entertaining their
clients, getting drunk, and listening to 'erotic' tapes. They frothed
with excitement over Jane Birkin's breathy bedroom ditties which
not even the BBC would consider too risqué for their radio
audiences. The low level responses of this group of international
merchants which was dominated by an inane blubbery Asian, were
at curious variance with the sensuality of Brazil's normal lifestyle.
Feliks reported that upstairs, the room service boy flirted quite
provocatively with him every morning when he brought his
breakfast. The maids did likewise, and one of them, Maria, decided
to celebrate New Year's Eve with me while her floor boss was
downstairs collecting more bed linen.

All in all there was a feeling of hustling loveless sexiness about
Manaus. In one square around the corner from the hotel, lithe

young boys in satin shorts and tight T shirts hissed, 'Hey, my friend,' as I walked by alone. Further on, girls, mostly in their mid-teens touted for business and wore the tiniest miniskirts and vests in the sweaty atmosphere of the tropical evenings. Off the main cathedral square, by the port area, a veritable living theatre took place every day from three in the afternoon to four in the morning. This tough, cheap-end-of-the-market red light district covered four blocks and some 200 girls stood leaning against walls and in doorways, or sat on low walls and doorsteps. Girls of all ages, shapes and colours where dressed in slacks, skirts or shorts and blouses, T shirts or halters. All over Brazil though, dress for everyone was the skimpiest possible; usually bathing trunks and bikinis were enough. Here the girls talked in groups or discussed prices with passing men – usually the equivalent of £2 or £3. They all frequented the bar on the corner, and it was here that I settled for a few hours to watch the evening drama, nursing a litre of beer.

There was sawdust on the floor, with spilt beer swilling between the plastic top tables. Paper peeled off the walls. At first, everyone seemed rough and intimidating, and I wilted under the hard stares and casual glances that a stranger inevitably attracts. The hookers looked mean, and their customers looked worse, but after a while I began to relax and realised that they were not as hardbitten as they tried to appear. But they had clearly been in the game for a long time. They were pros and on the whole, they were far less attractive than the amateurs I had seen out on the streets earlier in the day. Everyone spat on the floor, a national trait I remembered from my first visit to Brazil, and none more frequently than the drunk young man next to me who was passionately pursuing a rotten-toothed drunken harridan. She could, I suppose, have been his mother, but I was more concerned by the slimy globs that just missed the end of my shoe each time he spat. They had built up into an unattractive little pool by the time I left. Maybe after all, he was just a nervous suitor.

Most of the regular girls were fat, pot-bellied and toothless, but they were having a lot of fun. They punched and chased and tripped each other to the accompaniment of raucous laughter and hearty curses. Some of them harassed one handsome young waiter unmercifully. One butch girl in shiny shorts with a boyish haircut paid a lot of attention to another younger girl. A woman in a black bra and see-through white blouse, had a pretty face and large sagging shape, while her small black girlfriend, whom she protected vociferously, wore fashionably long, white cotton shorts. The plump young waitress waged a constant war on another waiter. The currently popular juke box tunes, always the same ones played in all the bars of Brazil, ground repeatedly on. One man acted out the role of tough guy – sour, silent and brooding. He ordered drink after drink, but ultimately appeared too nervous to choose a girl. Another much older man played up to an attentive young girl, but she seemed more interested in the cigarettes and beer he kept pushing on her than she was in him. 'She won't leave with him,' I thought; but she did.

Girls came and went and returned again after they had turned a trick or two. It only took a few minutes, in one of the sanitised, spotlessly-tiled in yellows and blues, brightly-lit, musically-accompanied, plastically sheet-bedded cubicles and hotel rooms that overhung the adjacent streets. The bar smelled of piss and sick, and there was an unexpected, if slightly exaggerated, bonhomie amongst the clientèle, complete with vigorous back slapping. The beer cost ten cruzeiros (it was forty in the hotel).

Outside, rats scuttled across the road unnoticed. I walked back through the dark silent town, and, curiously for such a tough place, felt no threat from approaching people. Even the shanty homes, nestling in the hollows below the level of the road on either side, did not seem to harbour ill-feelings. A couple made love noisily in a parked car, and a mysterious girl in black sat on a first floor balcony parapet, watching them. The free Brazilian spirit suited me well, and its out-in-the-open bawdy street life appealed to my curiosities in those nineteenth century style demi-monde antics that had been stifled and legislated out of contemporary European societies.

Another night, outside the bar, there was a fight. A lot of men, some quite young, wandered the area as usual. Then, without warning, one with a goatee beard lashed out at a girl, and she went for him with the heel of her shoe. The other girls came running to see and gathered round. A big older girl moved to defend the first, and was tripped up by a friend of the goatee who continued to spar with his protagonist. Then the boyfriend of one of the newly arrived girls decided to challenge the goatee, and they circled each other, lunging back and forth, moving up the street. Goatee got the upper hand and began to give the younger lad a kicking. Others moved in to help, but goatee, despite his scrawny, thin appearance, was a tough operator and the crowd hesitated. Some of the girls pulled their pimps and boyfriends away, and goatee brushed himself down and walked off. We had moved some 140 metres up the street.

A pretty girl with a beer gut pulled her jeans down and squatted for a pee without breaking her conversation with three friends. A few minutes later, she rounded on a man and began to abuse him ferociously. The first fight had got everyone charged up. He attacked her, and again a crowd quickly formed. For a brief moment everyone seemed to join in: thirty hookers and maybe fifteen prospective clients all hitting out indiscriminately. But finally the first attacker allowed himself to be walked off and people began to disperse. Then the girls all rushed off down the road towards the bar, and a couple of minutes later came racing back up the street again. In the middle of all this, a taxi pulled up looking for girls and three climbed in and drove off. A crazy girl kept lying down on the ground, rolling about, pulling up her sweater, and getting very dirty. More taxis arrived, discussed prices for clients, and took girls away. Round the corner, two policemen were interviewing the second attacker and the pot-bellied girl he had been fighting.

It was just another normal night on the street. Mostly they were local girls who had come in from the surrounding villages, young girls, screaming shrews, learning the ropes quickly; but a few had come from as far afield as Rio and São Paulo because they had heard that the pickings were better in Manaus.

We were searching for a remote frontier outpost as a film location, but although we visited various possible outlying towns, it became clear that the influence of Manaus had spread far and wide and all we found were polite suburbs: Amazonia suburbia. Even our excursions up and down the river's many off-shoots, failed to produce the thick overhanging forests that we had seen near Leticia and we had to settle for second best. One boat driver we hired seemed to have very little knowledge of the region. 'You're the most demanding clients I've ever had,' he complained.

While we were filming our boat excursion sequence a few days later, we were caught in mid stream by the most violent thunderstorm, much to the amusement of a schoolroom full of children in a shack high on a bluff overlooking the river. I dived overboard for a swim. With my eyes at water level, I could see the rain bouncing off the surface of the river like tiny silver drops; they caused dozens of miniscule rainbows to form for an instant and then disappear. The children ran down from their classroom to join me in the water.

In all our travelling we had seen no wild life, apart from some tame monkeys, parrots and the herds of llama and alpaca up in the mountains. Feliks felt particularly cheated and so, to satisfy our 'fauna' hunger, we made our way to the zoo of the Hotel Tropical, considered one of the world's great hotels. A palace set in extensive grounds on the banks of the Rio Negro, the Tropical possessed every possible modern convenience, a golf course, shopping arcades, a strident band playing beside a huge crowded pool, a beach and, most important for us, a zoo of its own. Here the monkeys insisted on taking Feliks' pencils and drawing his sketches for him. The absurd male tapirs found it hard to walk because their huge cocks dragged along the ground and kept getting caught in the shrubbery.

The military zoo on the road home had a more fulsome selection, and although Feliks thought we should film the zoo as such to highlight the irony of our search, the suggestion was rejected along with many of the personal touches we were always trying to introduce. We feared that the film was beginning to look too much like a dull travelogue, and for a while we became fretful. But there were compensations. Out drawing at the opera house on his own one day, Feliks got into conversation with three English girls. They were staying with Mark, a young Englishman, who it transpired was a friend of Feliks' London friends. We had tried but failed to make contact with him earlier in the week. Mark enjoyed having company from home, and it arrived on his doorstep in abundance during Christmas. The girls were an interesting trio. One was an artist who had been exhibiting her work in Lima while we were there, and who had come to Manaus for a few days on her way to join the controversial Fitzcarraldo film set of the German director Hertzog in Iquitos. Another worked in São Paulo and had brought her visiting college friend Carina. They were planning a long trek across the continent together in the New Year.

Mark had been posted to the Manaus branch of the bank he worked for, and was counting the days until he could return to Rio. But he had carved a niche for himself in Manaus, and although he found it a mercenary town, he enjoyed his Brazilian friends and resisted the temptation to sink into the usual insular expatriate cliques that always develop when people find themselves in foreign places.

Our new film crew, the brothers Carlos and Georgio the sound man, joined us for a days' filming in Manaus before we set off eastwards. They were a welcome addition to our little party, and were an informal and relaxed pair; it was a pleasure to watch our Brazilian experience unfolding through their eyes. I spent many late nights walking and talking with Georgio, visiting the unexpected out of the way nooks and crannies of the many towns we visited as we hopped by air across Brazil from Manaus eastwards.

First stop was Santarem, the next large downstream town, half way to Belém, where the Tapajos river flows into the Amazon. The huge extravagant luxury Tropical Hotel, standing almost empty and insensitively incongruous amid a sea of little poverty-stricken hovels, had been built in anticipation of the flood of tourists which were predicted would come flocking to Santarem, the moment the tourist department printed the relevant leaflets. But this was just a stopping-off point for us. Our film director had arranged to hire a small six-seater plane the following morning to take us to Itaituba, 320 kilometres to the south, also on the Tapajos river.

Itaituba was the modern-day 'wild west' pioneering town we had been searching for. It owed a sudden burst of popularity to its proximity both to recently discovered gold deposits, and to the Trans-Amazonica Highway which crosses the continent from the Atlantic to the Pacific, and which was nearing completion. The presence of gold-miners or 'garimperos', with money to burn, and the fast-growing traffic along the Highway attracted the 'servicing' industries in droves. The little dusty wooden town was growing up fast, even though it did not yet have a tarmac road, that true mark of progress.

Business was excellent for the local shopkeepers who supplied the needs of the mass of garimperos arriving regularly by air taxis from the mining areas to sell their gold and sow their wild oats. It was booze and women, and the women arrived from as far afield as Rio, to swell the numbers of young girls from the surrounding countryside. Students, sociologists, qualified doctors, it was said, had given up their careers, albeit temporarily, to cash in on the easy money to be made out of whoring for the garimperos. For all but an enlightened few, the miners could think of nothing else to spend their money on, and were ill-prepared to put the large sums of money they were making from the sale of their gold to better use. The miners mined the gold fields and the hookers mined the miners.

There was also a nervous middle class in Itaituba, which eyed the rough outsiders with a mixture of anxiety for their own safety, and hunger for their gold. But the garimperos on the whole kept themselves to themselves, hanging out in their own bars on the edge of town, where whole villages of brothels had set up along the Trans-Amazonica. Every now and again, however, a garimpero might try his luck with a local daughter of the bourgeoisie, and then there would be trouble. Gunfights over girls as well as over gold were common, and sudden violent death was part of the rhythm of Itaituba's daily routine. Indeed it was famous throughout Brazil as a centre for malaria, gunfights and the clap.

Staying in our ramshackle hotel above the pharmacy was Ajo, a striking slight girl in her twenties, with very clearly defined Indian features. She carried herself with that easy confidence that successful hookers have, who know how to take care of themselves. But Ajo was not a hooker. She was a garimpero. There were only two female garimperos in the region, and in the most macho of all possible macho worlds, Ajo was unique. She was a diver, perhaps the hardest job that a garimpero could do. You only worked a few days a month, for three hours at a time, because it was so tough. Working with an underwater hoover she scoured the river bed for gold, risking water snakes, piranha fish, crocodiles, rock falls and bursting eardrums. But the worst danger came from the mad-toting gold diggers who thought that Ajo was an easy touch. However she had friends a-plenty both in Itaituba and out there where she worked, and what she couldn't handle herself, they took care of for her. She could usually make 40,000 cruzeiros ($800) a day, she told us. That was for 150 grammes of gold, of which she could keep a third. At that time, her 150 grammes were earning over $3,000 on the international market.

Not everyone was convinced by Ajo. Our urbane pilot smiled indulgently when we spoke to him about her. 'Don't be so innocent. She makes her money using her cunt,' he insisted bluntly, reluctant in his male vanity to believe anything else. He had an axe to grind anyway, because he was suffering from the clap, and found little good to say all day.

Ajo spoke very intensely and in great detail, about her work, and her life. She liked the independence. 'I am an Indian,' she said, 'I like to feel free as the forest.' She had three children by a man who had left her. They were with her family now in Santarem, and she was determined to give them a good start in life, by buying a shoe shop there and settling down, once she had earned enough money. She was not, she said, going to drink and fuck it all away like the other garimperos.

Generally the garimperos never saved. One who did was Alfredo a wily man in his fifties who flew out with us next day. He owned land, farms and houses. He had just sold a kilo of gold and had over $50,000 on him. 'We all carry this sort of money with us,' he said. 'It is safe. There is honour amongst garimperos.'

We spent a quiet (apart from the midday thunderstorm) Sunday filming a lazy, drifting day in Itaituba. Two men sat by the riverside, playing flutes and singing, while the towns taxi-drivers washed their cars below. Young boys dived off the jetty into the fast running stream, daring each other to greater feats; and the rain poured down. Then we took a short drive out of town to the Trans-Amazonica – a thin muddy red ribbon snaking away through the trees into the distance, pot-holed and puddled, with the wooden shacks of the brothels lined up on either side, backed by the verdant rise of the forest.

On a wet Sunday afternoon, the action around the bars was muted, but the people who were there, clients and girls alike,

Goldrush brothels, Itaituba

extended a welcome of proffered beers and lively conversation from beneath a thatch-covered open-sided bar. They were flattered by our interest and posed enthusiastically for Feliks. A peroxide-streaked blonde girl with a shining gold tooth and a rag doll, moved raunchily from lap to lap amongst the rumbustuous miners. The Madame, a young and pretty woman, swung lazily in a hammock. Upstairs four little girls, the eldest no more than eleven, played at being prostitutes and flaunted themselves from the window. They were, we were told, the children of a customer who had gone away on business for the day, and had left them in the care of the Madame. There were sly winks and nudges which suggested otherwise, but the story was offered probably to parry any official enquiries. Two of the regular girls responded to our request to film them by staging a mock boxing match, which jarred somewhat with the relaxed atmosphere of the afternoon.

We learnt next morning that unexpectedly the garimperos were going through a rough time financially. The recent fall in the price of gold on the international market had ricocheted disastrously in Brazil. The government had decided to curb the amount of gold it was releasing worldwide and had closed down all the private shops which bought gold from the miners. Only the government-owned shop was allowed to trade, and we watched a long queue form outside it as the angry garimperos, denied their usual outlets, waited for opening time. They knew that the price had been set artificially low in the knowledge that they had to sell their gold anyway. It was illegal to sell privately, or to take the gold to another location for sale abroad. So they were stuck. 'We are being humiliated,' said one garimpero in the queue; and indeed so it appeared, as they waited disconsolately to hand over their little bundles of gold dust.

When we first arrived, I had noticed three girls shopping in the chemist beneath our hotel. We exchanged smiles as they were leaving and a few moments later, a boy ran up and handed me a note. 'We think you are very pretty,' it read. 'We would like to meet you.' They named a time and place. I saw them driving off in a taxi, and they waved as they passed. I waited at the appointed time and place, but as usual no one showed up. Later while Georgio and I were drinking a beer at an open air cafe frequented by the townspeople, a girl came over to us and sat down. She was one of the three from the chemist shop. I asked Georgio to ask her what had happened to them earlier. 'A Brazilian would never ask her a question like that,' he said. 'Only you Europeans worry about such details. She's here now, isn't that enough?'

Georgio's tactic for making me practise my Portuguese was

simple. He refused to translate our conversation with Leila. She had been born into the Itaituba middle-class, and many of her contemporaries had gone to universities further south. But now there was widespread unemployment here and some of the local boys with university degrees were even going to work as garimperos. She said she and her friends didn't mix much with the miners, but whenever the two sides did meet, it generally resulted in fighting. The present tension over gold prices was bound to explode soon she thought. What in fact happened a couple of days after we left, was that violent storms flooded the area and rendered thousands of people homeless, no doubt dampening down the anger of the disaffected garimperos.

Our journey continued on through Belém, a large imposing red-tile-roofed colonial city built on the banks of one of the many mouths of the great Amazon. The town was encircled by the familiar, dishevelled, matchbox-shack life of tropical South America: dilapidated windows and doors hanging open; hammocks swaying; barely-dressed people lounging and talking; lithe girls swinging their way down the street or waiting for buses, a lift, friends or customers; samba sounds issuing from a million radio sets. It all gave a sensual laziness to the human tableau. And in the town centre, outside the grandest hotel, stood a trio of sad patient goats, tied to a parking meter, while their peasant owner negotiated their future with the hotel cook.

I now looked forward to the prospect of revisiting the cowboy 'vaqueiro' country, where eighteen years earlier as a schoolboy, I had spent four months on a film-making expedition with six colleagues. Flooding back came memories of hot dusty days riding the dry woodlands, rounding up, corralling and branding the cattle, and of nights spent in hammocks in open-sided mud and wattle huts, and waking in horror to find vampire bats nestling snugly on to my face as I slept. I remembered the hair-raising landrover journeys across virgin land, the encounters with alligators, scorpions, piraña fish and snakes, and the friendships that developed with the gruff cowhands, the Norestinho vaqueiros, of the remote ranch where we stayed on the Brazilian highlands.

We flew south to Teresina from Belém leaving the jungle behind and crossing into the dry red stubbly hills of Piaui and Maranhão criss-crossed by thin wriggling trails. Neat, comfortable Teresina had recently been blessed with a visit from the Pope, whose holy presence had led to more local government spending and activity on the town's amenities in six months than any of the local people had seen in the previous twenty years. We drove south through palm and banana plantations. This was unfamiliar terrain because

we were on the northern edges of the highlands, while my earlier visit had been 400 kilometres further south and on higher ground. It was a different season too. But I was not prepared for the first sight of my romantic fierce, independent vaqueiros that greeted us as we rolled into one of the small villages on the outskirts of their territory. Three vaqueiros in their distinctive battered leather hats stood talking on a street corner, politely leaning on their ... pushbikes. Behind them, a cow was tethered to a 'no parking' sign. They wore jeans and T shirts. I was stunned.

Piaui was supposed to be one of the poorest regions of Brazil, but the little settlement in which we now found ourselves belied the statistics. The neat brick, wood and mud-walled houses in and around the village were luxurious compared to their equivalents on the western side of the continent in Peru and Bolivia.

I comforted myself with the thought that further south, deeper into the more remote highlands, the vaqueiro were probably still as I remembered them; but for the purpose of our film, it looked as if we would have to reconstruct those raw vivid images.

What we finally found, in the late afternoon, was a family homestead, with goats and pigs grazing in the spreading meadow in front, bicycles propped against the wall and a white-haired grandmother sitting serenely on the front porch with her offspring in the glowing orange warmth of the setting sun. Her sons and grandsons were persuaded to dig out their vaqueiro leather coats, hats and flaps, and to saddle up their thin rangy ponies. Quickly they were transformed from a group of casually dressed, lazing farmworkers into dashing mounted cowboys. We proceeded to film them chasing cows, catching them by the tail and sweeping them off their feet, ready for branding. The dogs, thinking the show was for real, threw themselves into the fray, harassing the unfortunate cows, hanging by their teeth from the bovine muzzles. The eldest vaqueiro, a battered, unshaven old-timer, sang a brief round-up chant. Feliks was delighted. He had known of the vaqueiros only through my experience, and this brief conjured-up tableau was everything he had imagined. He found the colour, dash and design of their costumes reminiscent of the seventeenth century ragged mercenaries of the Thirty Year War, immortalised by Rembrandt in his 'Polish Rider'. But for me it was a pale, seemingly amateur reflection of the hardy team of full-time cow herders, living in the tough remote territories to the south west, that I had known all those years before. But although this might have been a little genteel, there was still enough of the vivid sense of roughness and colour to set the pulse racing.

The family, so brusquely imposed upon, was dignified, polite and helpful, and remarkably good-natured in view of the way we arrived out of the blue, asked to film, set up the camera, shot our sequences, and then departed, all in the space of a couple of hours. How much I wished I could have arrived gently, stayed longer, spent the night, spent the week, and gained something more lasting from the experience – and given perhaps something of value in return. Instead we raced back to the security and comfort of Teresina.

CHAPTER 12   THE EAST COAST: pulse of Brazil

All that remained now of our South American trip were the great cities of Brazil's east coast – the sites of the earliest colonial settlements, where the black slaves had first been introduced. We hopped through Fortaleza, Natal and Recife on the easternmost edge of the continent. The landscape changed all the time, becoming dryer and less forested as we travelled south into more open, cultivated territory. We arrived in Salvador, Bahia to the echo of a cheering Brazilian nation as their team scored a 4–1 win over West Germany thus earning enough points to reach the final of the 'Little World Cup' at the expense of the hated enemy Argentina. Enthralled crowds gathered round portable TV sets in the airport arrival hall. The frenetic radio and television commentators maintained a continuous horse-race style commentary for the full ninety minutes of the match, heralding each goal with a climatic, long drawn out 'GOOOAAAAAAAAAAAAAAAL' which rang out and finally faded over a triumphant fifteen to twenty second howl. Our Brazilian cameraman Carlos was convinced Argentina would survive while our Argentine born director thought Brazil could not fail.

Salvador, once the capital of Brazil, had changed a lot since my last visit in 1962. Wide avenues and modern high rise blocks and big luxury hotels dominated the skyline. Bronzed, leggy youngsters thronged the beaches, mostly Southern Brazilians and Argentines come north for the Christmas holidays. At first I was disappointed with this new modern Salvador, and it took quite some time and a lot of walking to find the old town and the port-side that I remembered and which gave the city its unique flavour. Beyond the tennis-playing beach adoni, the lazing bikinied nymphs combing their long black tresses watched by narrow-eyed hopefuls and the enfants dorés cruising the smart cafes where 'everyone' gathered, were the crumbling unkempt streets and squares where the predominantly black population of Bahia lived and the hippies hung out and sold their trinkets. Here were the bordellos and the bars teeming with sellers and buyers, dope pushers and the black magic mysteries of condomblé.

In the late evening, as I continued to explore with Georgio, small unexpected vignettes unrolled as we passed, curious surreal moments which were utterly Brazilian, completely Salvador. A deranged young girl, the shoulder of her dress falling off to expose her breasts, stumbled about as if drunk, haranguing a group of amused men; a young hippie tried to sell half a bottle of wine, but the girl grabbed it and began to drink, and by the time the hippie retrieved it he had only the dregs left to sell. All this carried on as if in a bizarre street theatre. An aimless old man wandered in and out of the spectacle. A soft, limp, white man in his fifties, wearing blue shorts and sitting a few yards away on the steps of the closed theatre hall, oblivious to the scene being enacted around him, earnestly chatted up a fey, very black, teenage boy in a white vest and red shorts. After a while they walked off arm in arm.

Prostitutes discussed prices with the drivers of cars and taxis, which were yellow VW Beatles with the front passenger seats removed. The girls adopted the oft-repeated stance, one arm resting along the roof of the car, bottom stuck provocatively back for any interest onlookers, one leg slightly bent, upper bodies leaning forward, heads looking in through the half-open windows. They literally hung into the windows to encourage the prospective customers in their negotiations, allowing his hands to fondle their offered breasts, and reaching in to the car to further persuade any ditherers with tempting caresses and squeezes. The girls were hampered by neither officialdom nor modesty in their pursuit of business.

We came to the Baixa, the lower part of town by the old river front that I remembered, steep and rambling and smelling of fish. Here Salvador was raunchy and flowing with possibilities. The tough older whores moved in, grabbing and fumbling, offering 'sucky' and 'fucky' right there on the street or in doorways, unzipping men's flies while at the same time trying to feel through pockets for spare cash in case, as was most likely, you refused their offers. In the confusion they probably made most of their money picking pockets in this way, since their charms were not difficult to resist.

Georgio was bent on finding the 'Holiday Bar' which had provided him with a good time some years previously. After a long search we discovered that it was in fact called the 'Sayonara'. We went inside, climbed a dark flight of stairs which led straight into a big hall with peeling faded wallpaper. A band was playing, and a few disinterested girls sat at the tables or propped up the bar. Some were painting their nails, others talked together or played cards and a few entertained some customers. It was pretty empty, but we were assured that it would soon fill up, so we settled down with a couple of beers. One or two girls came over to sit with us, but we were low on money and for a while too involved in our conversation. That was until a spectacular girl walked by our table.

She epitomised the haughty, splendid long-legged look of the Brazilian girls, with a thick cascading mane of dark hair, and an easy confident stride. I felt romance stirring. Instant desire, yes of course; happily ready for adventure. But there had to be something more to it as well; I had a plain uncynical need for loving, for some specialness and the softness of mutual affection in my encounters – however fleeting. Lusting for sure, but contact too. I was entranced and overcome with confusion. I waited nervously for her to come back. Naively I still hadn't come to terms with the idea that as long as I had the money she was mine. I was fearful of rejection and anyway, I was sure that I would not be able to afford her price.

Georgio became involved with a noisy, pretty youngster across the table, and paid little attention to Carmen when I asked her to sit down with us. She was enchanting, sympathetic and nineteen, and had been a hooker for three years. She explained that although she did not like the Sayonara bar she was inexorably tied to the place all the same. Despite language difficulties and the unconducive atmosphere, we made a contact of sorts. She was not allowed to leave the bar she said, but we could go upstairs. Her price was 1,500 cruzeiros but she did not seem to mind that I only had 500 left in my pocket. I left Georgio negotiating with his uncompromising friend, and went with Carmen out of the hall, up another flight of steps, to a big open-plan second floor which had been partitioned into fifteen or so compartments all fitted out with beds. An old lady indicated towards one of them, but Carmen preferred another at the far end, and there we stayed, unhurried, cocooned and content for nearly two hours. When it was time to go though, and I wanted to arrange a rendezvous in the town for the next day, she would name neither a time nor a place for us to meet, but suggested vaguely that I could find her at the bar again after seven o'clock the next evening. Her days were private and her own she said. But she was not there the next day, and I never saw her again.

Georgio had gone and it took me two hours to walk back through the deserted town alone, through streets that were deemed perilous by locals. A prostitute, talking to some friends outside a row of grubby shacks, stopped me for a cigarette. (I took to carrying a packet of cigarettes with me in Brazil even though I don't smoke, because everyone you met asked for one as a matter of course, and it seemed a necessary element in my night prowling equipment.) She was very black, young, short, plump and playful and wanted me to come with her for a few shillings. She fondled me lazily and absentmindedly as we talked with her friends until a drunk and pugnacious regular came and took her off. Further on, an expensive disco was still in full swing, with younger smarter girls hanging around the entrance.

There were many people sleeping out, sprawled on doorsteps or curled up on the pavements, and on benches. In the muggy heat though it wasn't such a bad idea. The street cleaners swept round the slumbering bundles. Late revellers spilled out of another disco and walked off noisily down the street. Brazilians liked to do everything at full volume and at full speed. A final hooker on a street corner of the smarter residential and hotel section of town, asked for a cigarette, and offered a suck in the darkness of the beach across the road. She was young and pretty but tough and scarred. I declined but we settled for a chat instead, she seemed glad to take a friendly break. 'The men I get at this time of night are usually pretty horrible.'

We filmed outside the port market, Mercado Modelo, next afternoon, not far from the Sayonara bar. During the day, downtown Bahia was colourful and busy and the atmosphere easy. It was a happy hunting ground for bargain seekers, Brazilian tourists and pickpockets. Behind a news kiosk on Praça Cairu, two men sang and played guitars. They were 'violeiro antadores' or 'repentistas', who sang improvised verses, alternating the singing from one to the other, using whatever came to their attention in the crowd as material for their humorous and inventive rhyming. We, too, became the subject of their satirical game and they gathered a large appreciative audience and a full basket of cash. I remembered similar minstrels on my trip eighteen years ago, who visited the facienda out in the bush where we were filming and living. These travelling singers carried news to remote and isolated places, rather like medieval troubadours or a singing telegraph service. Often they would be challenged to a singing duel by a talented local, who would match them verse for verse to the delight of his friends. The variety and originality of their singing was always critically scrutinised by aficionados. The two in the Bahia market were old-timers, experienced practitioners of the art. One was a pale unshaven mestizo, the other a black joker with only one tooth left in the middle of his smile.

A crazed, thin, ragged, grinning man stood watching the singers. In one hand he held the skinned, decapitated bloody corpse of a monkey. In the other hand a plastic bag containing its head. He swung the corpse at people in the crowd and they shied away, revolted. He laughed and cursed them. A girl in grey leotard and slacks and a band about her head watched him with distaste and us with interest. Her name was Beatrice and she was a dancer with an International Brazilian folklore group. She adopted us and stayed with us for the rest of our time in Bahia.

Salvador oozed soul and charm and history. I was feeling once more the lure of Brazil that I first felt as a seventeen-year-old. It was a place, perhaps more than any other, where I felt I could happily live. It was arguably the most engaging city in South America and lay at the very heart of that black African/Portuguese magic that makes Brazil such a spectacularly unique and enchanting country. It was from here that the vitality of the Brazilian character flowed, that satisfyingly exuberant and successful intermingling of African and Portuguese cultures and people; a harmonious racial hotchpotch. How attractively this amalgam compared with the morose and melancholic mestizo marriage of Spanish and Andean Indian on the other side of the continent. The mysterious occult undercurrents of condomblé and macumba, the crumbling downtown slums, the brothels and the sleaziness, the uninhibited spontaneity and outrageousness of the people, ensured that no one could ever get complacent or pompous about Bahia. The more time you spent there, the less you knew it. Nothing was predictable, save its unpredictability. Even Brazil's military dictators were often outflanked by their nation's natural irreverence and irresponsibility. Sometimes their own personal traits displayed that same irreverence and undermined attempts at military severity. The narrow noisy streets of Bahia belonged to another century and the people exuded an almost dreamlike quality of a different age.

That same spontaneous, unbridled spirit expressed itself everywhere I went in Brazil, and there was always a constant accompaniment of music and song to almost every aspect of social and working activity. Over and over again, we were told by shanty dwellers and writers, prostitutes and politicians, that Brazilians lived for futbol, samba, carnival and fucking and that for the men at least, the responsibilities of work and family life were subordinate to these. It was repeated so often to me, who no longer needed convincing, this glorification of the Brazilians' loose, pleasure-mad character, and with such intensity, that one felt it was part of their own desired view of themselves, part of a PR campaign to sell themselves to an envious world. Although much of it was true, they seemed still to be trying to convince themselves as much as the listener. 'Ah Bahia,' they would intone dreamily. 'Ah! Rio – there are three girls to every man.' 'Ah, their beauty, their freedom.' 'How you will love Ouro Preto and Buzios!' and on and on and on.

And, of course, there would be disappointment initially, since no one, since nothing, could ever live up to such a barrage of pre-publicity; but then, bit by bit, you would become seduced; their enthusiasm for themselves, for their way of life, was infectious and it washed over you like an intoxicating wave, until you, too, began to forget the bad days you might have had and remembered only the good. The poverty of the shanties in the hills around Rio, the despair of the harassed and disappearing Indians of the interior, the excesses of the military who 'disappeared' political dissenters, all receded somewhat from centre stage. Futbol, samba and carnival were the opium of the people and it worked. They, and finally we foreigners, believed in it, and we loved it.

I felt there was in Brazil a burgeoning joie de vivre and an optimism that was utterly convincing and captivating. I had only encountered such a feeling spasmodically on the coast of Ecuador, in Esmeraldas and on Colombia's Carribean coast, but nowhere else in South America.

In Brazil, their unfettered enthusiasm was given full rein. The Portuguese immigrants, poor peasants in the main, had intermarried freely with peasant African and indigenous Indians and this had produced a nation of people relatively uncluttered, at least on the level of social interaction, by the ugliness of racial disharmony and prejudice. There seemed to be an easiness in the hurly burly of everyday contacts and exchanges. But even more than that, there was less evidence of the bigotry that hampers relationships between the races in most other parts of the world. Yet, even so, racial inequalities did exist on a professional, economic and class level. Blacker was poorer, less educated, and whiter, although not as a matter of course, was usually better off. You saw mostly whites in

government, in business boardrooms, at the elegant parties and at
the big social occasions. Not that middle-class blacks would have
felt uncomfortable in these situations, or that there would have
been any overt opposition to their presence on racial grounds. It
was rather that the class structure, the way the society had
developed and the opportunities available for upward mobility
amongst the poor had not embraced full emancipation for blacks
until quite late. Blacks still made up the majority of the dispos-
sessed lower class within the context of Brazilian society, but more
by default than as a result of institutional or inherent colour
discrimination. Social contacts were courteous, uninhibited and
unselfconscious.

Instances of discriminatory behaviour still broke through,
particularly when corruptible, heavy-handed authority, backed by
military rule exercised its power. Driving back from a filming
session at a samba school through Rio's dark, deserted streets at
four one morning a few days later, we saw two blacks being
roughed up by the police. Carlos, our cameraman, was furious: 'If
they were white, the police wouldn't dare bully them like that.'

Salvador's oldest square, Praça de Se Terreiro de Jesus, was
hippy and ethnic, with crafts and clothes and jewellery for sale.
Long dreadlocked freaks faked anger at the tourists' cameras and
two girls fought tooth and nail in the dry bowl of the central
fountain, tearing at each other's clothes and attracting an enthusiastic crowd. No one tried to intervene, and one girl finally
turned on her heel and stalked off complaining. Whenever there
was a momentary flutter like that, or the squeal of brakes across the
square or a voice raised in argument, everyone would rush to the
scene with a cheer to see what was happening. Otherwise they sat
or stood, lazily watching the world pass by, just hanging out,
waiting for the next flurry of excitement to rouse the pulse.
Everyone was busy doing nothing, yet the atmosphere was charged
with unexplained anticipation. A huge-bellied, white-suited black
man in a white stetson, bearded and smoking a pipe, strolled about
the square, turning coyly away from photographers. He clearly saw
himself as the local celebrity. Two women, a mother and her very
pregnant daughter, sold tasty fish morsels cooked on the spot, from
beneath a protective canopy. They were dressed in the traditional
eighteenth century costume of flowing white skirts and full lace
blouses. Other large black women, or 'baianas', tended similar
snack stalls on street corners all over the city.

The festival of Bom Fim, when the church is ritually cleaned for
four days every year, provided a good reason, if any were needed,
for a party. As the sun set over the city across the bay, bathing

everything in an orange glow, the stalls which lined the streets around the church, began to fill with the drinking and eating celebrants. Fairground sideshows swung into life. In one, a girl changed into Dracula and then into a gorilla before your eyes. Lovely, grand old baianas prepared spicy foods and sold good luck charms, T shirts and holy ribbons.

As the church was emptying, following the service, one young girl, who had arrived late, edged her way through the departing congregation on her knees, up to the front door, where she stayed for some time, deep in prayer. A couple of her girlfriends waited for her, giggling at her devotion. Then she got up, dusted herself down, lit up a cigarette and went off with her friends to join the party.

Pretty girls were everywhere, dressed in skintight, shiny leotards, stretched over springy swelling bosoms, brown backs left bare and tight trousers, shorts or tiny skirts. Drummers and bongo players pounded out samba and reggae rhythms and at one beer-drinking stall, some people danced, most notably an extraordinarily lissom girl, double-jointed, who contorted and thrust her limbs about at high speed. She held a large crowd spellbound. She would stop every now and then and coolly return to sit with her friends. But the beat would draw her out again, sometimes accompanied by a man friend and she would launch once more into her dazzling routine. I would have to learn those samba movements if I was going to feel at all at ease in Brazil.

We arrived in Rio on the Saturday that Brazil was playing the final of the 'Little World Cup' against Uruguay. The streets were deserted, as the whole population huddled round television sets across the nation. We joined an audience of millions as we were booked (thanks to our TV Company) into the splendidly gran-diose, old-fashioned, Hotel Gloria. Unfortunately though, the inefficiency and the ill-manners of the staff were, by contrast, thoroughly up-to-date. We joined the 'futbol' audience in front of the screen and despite a hundred million hearts urging their heroes on, and despite the optimistic crackling bursts of triumphant firecrackers set off by impatient supporters all over the city willing their side to score, it was Uruguay who stole the game and the tournament from a lazy, lacklustre Brazil.

Rio was in danger of suffering from a severe case of oversell. Brazilians, in their enthusiasm, tended to devalue the place by overstating their argument. If a thing happened once in Rio, that was enough for it to be eternally true and representative of Rio. It became part of the city's folklore. Rio! City of sunshine and beautiful women. But it also rained in Rio, and there were days when nobody smiled in Rio, and you could walk for hours without seeing any of the legendary lovelies. For the short stay visitor, the reality often failed to live up to the promise. For Feliks, Rio's reputation was destroyed in the five days he spent there. He resisted the barrage of propaganda, all the hype that had been heaped upon us and took on the role of devil's advocate, pointing to the bare realistic truths of what had been sumptuously pre-sold and which failed to stand up to close scrutiny. I enjoyed Brazil, and that included the outrageous pronouncements of her people and their blatant misrepresentations. For me they were titillating optimistic embellishments, but Feliks found them mischievously misleading and the people smugly self-satisfied and superficial. With my more prolonged stay, however, I became accustomed to the haunts and the rhythms of the city and the habits of the people; I got sucked into the flow and in the end, all those superlatives that had seemed to deceive began, gradually, to ring true for me, too, although an impression naggingly remained of a people lacking perhaps a more serious, reflective side to their national character.

 There was no denying that Rio was spectacular, set about a series of sweeping bays, with those curious steep green and craggy grey hillocks poking up in such inconvenient profusion. Wide avenues swept along the coast line of Copocabana, Ipanema, Flamengo and Leblon, with the skyscrapers and the huge statue of Christ atop the 600 metre high Corcovado, facing out over the Atlantic and watching the constantly changing, flowing open-air theatre that paraded below all day and all night. Rio was a city that throbbed. Cariocas (the natives of Rio) lived on the streets and on the beaches. Everywhere, every day, normal dress for vast numbers was a bikini or shorts and a vest, whether on the streets, on the buses or in the bars which opened out on to the pavement. Part of Ipanema beach was topless, but generated little extra excitement, since the bikinis everywhere else were so miniscule they barely counted, and anyway the stunning prostitutes, many of whom were transvestites, usually stood bare breasted along some of the main roads of the city every evening waiting for customers on their way home. The beaches were very busy at night in this respect, but quite dangerous too, since the tougher hookers were not averse to knifing a naive client for the petty cash in his pockets. In the main tourist/hotel area of Copocabana, the nightclubs put on explicit sex shows, with eight or more teenage girls making love on stage to each other, or with well-proportioned studs who could turn it on, on the hour, every hour. It was hard to find work and earn money in Rio because the population was distending daily, fed by the flood of hopefuls from the provinces cramming into the teeming favelas that littered the hillsides. So there was never a shortage of uninhibited and beautiful youngsters to perform for the benefit of the tourist or local clientèle paying little more than the price of a beer for the pleasure of watching them.

In Rio, it was holiday for fifty-two weeks of the year. The ocean was always there, invitingly cool and tempting in the humid heat, and a large proportion of cariocas passed by the beach at some time during the day. Ritual jogging, roller-skating, cycling and gym workouts on specially provided equipment on the beach, were part of the see-and-be-seen evening parade. Looking beautiful was the essence, even when running. There was an excellent line in sexy, high-fashion-designed jogging outfits and skating gear for the precocious middle-class nymphets who flaunted and preened in pretty groups along Ipanema and Leblon at about five o'clock every evening.

Feliks found this atmosphere of constant 'holiday' irritating, partly because he disliked the concept of holidays altogether. There was a certain superficiality about a life which revolved around the daily visit to the beach. And indeed 'the beaches' were the main recurring items of everyone's list of Rio's top attractions and delights; the continuous invoking of their names sometimes became a little wearisome: 'Ah Copocabana, samba, the girls, the sun, the "Garota de Ipanema" – the famous song "The Girl From Ipanema" was written at that very cafe, you know.'

When I suggested to Antonio Collado a leading Brazilian writer, that cynics gave samba, futbol, carnival and fucking as Brazil's all-consuming interests, he shrugged in resignation. 'If we Brazilians could put half the energy and enthusiasm that we devote to those four things, into work and efficiency and developing the economy, we would be the greatest and most prosperous nation on earth.'

Yet the Brazilian lack of inhibition and formality was deliciously seductive. On a visit to the House of Representatives to meet a politician in the capital Brasília, I was taken to lunch in the members restaurant. There they sat, the nation's leaders, some tieless, some jacketless, others in sports jackets, eating their lunch to the accompaniment of loud canned music. And it wasn't subtle hotel lobby musak either; it wasn't even Brazilian batucada or samba. It was Stevie Wonder and 'Another One Bites the Dust' and Michael Jackson and the whole American hit parade. They tapped their fingers on the table tops in time to the music and clicked their fingers and even hummed along, the business of the day clearly out of mind during lunch.

While out filming along Ipanema one day we ran into a childhood friend of Feliks' who declared that in all his travels after leaving Poland, he had found Brazil to be the most tolerant place in the world. And it was in Rio that he had decided to make his home.

I enjoyed walking the thronging streets of Rio late at night, along the kilometres of seafront pavement cafes, joining the parading crowds, drinking with old and newly-made friends in the popular bars and flirting with hookers. They carried out their work on the streets of the centre of town, on the beach or in the cars parked along the front. 'Listen to the car doors slamming,' said one English friend, whose apartment overlooked Ipanema beach. 'The girls always open the door to spit it out. A blow job is the quickest, cheapest and safest way for most of the guys on their way home from work in the evenings.' Further down the street one block was all gay, the cafes, the people, the atmosphere, with everything centred round a gay theatre in the middle of the block.

Strolling home to a borrowed flat in Copocabana during carnival, a severe leather-clad, bare-breasted figure talking to a colleague, beckoned me over. She offered me the pleasure of either one of them, or both, on the beach, while fumbling with my trousers and giving me encouraging pulls and squeezes. While they considered and discussed my degree of readiness in deep voices, I felt a little uneasy about the rough way my leathery friend was handling me, and I began to excuse myself. 'I really must be getting along...' But she was not having that. She (or was it he?) demanded money, and began to reach purposefully into her handbag. A knife? A gun? Trying to appear calm, I told her I wasn't interested while I slowly backed away. Luckily she abandoned her threatening stance with a sniff. They may have thought I was one of the hundreds of thousands of Argentine tourists who had come across the border for cheap holidays and thrills. Brazilians held the old enemy in the same contempt that the Argentines felt about them. If the Argentines regarded them as racially impure, savage and undisciplined, Brazilians considered their southern neighbours to be tightassed, bigoted, arrogant snobs. 'Do you know the best way to get rich quick?' joked a Brazilian friend. 'Buy an Argentine footballer for what he's worth, and sell him for what he thinks he's worth.'

There were dozens of samba schools, blocos carnavalescos, frevo and rancho groups in and around the city, each representing a different district of Rio. The first division ten took pride of place and they spent months and months before the carnival, preparing their thousands of members for the great Defile dos Escolas da Samba on the Sunday night/Monday morning of the four-day-long festival. Their weekly full all night rehearsals took place all over Rio, like Mourisco near Botafogo beach. There they prepared their routines, discussed their theme for the year, designed the elaborate costumes and selected their new song from the many submitted, which they practised endlessly to the pounding of the bateria – the percussion section comprising two dozen bongos and drums. The fast excitement of the drumming was executed for the most part by young, laid-back, black teenagers, cigarettes hanging lazily out of the corners of their mouths, sweat pouring down their faces, who set down a wonderful throbbing samba beat à la batucada. Perversely this was mauled and undermined by the dirge-like, excruciating dull, slow, flat high-volume singing of the faithful old songwriters, exhibiting their work. 'They're not singers,' Carlos explained, 'there's songwriters.' It was all part of the mystique, and criticism would have been poorly received. Tradition was everything.

The passions aroused by the competition of the samba schools, often led to violent scenes, and few carnivals went unmarred by a death or two during the four-day pre-Lent festival. In fact, the morning after we filmed at one school, six weeks before carnival, the director was assassinated outside his home.

All Rio supported one or other of the schools, and they all had their own special colours, character and locations. Salgueiro, Beija Flor – the trendy one – Mangueira, Portela, Imperatriz, Leopoldinese, Imperio Serrano, Vila Isabel, Tijuca, Uniao do Ilha do Governador e Mocidade Independente de Padre Miguel were the main ones, each with 3,000 or 4,000 participating dancers. There was fierce competition amongst the many members for a dancing place on the day. A strict hierarchy prevailed determining your position in the parade and your status. Long service as well as your talent was an important factor.

We spent one night filming Salgueiro, the red and white school, practising in a large rough open-sided concrete roller-skating hall, under a corrugated iron roof. But it was not just a rehearsal; it was a party too, a night out to catch up on the gossip and meet friends. During the night, there were periods of desultory dancing to the continuous drumming and whistling and the toneless turgid singing, while most people talked and flirted over beers, and a few drunken oldsters demonstrated their fading prowess on the dance floor for the benefit of the younger members. One thin, white, old lady in pink trousers, clasped her handbag tightly under her arm all night, as she shuffled about with a spindly-legged, hopping black man. Another plump, middle-aged, peach-capped mulatta half waddled and half danced importantly about the hall to the music. But when the time came for a full run-through, the mood changed dramatically and everyone rose to their feet.

Athletic bounding boys, sinewy, high-bottomed black girls in the skimpiest all-revealing halters, leapt into action. It was as if a tap

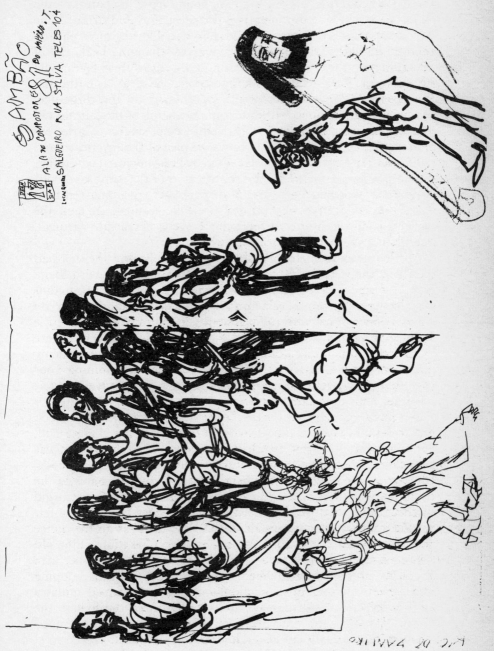

Samba school, Rio de Janiero

had been turned on. The music picked up, the sound of a thousand voices filled the air, and the whole company launched into a sweating, bouncing, joyous, frantic performance, working their way round the hall, in a long serpentining procession, led by the longest serving members and the most acrobatic dancers, their eyes wide and shining and their teeth bared in the widest of carnival smiles. For there was a definite carnival look, which clung to the faces of all Cariocas as they performed their ritual pieces, a fixed, huge, ear-to-ear smile, that seemed to be turned on and off at will. A glazed almost manic expression was the result. You just could not be seen without that grin, especially when the photographers were around.

The dance continued for an intense and exhausting half-hour of frenetic movement until the music stopped abruptly for the organisers to enter once more into their long discussions about the format of their show. Like puppets with their strings cut, the performers fell back into their resting or idling pose, waiting for the next half-hour of full effort.

On the balcony floor, the distinguished richer members of the club had their boxes, for each school drew upon all classes and racial groups of Rio society for their membership. There was every possible mixture of colour tones and physical features. In the samba school, a cat could dance with a king, and the great Adele Fatima, Rio's leading mulatta dancer and a famous blonde Brazilian actress, both proudly reaffirmed their Salgueiro membership. All Rio adored Adele, which was a great big plus for the rank and file of the Salgueiro school. She was one of them. And so the rehearsals continued until five in the morning. But that was Rio. The life at night was every bit as vibrant as it was during the day.

One morning, I went in search of a rowing club, and by chance came directly upon the leading one, the huge Flamengo club, complete with swimming pools, tennis and squash courts, gymnasiums, etc. It was also the home of Brazil's top football team, and was the most exclusive of Rio's social-cum-sporting clubs. The rowing fraternity is international, and I immediately found the Argentine sculler Ricardo Ibarra, winner of Britain's Henley Diamond sculls the previous year. He was training in Rio with the Brazilian national team under the country's top coach Booky and they were based at the Flamengo club. It was Booky who, two years earlier, had tried to arrange for Oxford and Cambridge to visit Rio for a re-run of their annual boat race and he now remembered me from the Moscow Olympics. Their training water was a perfect 2,000-metre-long lagoon, the Lagoa Rodgrigo de Freitas, a little polluted, but ideally placed right in the heart of the city.

I was given a guest membership and I felt immediately at home, settling happily to daily early morning sculling outings with the Brazilian national squad, before the sun became too hot. Later during carnival, I would go straight from the nightly celebrations to the lagoon, but only Ibarra trained diligently throughout the festival. The Brazilian team took the week off, and their general approach to training was pretty haphazard. Not one of them felt the urge to match Ibarra's devotion to duty. However much they admired him, they were reluctant to follow his example. Instead, to Booky's chagrin, they had a lot of fun. It was no surprise that Ibarra made the world championship finals later in the year, while the Brazilian selectors did not consider any of their rowers good enough even to be entered. In the Olympics the year before, the Brazilian teams' performances were universally dismal, although they were the most attractive team on view.

Street violence in Rio was as much a subject for daily news coverage as it was in Bogota. But here again, apart from my unfriendly leathery transvestite, I encountered few problems. We filmed at one beach, below the worst favela in Rio, which the Pope had visited by way of a special flight of steps cut into the hillside for him and where the recent murder of a naval commander had frightened the bathers away. The place was deserted, although it was considered to be one of the most popular beaches in Rio. Petty robberies carried out blatantly by the daring young toughs from the favelas were a constant source of public outrage, and the police were roundly criticised for doing little to stem the growing crime rate. But by the time I returned to Rio six weeks later, the crowds had returned to that beach as the pressure for space further along the coast during carnival week became too great.

Another of our filming sequences was a macumba ceremony. Unfortunately it had been laid on especially for us, in the small dark backyard of a polite semi-detached house in a quiet, black, slummy suburban street. Three men on bongos thumped away and after a long delay, six uninspiring ladies dressed in white robes, emerged from the house and began to circle a lighted candle placed in the middle of the yard. A man joined them, intoning monotonously and they answered, chanting according to their set routine. They were so obviously b-o-r-e-d by it all, and so theatrically amateur, that the whole exercise became embarrassing but we had to endure two hours of it while we filmed.

On the final day, after a film sequence in which Feliks and I had walked self-consciously along Ipanema beach towards a reclining woman with hard silicone breasts, which was supposed to display the beautiful bikini-clad cariocas at play, we repaired to a cafe across the road for an end-of-shoot celebration just as a thunder-storm burst over Rio. Feliks was holding forth eloquently about his disappointment in Rio and the stormy backcloth provided vivid testimony to his theme. The cameraman reached for his Arriflex and recorded what was probably the best scene of the whole Rio episode.

With that, Feliks returned to the hotel to pack, and we drove him to the airport. He felt his assignment had been successfully completed. We had travelled far in four months, and he had worked hard. He had produced a mass of fine drawings, and he wanted to get back to London to work on them, and to plan a sequence about the whole experience, to be included as a further element in his giant panoramic 'Memoir'.

He took all my photographs, and my diaries and I prepared to fly back across the continent to visit the Galapagos Islands off the coast of Ecuador. I then planned to pick up the journey overland through the Amazon jungle and again across Brazil but at a more leisurely pace, one with which I felt more comfortable. However I wanted to get back to Rio in time for the carnival six weeks later, before flying home to Britain to take up my coaching duties with the Oxford crew. I felt sad and suddenly alone watching Feliks' loved figure disappear into the departure lounge and wondered whether we had made the most of our experience together. We had not really talked enough during the journey, and although there would be time back in London, I hoped that he did not feel frustration now that the project was over.

MY LAST OF SOUTH AMERICA
Daniel's gesture, after our Rio airport parting, when he went off with the Brazilian brothers Carlos and Georgio, abandoning me in the queue at the passport barrier, a gesture of returning alone solely to give an intimacy wave and then run off.

I had a couple of days left in Rio before my flight to Quito, and I spent the time exploring the city, meeting friends and preparing the ground for the ten days I would spend during carnival. I sculled on the lagoon and on the last night, I teamed up with a student from Texas and two holidaying Canadian girls. We decided to go to a transvestite show at the Casanova in Cinelandia. Our taxi-driver strongly disapproved of our destination.

Out on the street, near the viaduct, the transvestite hookers stood on every street corner, their short skirts and evening dresses falling open strategically to attract motoring punters, and their see-through blouses showing voluptuous hormone-developed breasts.

It was an exciting display and the atmosphere was decidedly sexy, and full of promise. The most spectacular transvestites were the black and mulatto boys who thronged the doorway to the hall where the show was to take place. We were the only straights, and the only foreigners.

The venue was a gay disco hall rather than a theatre, and the show which consisted of samba dancing by boys in exaggerated drag, was far less exotic than the extraordinary members of the all male audience. They were outrageous, noisy and brash. They wore girl's panties, slips and blouses, tiny satin shorts and vests and bare torsoes and hair bands, and their hands were everywhere. A stream of two metre tall, coffee-skinned, big-breasted boys in low-cut gowns passed by our table on their way to and from the back yard where drink was being served, where couples necked furiously and where assignations were being made. It was impossible in the heady, surreal atmosphere to avoid getting caught in casual clinches and flirtations. I lost all sense of who and where I was. My samba improved by leaps and bounds as I sank into the hot sweaty sensuality of the moment.

At first the Canadian girls were frightened, and Paul, the beefy Texan, felt threatened by it all. But the crazy carnival fun of the place and the lack of inhibition of the people soon seduced them too, and Paul ended up wearing Norma's lace slip as he danced euphorically with a smooth-skinned mulatto giant. I danced with her(?) equally statuesque and equally captivating friend, who slipped the top half of her gown down to her waist and clasped my head to her full resilient breasts. It was a Bacchanalian scene worthy of Fellini or Russell at their self indulgent best. Only the waiter had shown initial wariness at our arrival, charging us 120 cruzeiros each for a beer. But within an hour we were paying the normal sixty. The atmosphere was intoxicating and I vowed to spend a night with a mulatto transvestite when I returned to Rio. I managed to talk with some of them but they kept disappearing and reappearing so often that I lost track of who was who. They spent the night busily turning tricks, and found the pickings at the club far more rewarding than out on the street, where the drizzling rain was ruining their costumes and hairdos.

It was the liveliest night I had had since the night at La Carlina in Santiago, and we made our way back to the hotel in the rain, soaked, happy and physically charged up. I was ready to return to Quito and the Andean west coast.

True to form, the hotel forgot to wake me at six, and at eight-thirty, I leapt up, grabbed my bag, raced from the hotel and fell into a taxi, convinced that I would miss the once-a-week nine-thirty

Quito flight. But just as true to form, chaos and inefficiencies at the airport had delayed departure until eleven o'clock.

Sitting next to me on the plane, twenty-year-old Marienis from Argentina, told me how she hated Brazil, how dirty and coarse the people were. Ah! the jealous narrow-mindedness of the Argentines. I sank into exhausted reveries.

CHAPTER 13   The Slow Road Back

It is comforting to return to a place in a foreign land that you already know and I felt immediately at ease in Quito's small-town atmosphere; and after the problems with the Portuguese language, I found that I could cope quite well with Spanish again. I was meeting Kate, a friend from America, who wanted to join me for a trip to the Galapagos Islands for a couple of weeks away from the sub-zero climate of Philadelphia, and our planes touched down ten minutes apart. We had to spend a day in Quito, because the TAME flight on to which we were booked to the Galapagos next morning was cancelled. 'There were only nineteen passengers,' explained the flight manager; and then remembering that low booking was not a legally valid reason for a cancellation he added, 'and there were some technical problems.' So we took the 'autoferril' train, a single carriage bus on rails, through the mountains down to Guayaquil where we could pick up the next day's flight for the last 960 kilometres over the Pacific to the islands.

We rode on the roof of the train to get the best views of Cotopaxi and Chimborazo volcanoes and the 3,500 metre high desolate wind-blown passes where the driver's assistant had to run ahead clearing away the sand that had drifted across the tracks. There were two elderly American matrons, a French couple and eighteen schoolgirls from Quito on board who were heading for Riobamba, a town I had visited a couple of months earlier. They sang and played games and wore funny hats and ponchos against the cold. It was their idea to ride on top, and while at first sight they had seemed to be a noisy crowd of irritating middle-class city kids, they turned out to be extra bright, indefatigable and thoughtful. As in Argentina, boys were conspicuously absent from this school outing. Luz, the sixteen-year-old 'leaderene' explained their purpose. She had met an Indian teacher at a student conference a few months earlier, and he had invited her to bring her class on an exchange visit to his village. 'It's a chance for us to learn a little about our own country for a change,' she said. 'I only hope he's there to meet us, because I've had no reply to my letters.' She and her friends were so enthusiastic and so positive about Ecuador. She had travelled all over the United States with her parents, but had had no desire to stay there. Kate, my American friend, was quite startled by their savvy and energy, and could not imagine American kids being so enterprising. Their enterprise was rewarded. The Indian teacher was there to meet them with a welcoming committee of five village peasant girls. They piled into the back of an old pick-up with their backpacks and drove off waving.

The driver of our little bus/train, sitting up in front with no steering wheel, manipulating his gear stick, had to slow and stop whenever we approached a road crossing because, far from the train having the right of way, all the road traffic studiously ignored us. The railway tracks ran down the main streets of little remote mountain communities lined with wooden houses and sidewalks. As we descended on to the coastal plain, the vegetation became thicker and the villages larger, set amid extensive banana plantations.

From the train terminal in Duran, we took the ferry across the bay to Guayaquil, past the slummiest rubbish-dump shanties in all of Ecuador, with rusty half-submerged ship hulls wallowing in the shallows beneath them.

The Galapagos Islands exist in a time warp, visited by a carefully controlled limit of 16,000 people every year, who arrive by air or boat as if from another planet. There are fewer than 4,000 inhabitants on the fifty-eight arid, volcanic and hot virgin islands and islets which are the summits of huge underwater volcanoes; some of them are still active. Plants and wildlife, unknown anywhere else in the world, have flourished in isolation there, adapting to the Galapagos conditions, different even within the archipelago, cut off from their mainland ancestors for millions of years. Reptiles dominate the scene as they did millions of years ago, since no large land mammals were able to reach there; it was there that Darwin developed his evolutionary theories.

The Galapogeans cater to the visitors, tend the flora and fauna of the islands, help the scientists run their studies at the Darwin research station, and live spartan lives mostly in the little port of Puerto Ayora on the main island of Santa Cruz. There are a few bars, three or four restaurants and half-a-dozen hostels which service the needs of the daily planeloads. It is from the harbour of Puerto Ayora that one rents cabin cruisers, sleeping six, eight, ten or more, complete with guide, cook and captain, for as many days as you want for a carefully orchestrated tour of the islands. The standards of the boats vary enormously as do the prices. 'Avoid the Cristal Rey,' we were told by one disillusioned group just returned from a scheduled week trip after only two days because the cook had served them fish heads for breakfast, lunch and dinner and the captain had refused to follow the itinerary they had agreed back in Santa Cruz before they started.

We were lucky. The moment I arrived, I began to negotiate. We gathered together a group of seven others and found an excellent boat and crew for an eight-day trip for $20 a day each. We left the next morning and discovered, only after we got back, that it was usual to spend a week or more getting organised for a trip unless you were with an official tour operator. The whole Galapagos experience was a tourist affair of course, but one very much for specialists and adventurers. I had been told for months as I travelled the mainland that the costs of the visit were prohibitive, but in the event, $140 covered my two-week trip, and it could have been done for less.

Kate and I teamed up with a sad-faced, Swiss girl called Ursula; a dour, obstinate, scrawny long-haired German boy called Norbert; Paul, an endearing, dry, diminutive bearded Englishman and his tall, humorous, prim Swedish wife; and a determined, serious, good-looking, tanned Dutch couple, Arnold and Cecilia, who insisted on visiting the most distant little rocky outposts in pursuit of Red Footed Boobies and the elusive thirteenth Darwin Finch. They had recorded the songs of the other twelve Finches and were desperate to complete what would, they assured us, be the only full set of Darwin Finch recordings in existence. Generally we were all having such a good time, watching the abrupt vivid sunsets, eating fresh fish and lobsters every day, playing with the dolphins and swimming with turtles and sea lions, that the long sea journeys involved in their solemn quest did not worry most of us too much.

But Norbert was incensed and nearly instigated a mutiny. He tried at one point to persuade the captain to turn back to closer and more popular islands and it took all the very best British diplomacy to calm ruffled feathers.

Ursula was seasick from the day we left Puerto Ayora to the day we returned. Norbert's spoilt whining ways became a source, first of irritation, then of wry amusement as we sought ways to thwart and punish him. His delight in the little misfortunes of others, the way he grabbed all the food, serving himself first and no one else, his chronic selfishness, united the rest of us in a campaign to teach the man some manners. It was with enormous satisfaction that we watched him drop his camera into the waves while we were making a difficult 'wet' landing in a turbulent sea, on one of the small rocky islets.

Generally though, we were a happy, if slightly formal little band. Some of us slept up on deck because the cabin was airless and claustrophobic and smelt of diesel oil. Besides it was cooler beneath the stars, listening to lapping waves, and the pleasure of watching the sun rise every day compensated for the hardness of the deck and the damp condensation in the early mornings. By day, out at sea, we soaked up the hot equatorial sun as we travelled through the archipelago. The salt matted our hair and we were constantly sticky because there was no fresh water. Two-hour walks on the islands in the burning heat were all that was permitted. 'We must not frighten the animals,' said César our guide; but we could swim in the volcanic rockholes pounded by the sea, nuzzled all the while by curious sea lions. One day the sea got so rough, that we nearly lost the dingy overboard, and almost everyone was sick as we hung on in the heaving waves.

And so, criss-crossing the equator, we island-hopped from Santa Cruz to Isabela to Floreana, Post Office Bay, Santiago, Buccaneers Cove, Tortuga Bay, Puerto Eyas, Espumilla, Espinosa and Plaza Sur with its friendly shouting sea lions, tumbling and flopping and necking, and its island iguanas and whirling birds, all unique to the islands and all stunningly unconcerned by our presence. Clearly, the streams of visitors were well behaved and observed the rules diligently. Shoes had to be carefully cleaned so that no plant or animal life might be accidentally taken from one island to another. No bone, no flower, no stone could be collected and taken away. No animals could be fondled. (Mother seals rejected their young if they smelt odd.) Tracks were strictly followed and straying was frowned upon. Every effort was made to protect the natural order of things.

The islands were an experiment in pure and uncontaminated living. No refuse could be dumped into the sea, and we trod everywhere as if on thin ice. Darwin would have been proud of us. But it had not always been so. Earlier sailors had introduced domestic animals, dogs, goats, rats and pigs which had run wild and threatened the native life of the islands. And passing ships, stocking up on provisions, had captured the helpless giant tortoises in their thousands for their meat, because they could be stored alive below decks, surviving for up to a year without need of food or water. They were piled one on top of the other and sustained the ship's crews on their long journeys. Six species of tortoise were now extinct, but fifteen types still survived on the islands, carefully protected and nurtured by the Darwin Station. The tortoises, some of which could live for over a hundred years, were at their most vulnerable as eggs, and as youngsters, and hawks, rats and wild pigs found them easy prey. But even the fully-grown, 180 kilogram adults could be overturned and killed by marauding packs of feral dogs, which the preservationists were trying to eliminate.

On other islands we saw marine turtles, pelicans, penguins, delicate pink flamingoes on their long thin stilts, mocking birds, an albatross, flightless comorants, flapping their stunted wings un-availingly, fur seals, brown land iguanas, lizards, approachable hawks, armies of multi-coloured crabs and thousands of dark grey, spitting, prehistoric marine iguana climbing all over each other and merging with the black basalt rock of the volcanic lava flows. Out at sea, schools of gentle leaping dolphins followed, and entertained us for kilometre after kilometre, and a whale, and less gentle sharks, their ominous fins slicing through the water, crossed in front of the prow. 'Look to your left, there,' shouted César, our roly-poly jovial and suggestive leader, pointing to two dark shapes in the water. 'Turtles! See! They are focking.' Deadly sting rays haunted the shallow waters around the islands; but when we swam out around the Devil's Crown, a full circle of rocks 800 metres off the shore of one island, the array of tropical fish was dazzling. An angry male sea lion snapped at me when his fifteen or so girlfriends swam too close. The turtles were fun to chase through the clear green waters, but were too quick to catch for a ride. We saw them in their greatest numbers as the females floated just off the shore, waiting for the twice-yearly moment when they would lumber ashore to lay and bury their eggs. Next morning they were gone, leaving behind their foot prints and litle give-away piles of sand half way up the beach.

On board, Augustin the cook, dissected lobsters methodically and ruthlessly. They had squirmed pathetically about on the deck for an hour until he was ready for them. Then he grabbed one and held it down as he hacked off the tendons holding the shell, which he then tore off. The tail went next as the unfortunate creature wriggled frantically to escape. Even when Augustin lopped of the head, and began washing the exposed corpse, the body and limbs continued to writhe. Two barracuda caught on the line the next day suffered similar treatment. They were beaten about the head with a bottle until they were dead. We never ate the same thing twice at any of the three daily sittings, for eight days, and my nine-year allergy to fish, which had developed after a poisoned meal in India, disappeared.

Other fellow travellers and visitors aboard our boat were flapping pelicans and elegant swooping frigate birds, and a chirpy, pushy young guide from another cruiser who took three of us back with him for a drink and a smoke on board the Lobo del Mar. Although his boat was larger and more luxurious than ours, his passengers, two girls and eight German and Dutch boys, sat glumly about the main cabin, smoking dope and strumming guitars. Our chatty little group did nothing to rouse them from their stupor, and their guide gave us a mournful look, raised his eyes to heaven and shrugged his shoulders. As he took us back in his dingy, we congratulated ourselves that even with the awful Norbert, we had managed to select a pretty agreeable bunch of shipmates.

Between island stops, I planned my journey back across Brazil: south through Peru and then on to Iquitos by river, down to Leticia and by rough track through the Equatorial jungles of the Amazon. But my long-trusted Bartholomew route maps (used for travels in India, Africa, the Middle East and Brazil eighteen years earlier) which indicated clear road passages eastwards, were to let me down badly. The tracks were imaginary and all that existed was impassable virgin forest. We discovered too on our return to port, that Ecuador and Peru had embarked upon a small-scale territorial war in their southern mountain borderlands, and the frontiers were closed. Not only that, but all the planes of Ecuador's domestic airline had been requisitioned for troop transportation to the war zone. We were marooned 960 kilometres out in the Pacific.

For the next two days we made periodic five-hour bus trips to the airport on Baltra Island for news of flight possibilities. (Galapagos residents rode in the front of the bus, tourists at the back; Galapageans got preferential treatment on the flights too.) But we also had time to explore Santa Cruz island. We stayed with Mrs Angemeyer, a delightful eccentric Ecuadorean who had married a German, and then promptly divorced him. She liked to dress in short, full, blue schoolgirl frocks and white socks and she ran the cheapest guest-cum-camping place in Puerto Ayora. Her rates varied according to whether you slept on the floor in the large communal rooms, or chose one of the small straw huts for two, sleeping on the ground with spiders, or took a luxury cubicle with wooden, mattressless beds, and netting over the windows for protection against the avaricious mosquitoes. On a whim, I had written a month earlier to book a space with her.

She was a mine of information too. When I told her of our luck on the first day in finding a boat owner whose Swiss customers had failed to arrive from the mainland, she laughed and replied: 'Oh they all say that, just to hustle you along.' Her cheeky fourteen-year-old daughter, who adored Kate, spied on us constantly.

News on the islands was sketchy and rumours of full scale war, border closures, emergency measures and the evacuation of foreigners were rampant since radio and telecommunication links with the mainland had been severed. Eventually a plane arrived to take us off, but even back in Quito reliable information was difficult to get and the situation remained tense. President Roldos went on television to address the nation with a powerful and emotional speech. He showed a charismatic and forceful side to his character which had not been much in evidence on the four other occasions I had seen him. Then he had seemed an insipid, humourless academic. Now he brandished his fist and thumped the table, his voice shaking with fury, as he told his countrymen to prepare for war, condemning President Belaunde again and again.

For South America's youngest and most liberal elected leader, this was a grave test. He saw no likelihood of any support from the five witnessing signatory nations to an earlier peace accord, the Rio de Janeiro agreement between Ecuador and Peru. Brazil, Argentina, the US and Chile were supposed to guarantee the terms of the treaty, but they were all pro-Belaunde. The view of repressive right wing militarists towards a moderate reformist democratic South American government was pretty clear cut. They were determinedly hostile to Roldos who was sternly anti dictatorships. The warm embraces he and Belaunde had shared a month earlier at Bolivar's anniversary celebration in Santa Marta now in retrospect seemed hollow and cynical.

Peru accused Roldos of illegally attempting to take possession of part of her remote Condor mountain territory, which she had won in the 1941 wars and which had lost for Ecuador valuable oil-bearing jungle lands. Roldos accused Peru of shooting down one of his helicopters, and then launching an air attack on an Ecuadorean border post, killing some of his soldiers. Roldos pursued his case through the United Nations while mobilising his army.

The tragic death of this champion of democracy in a plane crash a couple of months later, has still not been satisfactorily explained. The following month Panama's leader, who was in conflict with the

United States over sovereignty of the canal, also perished in a plane crash. Both these leaders had attended the Santa Marta presidential gathering. Spain's Prime Minister Suarez was to resign soon after, so that within three months of the Bolivar anniversary, three of the nine attending presidents had gone – a fitting comment on the instability of Latin power politics.

Alone again, I settled into the Hotel Sucre to decide my next move. Outside my window, overlooking San Francisco square, Quito life carried on as normal. The noisy street market below echoed to the insistent piercing cries of the trilby-hatted Indian women selling fruit, seeds, meat, chickens, vegetables, fish and drinks. One young girl's voice rose shrilly above the general hubbub from five every morning. Her penetrating call coupled with the all night drunken groaning, vomiting, copulating sounds of the man in the next room, and his girlfriend's patient pleading, served to give me a less than soothing reintroduction to city life after the tranquillity of the islands.

Journalistic instinct told me that I should stay to witness the denouement of the conflict in the Condor mountains, but I knew that that could take weeks. As it was, it was still possible to leave Ecuador by land across the northern border into Colombia; or I could fly. But the longer I waited the more difficult it would become, because Ecuador was getting jumpy. Sixty foreign tourists had just been arbitrarily rounded up in a drugs purge in the north, and had been held for a week. All were innocent, but I did not relish that sort of harassment.

Early next morning, I caught the bus to Colombia, and carried straight on without a break for two days, until I reached Cali. There I spent two pleasant days with my teacher friend Sara from our Christmas boat trip in Leticia. She was living with another teacher, an Irish ex-nun, in the apartment of an energetic, Jewish, half American – half Colombian theatre producer called John who was also a business man/singing teacher/landowner, and who had been educated in the States. John was quite a celebrity around Cali. He was in the process of building a new house to his own design, on the family finca (farm) two hours from town, which his grandfather had won in a poker game. We got on famously. 'You're the first Englishman I've ever met that I liked,' he declared. 'They're usually such jerks.'

I went with him to spend a day helping on the farm. We rode round his curiously wedge-shaped landholding, perched on a steep hillside, and he showed me the experimental agricultural techniques he was trying out, interplanting coffee with potatoes and beans, which he hoped would cut down blight. His coffee was flourishing. 'It hasn't been tried before,' he said proudly. 'I worked it out myself.'

The family which looked after the place, and helped him with the building, was unusual too. A couple in their thirties with two delightful children, they were alert and conscientious and they respected John not least for the way he respected them. They operated as a team. There was not the slightest trace of the usual master/serf feeling in the relationship, and the genuine warmth that existed amongst them was invigorating. The wife was a wiry, independent, handsome woman and she prepared potato soup and rice for us while we worked in the rain and mud on the building site. At the end of the day, I found it difficult to leave. John wanted me to stay on. 'It's so long since I've had such a rapport with someone,' he urged. 'You get on so well with everyone here. They enjoy the way you are.' He couldn't see how a few more days would disrupt the tightening schedule of my onward journey, but Sara understood. I was finding people more and more welcoming and as I covered the same ground for a second time, I felt increasingly at ease. Border crossings were easier since now I only had one bag and I knew where to catch buses; I knew the ropes. I could offer advice and information to other travellers. My Spanish was better too, and I began to regret that I could not dally longer in places like Quito, Popayan, Bogota and Cali. But once I started there would be no end to it and so I wrenched myself free from the comforting embrace of newly made friends and headed north for Bogota and Venezuela.

My stopover in Bogota was short. I stayed with John's two young cousins, who regarded me as a somewhat curious offbeat figure. They devoted all their spare time to me, questioning me about travelling, politics, love and everything that was happening to me in Bogota. They watched my behaviour with bemused fascination and I had to resist a temptation to act out more extravagantly the larger-than-life role that they were casting me in. For two good-looking Colombian boys, they led very quiet lives, studying by day and watching television and cooking at home in the evenings. They were as sorry as I was that my stay had to be so short, because it had been a funny distraction for them.

Before leaving Bogota, I made contact with the director of the newly-discovered 'Lost Cities of the Sierra Nevada' (Ciudad Perdida), that predated the Inca antiquities, and which were hidden in the high, remote valleys of the Santa Marta mountains. Although journalists and tourists were being refused permission to visit them he was willing to take me, by helicopter, on his next visit, during which he hoped to reach yet another suspected 'lost' city.

But since that trip was not due for another month, we agreed that I would try to return later in the year for a further expedition.

The long bus rides were becoming an endless day and night pattern, with occasional twenty-four hour stopovers. From Quito, up through Colombia to Venezuela and then down into Brazil to Manaus was about 5000 kilometres, some of it over very rough terrain, and I was slowly being overtaken by a 'journey's end' feeling – that this last lap was just a PS to the whole adventure. The circuit had been completed in Rio and I was now serving out my time following my personal stubborn commitment to do it by land.

Most bus and collectivo rides were punctuated by police searches, some cursory, others quite thorough. From the Ecuador border to Cali, we were examined five times, the last requiring all passengers to disembark, in the middle of the night, under the glare of flashlights, and to line up like criminals facing the bus with our hands up against its side. One by one we were body-searched and then made to show our documents. I never left my bag unattended because policemen were the worst thieves and made good use of situations like these. So my bag was thoroughly searched in the middle of the road.

On another occasion, soon after we had crossed into security-minded Venezuela on a sixteen-hour leg, I was admiring the technique of a sharp Romeo across the aisle, as he pursued the remarkable seduction of an apparently innocent prim plump girl, when we were stopped. A full search of the bus revealed some discrepancy. We were herded back on to the bus, and taken to the local army camp. One of the passengers, a nervous, middle-aged woman with a shopping bag full of provisions, was led off the bus. A policeman handed a rolled newspaper package shaped like a cone to the young overweight camp commander, who opened it in full view of the curious passengers still on the bus. We craned towards the windows to watch. Fully aware of his audience, the captain licked a finger and poked it into the package with a theatrical flourish. Then he put the finger to his tongue for a taste. With a dramatic grimace he spat out energetically, as if he had been poisoned. A great sigh went up from the bus-load of Colombian and Venezuelan passengers. The man next to me who had been playing Lennon and Queen tapes very loudly on his machine during the ride, said: 'He would have done better to sniff it,' and made a coke snorting movement. Everyone laughed.

The unfortunate dope smuggler was escorted to an office for interrogation, and we thought that that would be the end of it. But no. There followed a full scale, four-hour search. While the soldiers went through every piece of luggage and every bit of clothing, the usual peasant patience and resignation prevailed. This was normal practice. The searches in Venezuela were far more thorough than anywhere else on the continent where the main aim usually seemed to be general harassment.

When we got going again, Romeo turned once more to romance, and soon the girl was lying full length across the seat, her head on his lap as he caressed her hair with one hand and her body with the other. When she arrived at her town, she transformed herself abruptly back into a retiring schoolgirl and left the bus to join her waiting parents. As she walked away with them, she turned back to give him a shy little smile and a surreptitious wave. He and I sat together from then on until he arrived at his destination. He was Venezuelan but perferred to live in Colombia. 'The girls are much friendlier there,' he said. 'In Venezuela it's money, money all the time.'

At another stop, we had a half-hour break for a snack of eggs, bread and tomatoes, washed down with beer. Opposite me, a man in his fifties wearing a cowboy hat with eight empty beer cans lined up on the table in front of him, drunkenly chatted up a plump girl. Shoeshine boys and Marlboro cigarette sellers streamed in and out, and I kept the strap of my bag wrapped tightly around my legs for safety. Each bus ride held some peculiarity to make it memorable in some way, be it a squawling kicking child, an old arguing couple, a beautiful girl, a goat in the next seat, loud music, breakdowns, collapsed roads, police searches, dramatic landscapes or failing brakes.

I bussed north to Cucuta on the border with Venezuela, through lands where the people wore stetsons, and tethered their horses to hitching rails, and where the 'policia' lounged about outside their offices on the dusty, untidy main streets, guns slung low across the hip.

I had been discouraged from visiting Venezuela by many who had been there and from going to Caracas in particular. Unfriendly, high cost, high speed, ugly uninteresting city, I was told. But as I raced through the rich countryside, with mountainous tropical forests, waterfalls, white-sanded Carribean coastline, and English-speaking Trinidad, Guyana and Jamaica just a hop away, there was yet again evidence for never accepting anything on hearsay. It was a varied and appealing land, and the people I met were open and talkative. Caracas, tucked along a narrow strip of land between the coastal ranges of steep hills, was indeed a mini Manhattan, huge, rich, and smoky, but it was a lot more besides; I was urged to give the city a chance. 'To know Caracas is worthwhile,' said Sylvie, a Caracas lawyer, 'do not just dismiss it.' I felt instinctively that a longer stay would not have been unrewarding. 'A working girl here is not looked down on,' Sylvie continued. 'She can live alone too. But in Colombia people would be appalled.' All the same Venezuelan men preferred Colombian girls, possibly precisely because they were less liberated and independent.

Venezuela's thirteen million people (300,000 unemployed, ie half Britain's rate) enjoyed the highest living standards in the Latin world, and was one of the most stable democracies. On the other hand local criticism pointed to the fact that television was in private 'establishment' hands, that the police were corrupt, that there was little power-sharing and that opportunities were limited. But press and political freedoms were taken for granted. Venezuela was beginning to take a responsible role in the affairs of the region too, but was realigning itself alongside the powerful United States, Mexico, Canada, Brazil and Argentina, and drawing away from its long-established Andean Pact Alliance with weaker Peru, Ecuador, Bolivia, Colombia and Panama. There was talk of granting special oil concessions to the rest of Central America. Many people I spoke to resented the support the government was giving to the El Salvador junta, and put it down to personal friendships: Duarte had spent ten years in exile in Venezuela. The 'people' I was assured, supported the rebels, as they had supported the Sandinistas in Nicaragua. The government at that time had supported the Sandinistas as well, and there was criticism of its lack of consistency.

In Caracas I was able to take long overdue showers, and rest, but I felt healthy, if a little unfit from all the buses, despite the gruelling travel pace. I found that when I was on my own I ate far less and as a result suffered less from the usual travel queaziness. Because fruit was so varied and so accessible, it was easy to base one's diet entirely on it and overeat, but I found it to be a major cause of stomach problems and mouth ulcers, so I cut down, and although I lost weight, I felt better.

The journey east along the coast and then south, took me across the llanos plain, over the broad Orinoco river to Ciudad Bolivar, which was really four towns being merged into one, and was Venezuela's fastest-growing metropolis with over half a million inhabitants.

It was impossible to find your way between these towns, and everyone I questioned for the onward bus south gave me a different answer. The bus from Caracas dropped me at eight o'clock at night at a crossroads in a suburb called, I thought, San Félix, and as I got off I asked the driver for directions. 'El Dorado bus? Oh yes. Si si muchas busetas. Pero manãnã.' 'De donde?' I asked. 'San Félix.'

'Este no es San Félix?' 'No.' A group of taxi-drivers all gave different replies: 'A bus will pass at three in the morning'; 'Nothing until tomorrow'; 'It will leave from here'; 'It will leave from San Félix, ask for the Orinoco and Maturin bus company.' I left them arguing. So I took a buseta to San Félix across the river. But no one knew of the bus station I was looking for, and they found it all terribly funny, this lost gringo. Two men tried to send me back to where I had come from, a girl said it was down the road, and the desk sergeant at the police station pointed down yet another road. I tried; no luck. 'Long way,' said a slightly drunk man. 'How long?' 'Quatro manzana' (four blocks). That didn't seem very far; maybe he was very drunk. The grubbiest hotels cost $10 or more, and were all full. I kept being directed towards rougher and darker areas and I got approached by more and more 'friendly' drunks. Holding tightly on to my bag, I returned to a well-lit, little square and tried another hotel. A man and a garishly-painted girl booked in ahead of me and the proprietress called her eight-year-old daughter to show them to the room. But she had no room for me.

Out again, I headed down the rough dark road by the river Orinoco. At last the caretaker of a dingy little hotel, an old one-eyed man and the resident hooker offered me a room with a fan off the central courtyard. Why not a shower and a clean-up before continuing my search for the elusive bus station? As I prepared my toiletries, a smartly-dressed group arrived at the front desk. Were they tourists? Decidedly not. Five men and one prostitute perhaps? No; one appeared to be a policeman. A minute later they swept into my room. My papers? Of course. A pretty smart young woman, five men and a couple of less elegant ladies waited as I sorted through my security belt. 'It's an inspection,' they explained and intro-duced themselves. 'This is the police chief, this is the head fireman, and these gentlemen are representatives of the military.' 'And the pretty lady?' I asked. 'Your passport and papers please.' Oh oh a journalist. They looked at each other. (What on earth is he doing here, in this hole? in this town?) 'OK! Gracias, adios,' and off they went to continue their 'tour of inspection'. I continued to get ready for my shower. I got Mr One-eye to replace the broken bulb in the shower cubicle and finally began to wash my grimy hair in the cold dribbling water. There was sudden shouting outside, the door in the shower banged open, and a soldier with an automatic rifle barged in. Oops! sorry: 'Mea cupa,' he said. 'That's OK,' said I, and he rushed out. Ten seconds later, bang; the door flew open again and this time a policeman with a pistol looked in, clearly hoping for a naked girl. 'Sorry.' 'That's all right,' I said, very accommodating. They crashed through the courtyard, banging on doors and shouting. 'If shooting starts, I'm a little vulnerable,' I thought, and quickly finished my shower. Pulling on my trousers I peeped out. Half-a-dozen soldiers and policemen trotted out of the courtyard empty handed; I could get on with my shaving.

A wizened Italian woman was convinced that I too was Italian, and told me about her time in Ethiopia, while I was shaving. As I left the hotel to find the bus station, old One-eye warned, 'Muchisimo peligro ciudado! Cuchillas, ataque.' (It's a dangerous town. Knives, attack.) It was dark outside the hotel, but round the next corner there were bright lights, a couple of rough, dilapidated, wooden shacks masquerading as late-night cafes, a group of large jolly, middle-aged whores, some taxi-drivers but no bus station. 'The taxi-drivers will know,' I thought. But no. They wanted to take me back across the river, and had never heard of the Orinoco and Maturin bus station. A few yards on it got very dark again, but following my rule that you never find out anything unless you try for yourself, I walked another few steps further and asked a trio of old gents having a smoke and a chat outside their front door before they turned in for the night. 'Bus station? Over there, where that light is,' they said pointing thirty metres on. And so it was. Beside the river Orinoco, a teetering bus shelter and office, with the destinations written on a board and the faded words 'El Dorado' just discernable in the gloom. The young owner of the crumbling hotel next door, confirmed a six-thirty am departure.

At last I could relax and I returned to one of the brightly-lit poky cafes for a chicken leg and a coke. The owner was a quiet, handsome black man who cooked for and served his varied clientèle alone: three abundantly overflowing, unpretty hookers, a pair of mulatto thugs in dark glasses, and an unexpected elegant black couple – she very tall in glasses and cocktail dress, he in a suit, middle-class, attractive and utterly out of place. The curious evening had unrolled as if in a dream. I was, and had been, an innocent 'candide' figure, both an observer and a participant in the whole series of eerie and surreal sequences. I walked back to my room, through the still threatening streets of this run-down-about-to-be-a-boom town. A couple of cars with blackened windows cruised ominously up and down. I went to bed.

The bus finally left at nine, and the tarmac road ran out six hours later in thick jungle just before El Dorado, a true one-horse town of impermanent bungalows, where Papillon's famous prison stood. The bus line ended here as well. Ahead lay the long gruelling haul up into the Guyana Highlands, out of the rain forest and up on to the vast Gran Sabana, with its distinctive flat-topped 'tapuis' mountains, like Conan Doyles 'Lost World' Roraima, rising starkly out of the flat, undulating, treeless plateau. In the middle of this wild remote land was the isolated Venezuela/Brazil border town of Santa Elena de Uairen. From there the trail plunged down again into the immense impenetrable Amazon basin itself. It was 1,600 kilometres to Manaus by a pot-holed track, which cut a thin, rust-red streak through the landscape. This was the northern link of the great Trans-Amazonica Highway which will one day inter-connect the isolated far-flung outposts of Brazil's vast jungle territories.

Virtually the only transport using this route were the 150 or so Brazilian timber trucks that made the bouncing wearisome week-long journey to Venezuela with logs cut from Brazil's huge forests. Venezuela wisely preferred to preserve her own extensive forests and buy instead from her giant neighbour. The drivers, working usually on their own, earned $600 a trip and made three a month. But it was painful and frustrating going and the appalling track took a terrible toll on their precious vehicles. They returned empty from El Dorado and, although they were not officially supposed to take passengers, I was able to hitch a ride with Gilmar, a quiet, pensive, blond, unshaven Brazilian of Italian parentage, to the remote cattle town Boa Vista, a curiously confusing settlement, part wild west, part space-age in style.

From there I teamed up with Aaron, for the thirty-hour run to Manaus through dangerous Indian territory. His old leaky truck had to be watered every half-an-hour from roadside streams, but the stops provided an opportunity to swim beneath occasional, spectacular, crashing waterfalls. At ferry crossings, vicious midges bit mercilessly, drawing blood and raising large welts. Again my back seemed to provide the tastiest feast and I itched for days afterwards.

Aaron was older and brasher than Gilmar, with a coarse humour, fat beer belly and a boorish manner. He was a German/Brazilian who had worked the route for some years, but was now ready to settle down. He had bought a three-kilometre-square plot forty-eight kilometres south of Boa Vista, which he intended to clear for cattle rearing, and where he planned to live with his Japanese/Brazilian wife and their three children. This was to be his last timber run, and he cursed each bump and pot hole as we crashed along. He would never pick up the Indians trudging along the trail who called for a lift, and the few mulattos and whites he did pick up, he would drop off well before any settlement in case the police decided to hassle him. For some reason I was considered all right.

Whenever he felt too tired to continue we would stop to rest. While he slept in a hammock slung under the tailboard, I slept in the back of the truck on a tarpaulin listening in the thrilling wildness to the untamed night noises of monkeys screeching and crickets whining in the undergrowth. We ate at isolated little huts along the way where gutsy stalwart families prepared fine home cooking for the lone, long-distance drivers. There was a rough fellowship amongst these pioneers, born from their shared battle for survival in a hostile and lonely world.

None of the drivers I travelled with would accept any payment, saying simply that they welcomed the company. They drove usually within sight of each other south of Boa Vista for protection against raiding Indians who attacked these foreign intruders of their ancestral lands. Although things had become a little calmer of late, because the Indians had been settled on to protected reservations, a dozen road workers had still died in the few years previously, and the attacks had delayed completion of the road. But angry Indians were not the only danger. Rockfalls, collapsing rotten wooden bridges, highway robbers, and forest fires were additional everyday risks. On one occasion, around midnight, a thin, red line in the far distance grew hugely as we approached into a vast, uncontrolled, bush fire, stretching four or five kilometres to the east and west of us, straddling the road. The flames leapt high into the air, and the heat intensified, but rather than stop to assess the situation, Aaron gunned the engine, and with a wild whoop, we burst through to the other side.

An account of this journey alone could fill a book, but suffice it to say that the crossing of the wild savannah lands and the jungles of north Brazil reaffirmed my enthusiasm for the rough riding type of adventure travel, and redressed the balance against the hectic, plane-happy, accompanied, filmed journeying that had dominated so much of the earlier journey.

The vastness of Brazil became increasingly daunting. The 800 kilometres from the northern border to Manaus was now to be followed by a further 600 south to Porto Velho, and then a difficult stretch east for 1,700 kilometres to Brasília, which because of rains and poor road, I was told could take up to two and a half weeks to travel; then there was another fast leg of 800 kilometres on good roads down to Rio. Beyond Rio, it was a further 1,000 kilometre run to Brazil's southern border with Argentina and Uruguay. To cross the country from east to west meant a journey of 4,000 kilometres. Four thousand kilometres by 4,300 kilometres: Brazil was really four or five countries rolled into one, and I could see that, if I held to my overland plan, I would miss carnival in Rio. It was the Porto Velho-Brasília leg that worried me. Finally, after much heartsearching, I succumbed to necessity, and booked on to a flight to the capital Brasília, which I had been commissioned, back in London, to photograph.

CHAPTER 14 BRASÍLIA: the coming of age

Brasília stood majestically across the lake from the airport, its elegant skyline reflecting glowingly in the setting run through the crisp clean air. It had filled out considerably since I was last there in 1962, only a couple of years after it had been officially declared the capital. Ever since then Brasília had been constantly heckled as a white elephant and a waste of money. No one came to Brasília, it was said, and no one wanted to work there. Yet here was a burgeoning city, with three quarters of a million inhabitants and a developing character of its own. It was in fact in serious danger of coming of age and becoming a fully-fledged capital. Diplomats, government officials and natives of the city took great trouble to list all the advantages to life in Brasília: its undeniably efficient layout, the clean air and healthy climate, the peace and calm, the space, the easy access to adventure safaris in the bush, the lack of street crime, and the uncluttered transportation system, often on roads sunk into ditches below eye-level. They also enjoyed the company of like-minded people. Contrary to popular opinion, all the locals I met were loyal and defended their city vociferously; and contrary to the universal myth, they had no desire to rush off to Rio for coastal weekends. They rejected the cliché criticisms of the international, Rio and Saó Paulo press who still insisted that Brasília would 'never fly'.

'Those glib detractors are out of step,' said the new head of the national press agency. 'Most of them have never travelled around Brazil and don't realise that civilised life doesn't end outside São Paulo and Rio.' But one departing ex-president was reported to have said as he flew out of Brasília for the last time, 'Goodbye city without a soul.' And he hasn't been back.

Green grass had replaced the great tracts of bare red earth, and the yawning gaps between buildings were beginning to be filled in. The series of residential, self-contained six-storey apartment blocks, the Super Quadras, raised on stilts and complete with their own shopping centres, stood at either end of the two wings of the city which had been designed in the shape of an aeroplane. There was an overflowing hotel sector near the centre, and elegant red-roofed, private villas surrounded the artificial lake. The business sector of town was busy by day but it quickly emptied at dusk as the while collar workers converged on the bus station for the rush homeward to the Super Quadras and the satellite towns half an hour away.

What was missing though was a heart, a tangible focal point for people to hang out, and to 'paseo'. A huge open space and a network of roads dominated the centre of Brasília, creating a vacuum where a human bustling city should have been. Only the isolated below-ground-level bus terminal, and two gigantic covered shopping-cum-cinema-cum-restaurant complexes (Conjunctal Central and the Centro Commercial) gave it any sense of being lived in. It was a difficult city to walk in too because the distances were so great. Trying to photograph crowds proved difficult and I kept returning to the rush hour scene at the bus station. Friends laughed when I asked where people gathered: 'People? What people? That's what we like about the place.'

In design-efficiency terms Brasília was excellent, but over-planning had produced a coldness, a lack of humour which made it an all work no play environment. Although there were wide impressive avenues and magnificently created buildings by Oscar Niemeyer, there was a crying need for the courage of a decision to re-design the centre.

Brasília's 'heart' was in fact spread out like so many pulses around the city, banished to the outer edges. In order to find a place to sleep without paying $100, I had to take a half-hour bus ride to Banderante, one of the four or five depressing out-of-town satellite 'nucleos', which was the first settlement in the region twenty-five years ago, built in shanty fashion to house the workers who were building the city. All Brasília's slums were conveniently placed out of sight behind the landscaping; they were home for those workers who had created Brasília and who were now unable to find proper employment, performing servant tasks and menial work in and about the city. On the bus to Banderante, I fell into conversation with a student who had lived in Brasília all his life. He was one of the few natives of the new capital. He was born in October 1962, two weeks after I first visited the place. It was changing fast he said, improving all the time, but it still lacked warmth. He took me to a comfortable clean $5-a-night workers' hostel.

Next day, I joined the early morning commuters for the bus ride back into town to take photographs and meet some government officials and British council and embassy staff. The Brits had been advised of our possible visit, and they were disappointed that Feliks had not come. The council had planned receptions and tours for him, but they were kind to me all the same, and offered me a car and a driver so that I could get round to all the various 'sectors' – bank, hotel, sport, newspapers, TV and radio, cinema, embassies – to take my pictures more easily. For three days I luxuriated in pleasant informative dinners, lunch at the House of Representatives, to the background music of the current American pop hit parade, and the hospitality of one of the embassy staff who invited me to stay at his lakeside home.

Officials presented their city's credentials. They explained that Brasília was helping to open up the interior of the country, and light industry and agriculture were being established to make the region self-sufficient. In fact manufacture of the new revolutionary sugar cane alcohol fuel, invented and being developed jointly by Brazil and Cuba to replace petrol, was to be centred in Brasília, and already, the numbers of cars running on the cheap fuel were causing a minor pollution problem. There was pollution too in the lake which was inadvertently serving as a collecting bowl for the city's waste. The drainage system in this super-designed metropolis was hopelessly inadequate.

The Spanish-speaking countries of South America were becoming fearful and suspicious of the rapidly growing wealth and influence of their giant and thrusting neighbour, and Brazil's president, Figueiredo, was hard at work touring the continent trying to placate them. He protested that Brazil was not interested in leading or representing South America, nor indeed in expanding territorially. She was big enough as it was he maintained, and her economic interests lay towards the American north, Europe and Africa. A leading journalist in Brasília hastened to point out that although the United States and even some over-zealous Brazilian leaders, were avidly trying to portray Brazil as the developed world's newest member, arguing that she no longer needed aid and loans, she was in fact still very much a Third World power. 'Brazil should not be trying to run before she can walk,' he said. 'We should be developing a relationship with Africa's Portuguese-speaking countries and with Portugal herself.' Brazil's present government was, he said, less militaristic, and more Brazilian in character than previous regimes, and Figueiredo had set himself upon a course of liberalisation. In typical Brazilian fashion press censorship, as far as the president was concerned, had ended in 1978 but his military colleagues still insisted that the newspapers 'respect' the dignity of their positions and refrain from criticism. There had been a general amnesty some months earlier and there were investigations currently underway into past police brutality and corruption, although these were being strongly resisted.

Twelve bus hours south of Brasília, through Minas Gerais, one of Brazil's richest states, and beyond Belo Horizonte, stood one of South America's most beautiful colonial towns, a national monument, and the complete antithesis of modern, over-planned Brasília. Ouro Preto, was perched deliciously atop and around a group of steep green hills, watched over by a plethora of loftily-sited, magnificently-preserved churches. The whole combination created a harmonious splash of white and orange/red amidst the lush verdant landscape. It was proudly and unashamedly a tourist trap for Brazilians and foreigners alike, and the international hippy community adored its steep, narrow cobbled streets and curious shops of arts and crafts. It was also a centre of Brazilian academic and artistic life and the place thronged with students. I spent two days as a guest of a household of students exploring one of the most appealing towns I had ever seen and enjoying my last moments of ease out in the countryside before launching into my South American finale – carnival in Rio.

I had been well prepared for the glamorous spectacle that the carnival always was in Rio. But for some cariocas it was too hyped up and they preferred the earthier carnivals in Salvador or Recife which were more informal, more street-based. But every town and village in Brazil celebrated carnival, and as a national unifier, it was wholly successful. Far better to focus a country's passion and nationalism on the creative exhilaration of carnival, football or samba, than on the destructive militarism and war-like posturing and territorial claiming that most countries use to stir up their people. But all the same violence was never far from the exuberant festival of carnival, and many cariocas locked up their homes and took off to the coastal resorts of Buzios and Cabo Frio for the duration. I, on the other hand, had looked forward to the 'Queen of Carnivals' for months and I was determined to enjoy myself thoroughly.

CHAPTER 15   Carnival in Rio

Although carnival was still a week off, the celebrations were already well underway with private parties and balls held every night. Rio was brimming with expectancy and visiting high fliers filled every hotel and guest house. These had been booked up many months in advance so I took advantage of kindly offers of hospitality and stayed during the fortnight with a wide variety of households. Sleeping was impossible of course; there was far too much going on, but it was good to have somewhere to bathe and change and to doze for an hour or two every now and then.

My hosts were very understanding and seemed happy to leave me to my own devices. Tadeo, a rowing colleague and his wife gave me the spare room in their Leblon flat for four days until they took off on a European tour and left the flat to their in-laws; Marcello, another rower and part-time model, transferred me to his parents' home on the slopes of Corcovado hill and left his battered Ford Mustang and family in my care while he went off to Buzios for carnival. When his parents also took off for the cooler mountain air south of Rio two days later, I moved in with Maria, a delightfully spry friend of Feliks' from his pre-war Warsaw days, who lived in the heart of Copacabana's red light district. And when Maria's live-in companion returned after carnival, I spent my last two days with an ex-patriate Englishman, staying in the basement of his lovely colonial house on bohemian Santa Theresa hill in the city centre with its steep narrow cobbled tree-lined streets and ancient trundling trams.

The beaches along Copacabana, Ipanema and Leblon were packed every day all day and the sand burned hotly underfoot. Aside from the brash ice cream and trinket salesmen who patrolled the shoreline, outrageously costumed, extrovert drag queens, very different from the convincingly feminine transvestites of Cinelandia, regaled the languishing sun-worshippers with salacious songs and high-pitched squealing banter. They were an integral element of the carnival scenario and invariably sported a week's stubbly growth under their extravagant make-up. One ice cream seller boosted his sales by combining two roles with great aplomb. He minced along the beach in a pink frock pursued by a horde of kids and his incessant line of ribald chatter enlivened Copacabana from end to end.

The bronzed locals exercised on the specially provided gym equipment; played beach netball and kept their eyes out for a pretty pass. They stood in the popular way along the water's edge, gossiping and being seen. On the whole only the tourists swam in the dangerous crashing surf.

A young French hippie drew portraits on the topless section of Ipanema beach. I had met him first in Asuncion the day I was released from prison. He had lost his passport there and had spent four months stuck in Paraguay. We had a drink at the famous Ipanema de Garote bar where an impromptu Sunday afternoon pre-carnival celebration exploded into life. The street was quickly blocked with dancing, drinking, bikini-clad cariocas. A rough and ready band kept a pounding samba beat throbbing through the afternoon. My artist friend was not fully convinced by the Brazilian display of exuberance. 'Yes, they have vitality and madness,' he ventured thoughtfully, 'but don't you think they are too aggressive, too macho? They treat women like meat here and they seem very superficial and immature. I think Europeans are more subtle; we value relationships more; perhaps we are just a little less primitif.'

One late afternoon in Leblon, I joined a dancing throng of hundreds winding its way for hours through the streets in the wake of a band, all of us packed tightly together, jigging and samba-ing for all we were worth. Open cars cavalcaded daily down the main streets, the drivers steering recklessly while their passengers, mostly young girls, crowded in near hysteria on the backs of the seats behind. The sidewalk pedestrians urged the girls to bare their breasts – a carnival obsession. And the girls obliged, some boldly and enthusiastically, lifting their T shirts high, enjoying the wild roaring approval of the men in the mob. Others were less daring and needed persuading; one demure beauty, resigned to the display, shyly unbuttoned her blouse to show a breast, and then when the crowd surged forward demanding more, she closed her eyes, gritted her teeth and pulled the blouse wide open for a moment, before covering up and begging the driver to move quickly on. The rabble bayed lustily as she disappeared up the road. Bosoms and bottoms were everywhere. Carnival seemed to be all about women presenting their bodies for the perusal and approval of lecherous men who invariably grabbed and fondled and probed wherever they could get close enough to make contact. The newspapers hailed the least violent but most decadent and obscene carnival of recent years, with pages upon pages of explicit photographs depicting near-naked girls being manhandled, and drugs being ostentatiously used. Even the septuagenarian boy-friend of my Polish hostess Maria, himself an inordinately hedonistic Viennese, who had directed the Brazilian national dance troupe for many years, was shocked by the rapacious scenes shown on television during the samba school parade. 'They are losing all self control these Brazilians,' he complained mournfully. 'I saw a man masturbating one of the dancers right there in public for the whole television audience to see.'

All Rio throbbed with Bacchanalian sensuality, made all the more intense by the steamy, sweaty, summer heat. My days and nights fused into a multi-coloured array of images and experiences, all merging irresistibly into a blur of semi-comatose impressions.

The night before the four-day festival proper began, I was taken to one of the many grand soirées that were reported daily in the gossip columns. Pélé, Robert de Niro and Brazil's favourite movie star Florinda Balkan were the guests of honour, but foreign visitors were equally lionised by the anxious-to-be-international-jet-setting carioca high society set. The daily *Globe* even ran a story on the visiting Oxford coach and writer Daniel Topolski. That did my standing in the social merry-go-round no end of good while I remained in Rio.

Our film cameraman friend Carlos had invited me to play the role of a foreign visitor to carnival in a documentary film he was preparing with his French director colleague for American cable television. In it I was to be given an unorthodox 'alternative' view of carnival by a leading Brazilian film actress called Itala Nandi. It seemed like a good way to see the festival and to earn a little money at the same time, so I agreed; but I had not reckoned with the natural helplessness of my Brazilian friends in the face of decision-making and organisation. We fell out. I was not prepared to spend half of each day and most of the evening sitting in their office or in a bar waiting for them to sort themselves out while the celebrations raged outside; they for their part decided after five days that they did not want me or the character I was playing in the film after all. So a fight over the desirable Itala was scheduled between me and the other actor (in fact the director) on the dance floor at the Monte Libano Ball which I was to lose. I would then sulk off into the darkness never to be seen again. Thus I was written out of the script, unpaid, but free to enjoy the rest of the carnival as I wished.

Before our association finished however we did film at one of the best balls of the year – the Vermelho e Preto (Red and Black) held by 'my' club, Flamengo. In a vast hall decked out in shimmering red tinsel and black drapes, upward of 2,000 near-naked people – also done up in red and black bits – heaved and panted to a hectic samba rhythm. The men had paid over $100 a ticket just to get in (you paid extra for food and drink inside) but they were allowed to bring in two women – a curious recognition of the fact that women are supposed to outnumber men in Rio by two to one. Young girls, hoping to be picked up and taken inside, hung around the entrance amongst a tense, struggling mob who, having failed to secure a ticket or been unable to afford one, fought tooth and nail to gatecrash. (Indeed one person was killed in the mêlée.)

Inside, the dance floor was a veritable bear garden. On two balcony levels overlooking the dancers, fellow partygoers watched, drank and preened. Up there the women, some of whom were hookers hired for the evening, were flamboyantly salacious, the men leery and beery, gawping and grabbing. Whenever a camera was produced people came alive. They were ready to do anything to get noticed. They posed unashamedly for the cameras, dressed for the cameras, discarded clothing for the cameras, bared bottoms and breasts lasciviously for the cameras. Echoing Andy Warhol's adage, everyone wanted to be a star for a few moments, to produce an image momentarily unique enough to feature next day in the photographic displays of the city's newspapers and on the nation's television screens. Just lifting my camera to my eye was enough to produce a panorama of exposing, thrusting, beaming boys and girls flashing that manic carnival *smile*, vying with each other for attention. They were gloriously rude and brazen.

One girl gyrated her bottom lewdly at me from the second floor balcony, straining backwards, hanging her stretched buttocks over the edge of the sill. To ensure that I recorded her fully, she reached behind her and, tugging the tiny panties deep into her crotch, pulled the bared white cheeks wide apart. The gazing spellbound men urged her on and begged me to keep on photographing her for fear she would stop. Again and again she did it, while other girls on the first floor balcony wriggled and pouted wantonly, taunting the men on the floor below. Phials of amyl nitrate were freely circulated, heightening the tension all round. After a while the straining men began leaping up, reaching out to touch the girls who pulled back in teasing horror, laughing challengingly all the while. When one or two of the fellows succeeded in realising their goal, the mock horror turned to genuine anger as the women struggled to free themselves from the lusty attentions. However, as the evening wore on, the games took on more serious intent as some people got fully to grips; costumes were shamelessly pulled aside and couples fell on each other in dark corners of the big hall and in the gardens outside.

'Brazilian men do not know how to direct their sexuality,' claimed Itala as we clung and slithered together amongst the slippery, sweaty bodies entwining and gyrating on the floor. 'You know who and what you want, and how you want it. You understand your sexuality; but they have no control over their desires.' I was baffled. What on earth could she mean, I thought, as we squirmed about in a pretty fair imitation of advanced foreplay. 'Brazilian men never take responsibility,' she continued. 'They behave always in this Peter Pan way.' Later she expanded further on her critique of the Brazilian psyche. 'Brazil is always said to be the country of the future, never of the present. When will we ever grow up?'

We left the ball in full swing to film in Cinelandia outside the 'gay' Teatro San José in downtown Rio. As people thronged the entrance, a predatory thief squatted next to a dozing, drunken reveller sitting on the front steps. I watched in fascination as he casually and systematically went through the man's pockets, pretending for the benefit of the passing glancer to be a friend of the victim. Failing to find anything worth taking he began to pull at a ring on the man's finger. The drunk groaned and stirred and looked up for a moment but then fell back into his stupor. I got Carlos to turn the camera and lights on to the scene since I suspected that any personal intervention would surely have resulted in knives and bloodshed. The thief, caught and dazzled momentarily in the spotlight, drew angrily away along the step; but the moment the camera turned away, he boldly returned to his task, attempting again to ease the recalcitrant ring from the drunken finger. After a while he gave up, shrugged, and wandered off looking for pastures new.

The crew had meanwhile turned their focus on to a plump, white, unpretty shaven-headed queen who was rushing about the road in hyped excitement, leaping on to the bonnets of slowly passing cars, there to sprawl in mock seductive pose, yelling and squealing with delight at the attention he was getting. He was covered in blue bruises and love bites; he'd lost one of his high-heeled shoes, his mascara was smeared down his cheeks and his ball gown was torn, but he was having a whale of a time. Carlos persuaded him to calm down for a bit and began an interview which charmed the whole film crew. The man was witty and frank and, according to Carlos, articulated his view of life, love and homosexuality in the most original and intelligent terms. He told us that in his 'other' life he was a successful city businessman. He and the film unit were so taken by each other that they decided there and then to make a full length documentary about him.

One the way home, the city still dark at five in the morning, we passed a group of twenty or so boys, stripped down to shorts, playing a football match on an open space of rough land by the light of a couple of street lamps. The occasional early morning jogger trotted by: a night cap run? or a first thing in the morning wake-me-up?

I ran into Carlos and the team by chance a couple of days later filming outside the entrance to the Grand Gay Ball. A long catwalk had been erected along the front of the hall for the benefit of the public and the television cameras, and all the arriving celebrities and guests had to parade their extravagant fancy dress costumes before a panel of judges. They were so theatrical these Brazilians. A large crowd had gathered to watch the free show. And what a show it was. All Rio's most glamorous transvestites were there for their big night of the year, shrilly demanding attention, and dressed – or undressed – to kill. I even spotted my huge mulatto dancing partner from the Casanova evening six weeks before, looking magnificent. Twelve dwarves arrived in Snow White costume, and some women dressed as men, or tried to double bluff as larger than life drag queens. But no one could match those mulatto transvestites for sheer panache and daring.

I continued to cruise Rio at the height of its carnival madness. The dockside sailor bar area at Maua, considered highly dangerous for solo out-of-towners, was awash with celebrants and devoid of any threat or nastiness. The topless shows and the whoring had been abandoned so that everyone could join in the fun. While most people leapt about in the streets, some gathered in the bars along the front to watch the continuous all night coverage of the main events – like the Gay Ball I had just left – on television.

I returned to the city centre by way of Cinelandia. Round the corner from the Teatro San José, permanent heart of Rio's transvestite operations, a small square was alight with fairy lights and a street party and band was in full cry at four in the morning. Drunks and tarts milled about happily with transvestites and transexuals in scenes of such licencious libertism that they out-Fellinied Fellini and left Ken Russell standing. Everyone sang the most popular samba songs of the carnival – Portela's 'Oh Mario' was a favourite – wherever there was music. The boy/girl hookers primped and flirted and occasionally fought. One was slashed by a slighted lover and, with blood running down her face, she and her friends set off down the street after him. But he got away. Another transvestite held firmly on to her pretty boyfriend in tight satin shorts. On the pavement opposite the band, six men were trying to force their libidinous attentions on a sturdy, robust, pale-skinned young girl dressed rather incongruously in a sensible skirt and blouse and with a big school satchel slung over her shoulder. Clearly she wanted to dance with one of them but whenever she made her choice and began to samba the others moved in close grasping at her from all sides, pushing her back into a shop doorway. Over and over again the charade was repeated. She pushed them away, then chose one again and began to dance, pressing up against him, taunting him until, vicariously enflamed, the others would crowd in once more. How she escaped them with the game she was playing was hard to see, but since they were all so stoned they probably did not realise quite what was happening, and after a while she got bored and wandered off.

Some of the transvestites were very beautiful, and clearly desirable as women, so different from the mocking vulgarity of the drag queens of Ipanema, who were so obviously men. They were mostly 'working' boys, but it was a tough area and I was a little hesitant about getting myself caught up in something I couldn't handle. Still I had promised myself a transvestite (or would it be more accurate to say transexual) adventure and besides my curiosity was aroused. How in practical terms was a half-way-to-being-a transexual put together? How did a transvestite operate? When I caught the glance of one particularly tantalising mulatta for the third time, she came over to say hello. 'I am called Mara,' she said. 'Do you like me?' Faced with a willowy, full-breasted, half-naked beauty the answer was obvious. For better or for worse, I was hooked.

She took me down the street, away from the party and the lights, to a small hotel. We went up to the first floor where the receptionist, a bleary-eyed geriatric, took the money for the room and handed Mara a key. The room was small and neat with a big circular bed in the middle. We undressed. Mara was all soft and willing, her hips slim, her legs long and her bosom large and firm; no silicone implants, no unseemly lumps or scars. A course of female hormones had fashioned an exquisite mulatta woman. She also had a disconcertingly well-developed cock, which to my surprise and confusion perked up as I caressed her breasts. Somehow I suppose I had expected her to have pygmy-sized shrunken male genitals, or to have undergone the full transexual operation complete with artificially rebuilt vagina. Instead I was presented with a whole array of inspiring variations. I was not too sure where to start, but Mara showed no impatience. On the contrary she was possessed of a gentle and affectionate nature which was very reassuring in the circumstances. She led me through an enchanting range of hedonistic exercises.

The climax to carnival was the parade of the samba schools – a fourteen-hour extravaganza that encapsulated and expressed the whole theatrical exuberance of Brazil in one surging once-a-year event. The drama, the colour, the size and beauty of it all, the dancing, the costumes and the music were overwhelming. A vast battery of overhead lights turned night into day and packed multi-tiered stands lined the two kilometre route. The society elite occupied comfortable boxes on one side and faced a vast bank of seats rising high into the night sky across the road. The journalists had their own enclosures ranged alongside specially reserved boxes for high-paying Rio companies and organisations. The fight for simple free cups of 'Press' coca cola was little easier than the battle to gain access into the heavily-guarded venue itself. The editor of Brazil's leading colour magazine *Manchete* had kindly given me his personal 'press pass' and although I in no way resembled his photograph, no one seemed to pay any attention to such details. Once past the barrier, I was free to roam wherever I wished; I spent the full fourteen hours down on the piste amongst the samba school performers as they paraded by.

One by one they came, each school 3,000 to 5,000 strong: Imperatriz the eventual winners, sexy Unidos de Vila Isabel, Mangueira costumed in pink and black, Imperio Serrano in white, the superbly luxurious Beija Flor, the multitudes of Portela in blue, and as dawn broke, my favourite Salgueiro in red and white. They were followed by Governador, full of unexpectedly plain performers probably tired out by the long wait. Up close the glorious effect was no less devastating than when seen from the stands. Each school took well over an hour to pass by and in the half hour between 'acts' the gilded international celebrities, the local big wigs – and we photographers – sauntered around, showing off and waving to friends in the crowd. There was Pélé again and de Niro and inevitably Florinda Balkan who was adored by the Cariocas as a home-grown girl who had made it big in the outside world. 'My God Daniel,' cried London socialite Vivienne Ventura, an old French Lycée school friend. 'What on earth are *you* doing here?'

One after the other the schools lined up at the far end of the parade street awaiting their turn. Then at a given signal, their 'baterias' opened up and they began their splendid advance down the piste, preceded by a 'sweeper' row of security men clearing the way. This was the stuff of fantasy. Huge, garlanded floats, some with fountains playing, inched by bedecked with twirling, thrusting, sequined and spangled mulattas and wildly-feathered and shimmeringly-costumed men and women. Acrobatic dancers performed as though their lives depended on it. A tiny, completely self-possessed eight-year-old girl led the brilliant Salgueiro school with a breathtaking samba display. Behind her, ranks of fine-featured, white-suited and top-hatted young men strode in perfect harmony to the throb of the bateria. Flamboyant aged Bahiana-style women, in blocks of 400 or more, elaborately dressed in full skirts and bodices and teetering head dresses, filled the street as they swept imperiously by, confident in their long-serving roles within the samba school tradition. The detail and the sheer size of the presentations were a glittering tribute to the months of painstaking work and money that had gone into the preparation of each Escola. As the night wore on some people in the audience dozed off where they sat or slumped against the railings; but most were hyped-up and speeding too fast to stop. By daybreak, the smiles were wearing thin, the mascara was streaking down cheeks, and the costumes had lost their crispness. But still the last three schools were to come. They had waited all night for their moment and now they had to rouse and galvanise themselves for action. The crowd was punch drunk by the end and hard pressed to receive the striving tail-enders in the manner they deserved. But like professional stage entertainers, audience and performers alike rose to the occasion and they passed to rapturous applause.

By ten o'clock I could take no more. Although there was still one school to go, I staggered off to find my borrowed car. Like the Lord Mayor's show in London, once was surely enough; but it was a glorious uplifting finale to my South American experience. I was ready to return to Europe.

EPILOGUE

Reading back over *Travels with my Father* there is a troubled thread running through the narrative. I would not wish to deny the good people we met throughout Latin America and the warm friendships that we established there. Equally it would be impossible to reject a continent so rich in texture and detail, so generously endowed with physical splendour and so abundantly peopled by such a variety of cultures and races. However, overall, and common to all the countries there, despite their separatist nationalistic posturing, was that uneasy sense of threat, of a population mass muzzled and in thraldom. The Brazilian writer Antonio Collado expressed it to us thus:

> Latin Americans get very annoyed at being lumped together as if there were no differences between them; but although they are right in many ways, when you look at them now you will find degrees of poverty, degrees of wealth and more or less advanced countries throughout the continent – but fundamentally there is a sort of tacit agreement between them that their peoples are not going to participate much in what happens. That seems to be almost instinctive and I would say it happens from Mexico to Tierra del Fuego. You will always find a very well-off group, the ruling classes, and a tremendous gap between them and the mass of people – far more than you find in Europe or the United States... I suspect we are like India in this respect. South America is still very much a colonial area... Europe and North America have gone through a long period of civilising themselves, getting ready for a big expansion, but that period of transition to democracy is a price Latin Americans don't want to pay.

There was a harsh brutality and a lack of tolerance and simple humanity that coloured the reactions of those in power when faced with non-conformism or diversity of opinion. Within three days of arriving in South America I knew how tenuous life could be for ordinary people, and little that subsequently happened altered that view. It was a sensation I had not felt so acutely anywhere else in the world, be it China, the Middle East, Eastern Europe, Africa or India. You might be stopped in the street and people would watch curiously and, as you were led away, they would say to themselves: I just saw a terrorist/criminal being arrested. Yet it could so easily have been them – and would I have thought any differently about them if the roles had been reversed? In prison everyone became unshaven and grubby, even those who made an effort to stay tidy. And if a high-born Latin, or that Argentine businessman I'd met in Asuncion just before I was arrested, were mistakenly apprehended he would probably get out by pulling strings the way I did, and he would say: 'Disgraceful; me thrown in with common criminals.' Would he have realised that many of them were innocent too? Would he have spoken to them? Too easy to think that everyone else was guilty, at least of something, and that you were the only innocent. It was all so arbitrary. One lived it seemed at the whim of those in power.

A professor in Brazil explained: 'The people in power see the population as their natural enemy, and the population regards those in power as the enemy. This is traditional with us Latins. We inherited this mutual fear and distrust from the Spanish and Portuguese.' He despaired of his system of government. 'We will never be able to grasp the concept of responsible and representative government – one elected to carry out the wishes of the people and to rule for the general good. It is not in our nature. We see the winning of political leadership as the opportunity to wield and manipulate power and people and to accumulate wealth.' The 'people' have no choice but to remain in permanent opposition, constantly denied a voice or the chance to influence the way they live. Is it any wonder that in the end they rebel. They have nothing to lose. Their one sustaining strength is their faith, yet even here there is uncertainty. The church is split. The lower orders live closely with their communities, identifying with their suffering and tend to be radical in their search for a solution. There are many priests involved in the resistance movements. Their superiors however side with the establishment to preserve the status quo.

The United States often via the multi-nationals is widely seen as colluding in the continuation of this self-perpetuating scenario. A Bolivian diplomat discussed the frustration felt by Latin Americans: 'The United States offers succour to regimes which rule in a way that would be entirely unacceptable to the so-called Western democracies; Americans would rise up in rebellion if they were submitted to the inhuman treatment meted out daily to thousands of South Americans. And Washington, in its blinkered crusade to stamp out what it sees as Russian-inspired communist infiltration everywhere, refuses to recognise that in fact it is simply shoring up and aiding totalitarian dictators to suppress their peoples' attempts to win freedom and social reform. It took you in Europe hundreds of years to achieve those basic dignities and values that you take for granted and here we are being denied them by the very nation that professes to uphold them above all else. The United States is destroying its credibility as leader of the free world and forcing us to turn elsewhere for help.'

Ultimately, despite the dangers, it was impossible not to get drawn into the passion of political debate. The contradictions within Latin American society were reflected in the volatility of the people, which, like that of the very land itself, ensured that as a continent simmering away in the southern hemisphere, South America could never be ignored.

INDEX